The Lake English Classics

OLIVER GOLDSMITH

A BIOGRAPHY

BY

WASHINGTON IRVING

EDITED FOR SCHOOL USE

BY

GEORGE PHILIP KRAPP, Ph.D.

TUTOR IN ENGLISH, COLUMBIA UNIVERSITY

CHICAGO
SCOTT, FORESMAN AND COMPANY
1904

ROBT. O. LAW CO., PRINTERS AND BINDERS, CHICAGO.

TYPOGRAPHY BY
MARSH, AITKEN & CURTIS COMPANY
CHICAGO

PREFACE

The text of the present edition of Irving's life of Goldsmith is taken without change, by permission of the publishers, Messrs. G. P. Putnam's Sons, from the author's final revised edition. Irving's notes to the text are indicated by the star (*); additions by the editor to the author's notes are inclosed within brackets; the editor's own notes are indicated by numbers. Proper names are annotated only when the note serves to make clearer the point of an allusion in the text. The editor may say that he has edited the book with the main purpose of bringing out its value as a picture of eighteenth century literary life, rather than as an example of the work of Irving.

COLUMBIA UNIVERSITY,
New York, May, 1903.

CONTENTS

OLIVER GOLDSMITH

CONTENTS OF THE CHAPTERS

CHAPTER I

CHAPTER II

CHAPTER III

10 CONTENTS

CHAPTER XXXIV PAGE

CHAPTER XXXV

CHAPTER XXXVI

CHAPTER XXXVII

CHAPTER XXXVIII

CHAPTER XXXIX

CHAPTER XL

14 CONTENTS

INTRODUCTION

I. BIOGRAPHY OF IRVING

There is a familiar engraving which represents an imaginary gathering of Washington Irving and his literary friends **Irving and** at Sunnyside, the home of Irving's later years. **his literary** In the center of the foreground Irving is **friends.** seated, a somewhat portly, smooth-faced, and kindly-looking man of fifty or more. At his near left stands James K. Paulding, an early literary comrade and life-long friend. Near by sit Bryant, the poet and editor, Cooper, the novelist, and Bancroft, the historian. Somewhat in the background stands a younger man—Emerson, the poet and philosopher. On the right the place of honor is held by Prescott, Irving's friendly rival in the field of Spanish history. Here also are Halleck, remembered as the author of *Marco Bozzaris*, and, again in the background, several younger men— Nathaniel Parker Willis, William Gilmore Simms, Longfellow, Hawthorne, Holmes. But the center of the picture is Irving; all the other figures of the group combine to bring him out with special prominence.

This fancy of the artist pictures to us very well the place of Washington Irving in American letters during the later years of his life. Other names were becoming known— those of Longfellow, Hawthorne, Emerson—names that were destined to equal, some of them perhaps to surpass, his in renown; but they were the names of young men, candidates for fame and as yet hardly well breathed in the race. Irving was nearing the term of a long and prosperous career, a career

that covers one-half of our whole literary history. He could
look back to the time when American letters were not yet in
existence, for he himself was the chief founder of them.

**American
literature
before Irving.** Before his time, indeed, life in America had
not been of a kind conducive to the develop-
ment of a literature. Until within a few
years of the Revolutionary War men had been too much
engaged in clearing farms and building homes to spend much
time on the more leisurely pursuits of art and letters. There
were historians, for example Bradford and Winslow; and
preachers, for example Cotton Mather and Jonathan Ed-
wards. But often their work is crude in form and narrow
in subject-matter; when we read the writers of this period
now, it is with something of the antiquarian's pleasure in
their quaintness and archaisms, or the historian's interest in
the information to be derived from them. In a somewhat
later period the intellectual stir that preceded and accompanied the Revolution bore fruit in a plentiful yield of state
papers, speeches, pamphlets, and even poetry. Some of it is
extremely vigorous, and at its time it was effective. But, as is
almost always true of literature written for a special time or
occasion, very little of it has outlived the period of its production. With the possible exception of Woolman the Quaker's
Journal, the only American book written before the close of
the Revolutionary War that still holds a worthy place by
reason of its literary excellence is Franklin's *Autobiography*.
Yet nothing was further from Franklin's intention than the
composition of a work of literature. Franklin was statesman, scientist, philanthropist, all more or less consciously;
but he has come to be counted among men of letters almost
by accident. The first writer in America who deliberately
chose letters as a profession was Charles Brockden Brown,
a moderately successful journalist and novelist of the first

decade of this century. But Brown's work did not have sufficient power or originality to draw together and give form to the incipient literary tendencies of the country. Irving, the first American to gain wide reputation abroad, was also the first to gain a reputation at home that has proved lasting. Cooper and Bryant were his near followers; but all the other names in the first flowering period of American literature came into prominence only after his fame had reached its zenith.

Irving was born in New York in 1783, the year the Treaty of Paris was signed and the independence of the United States formally acknowledged. Washington, **Irving's birth.** for whom he was named, was inaugurated when Irving was six years old; and we are told that when he came to New York to take the oath of office as first President, he placed his hands upon the head of his youthful namesake and gave him his blessing.

That America of which Washington took control in 1789 was an almost inconceivably different country from the America of to-day. The settled portions of it were still a mere fringe along the Atlantic coast. Eighteen years were to pass before Fulton made his first experiments with the "Clermont" on the Hudson, and thirty-nine years before work was begun on the Baltimore and Ohio railroad, the first railroad to cross the Alleghanies. But perhaps the most astonishing changes of the past hundred years are those which have affected the cities of the country. When Irving was a boy in New York, that place was a town of less than 25,000 inhabitants. It covered only the lower end, the point, of Manhattan Island. The present Bleeker Street marked the northern limits of the little town.[1] Beyond that stretched the rocky, hill-broken farms of the Dutch settlers—the Wolfert Webbers whom fate

---

[1] Cf. Todd, *The Story of New York*, p. 438.

was to make rich in spite of themselves. The fashionable promenade was in Battery Park, now a region of grimy shipping and ugly warehouses; and William Street, in which Irving's father lived, now a street of tall office-buildings, was then an uptown residence street.

There was much in the life of this eighteenth century New York to excite the imagination of a sensitive boy, and Irving spent his time in exploring the secret places of his native city and in wandering through the half-wild regions beyond the Harlem. The wandering instinct was strongly developed in him, and when his explorations on land grew tame, he tells us he would go down to the wharves at the city's edge and watch with longing eye the great vessels sail slowly out of the harbor on their long voyages across the ocean.

His own first long voyage was one he never forgot. In his seventeenth year his parents gave him permission to make **Irving's first** a summer visit to his sister, who lived near **trip up the** Albany. In 1800 the best way to reach **Hudson.** Albany from New York was by boat on the Hudson River. Nowadays the distance is made in less than twelve hours; but then it was a long voyage by sail, and Irving tells with what anxiety intending passengers selected their boat and made all possible preparations for their comfort. This journey made known to Irving for the first time the beauties of the river that he never ceased to love. The depth and vividness of the impressions he received at this time may be seen from the following description written many years afterwards:

"What a time of intense delight was that first sail through the Highlands! I sat on the deck as we slowly tided along at the foot of those stern mountains, and gazed with wonder and admiration at those stern cliffs impending far above me, crowned with forests, with eagles sailing and screaming around them; or listened to the unseen stream dashing down precipices; or beheld rock, and tree, and cloud, and sky reflected in the glassy stream of the river. And then how solemn and thrilling the scene as we anchored at night at the foot of these mountains, clothed with overhanging forests; and everything grew dark and mysterious; and I heard the plaintive note of the whip-poor-will from the mountain-side, or was startled now and then by the sudden leap and heavy splash of the sturgeon.

" .   .   . But of all the scenery of the Hudson, the Kaatskill Mountains had the most witching effect on my boyish imagination. Never shall I forget the effect upon me of the first view of them predominating over a wide extent of country, part wild, woody, and rugged; part softened away into all the graces of cultivation. As we slowly floated along, I lay on the deck and watched them through a long summer's day, undergoing a thousand mutations under the magical effects of atmosphere; sometimes seeming to approach, at other times to recede; now almost melting into hazy distance, now burnished by the setting sun, until, in the evening, they printed themselves against the glowing sky in the deep purple of an Italian landscape."—*Life*, by P. M. Irving, Vol. I, p. 19.

Perhaps, as it so often proves with the recollections of childhood, Irving has unconsciously filled in the above picture from the recollection of his frequent later trips up the Hudson. Yet the fact that these later recollections all center around that first early experience shows that it was a profound one, and, in Irving's life, the most formative of them all.

But manifestly a man's life could not all be spent in idle wandering, however pleasant that might be. In the summer after this trip up the Hudson, Irving began the

Attempts at law. serious study of the law. His preliminary education had been very slight indeed. He had attended a boys' school for some years, and had prepared for entrance to Columbia College. Two of his brothers had attended this college and had been graduated from it. But, perhaps through negligence or a dislike of all formal study, Irving himself did not enter the college. In after life he always regretted the omission of the strict discipline of a college course in his education, for he thought it deprived him of an advantage he was never able to make up in other ways. With no more liking for the routine of law than for that of the school, Irving nevertheless gave his attention to the former subject for the next few years. Before he could be admitted to the bar, however, his health broke down, and in 1804, in hopes of restoring him, it was determined to send him on a voyage to Europe. Thus, though doubtless in a way far different from that he had imagined, a long-cherished wish was to be realized.

The voyage across the water was made in May and June of 1804, and proved to be the thing Irving most needed. When, after a voyage of six weeks, he left the **First journey to Europe.** ship at Bordeaux, his health was very much improved. For a year and a half, he was a traveller and sight-seer, visiting various places in France, Italy, and England, meeting many famous people, and passing through many exciting and whimsical adventures. He soon developed the true traveller's spirit, and took the buffets and the favors of fortune with equal good will. During most of these journeyings, he kept a diary in which he noted his opinions and observations and described the adventures of a traveller's life. Perhaps the most exciting of these experiences was an attack by Italian pirates. He was passenger on a ship bound from Genoa to Messina for a cargo of wine, and when several days out the ship was attacked by pirates, off the coast of Italy near the Island of Elba. Though the affair proved a bloodless one, it was not unattended with danger. The description of it[1] reads almost like an extract

---

[1] *Life*, by P. M. Irving, Vol. I, p. 65 ff.

from one of Irving's own banditti stories in the *Tales of a Traveller*, and often, in writing those stories, he must have thought of his early experiences in Italy. Fortunately no more serious adventure than this of the pirates occurred to interrupt the journeyings of the youthful traveller. He continued on his way through France and Italy, and passed the latter part of his stay abroad in England. He took ship for America in January, 1806, and after a rough voyage of over nine weeks, arrived safely at New York.

As soon as he had settled down in his old place, Irving again took up the study of the law, and after several months, in November, 1806, was admitted to the bar **Admission to** of New York. His admission, however, was **the Bar.** due more to the good-nature of his examiners than to the adequacy of his preparation; for we may well suppose that what little legal learning had found its way into his brain before his departure had been quite crowded out by the many new experiences of his two years abroad. Even after his admission to the bar, he does not appear to have taken much interest in his profession. To his natural dislike of the dry routine of business there was added the further distraction of an active social life. He had many graces of nature and of manner; his disposition was frank and kindly, and wherever he was known he was liked. His letters of this period from Richmond and Baltimore and Washington show with what ease and pleasure he took his place in the best social life of the community in which he happened to find himself.

About this time Irving made his first attempts of any importance at literature. Together with his brother William **Salmagundi.** and a young friend and relative, James K. Paulding, he projected a Spectator-like periodical called *Salmagundi*. The first number of this periodical appeared in January 1807, and nineteen other numbers appeared at irregular intervals between that time and the appearance of the last number in January, 1808. The purpose of the periodical as announced by the editors in the first number was impudent enough when we consider their age and inexperience: "Our purpose is simply to instruct the young, reform the old, correct the town, and castigate the age; this is an arduous task, and therefore we undertake it with confidence." The essays, broadly humorous and satirical, had the high spirits and unrestraint of youth. They secured for the writers a considerable local popularity, but they were ephemeral in character and Irving himself was soon quite willing to have them forgotten.

Irving's second literary venture brought him a wider and more lasting fame than the *Salmagundi* papers. In 1809 he published his *Knickerbocker's History of New* **Knickerbocker** *York*. This is a burlesque history of New **History.** York, supposed to have been made up from the writings of a Dutch antiquary, Diedrich Knickerbocker. It undoubtedly ranks as Irving's masterpiece of humor. Sir Walter Scott, who praised the book warmly, thought he saw in it great resemblance to the satire of Swift. The *Knickerbocker History*, however, is without the deep seriousness of Swift's satire; like *Salmagundi*, it shows more the high spirits of youth than the settled purpose of the satirist. At the time of the appearance of the book it was severely criticised by many of the Dutch families in New York, who felt personally aggrieved at the ludicrous figures their Dutch ancestry made in its pages. And in fact there was slight justification for such treatment of the burghers of New Amsterdam. Irving chose to present the unjustly exaggerated view of Dutch character that had long been traditional in British literature. In England, where the Dutch with their armies and fleets had several times so frightened the English that the English were driven to exaggerated satire to regain their self-respect, such a treatment of the subject as Irving's would have had point; but in America no more inoffensive and industrious race of people than the Dutch was to be found in all the Colonies. But neither satire nor history was the main object of the *Knickerbocker History.* Irving, writing in 1848, thus outlines the purpose of the book:

"It was to embody the traditions of our city in an amusing form; to illustrate its local humors, customs, and peculiarities; to clothe home scenes and places and familiar names with those imaginative and whimsical associations so seldom met with in our new country, but which live like charms and spells about the cities of the old world, binding the heart of the native inhabitant to his home."

How well the book accomplished this purpose can be seen by a glance at its present-day effects. In New York the Knickerbocker legend has worked itself into the very fibre of the people. Allusions to it are familiarly made by many who have never read a line of Irving. The name itself, by an odd change, has become a synonym for aristocracy. In a thousand ways the legend has preserved traditions and sentiments that otherwise would have been speedily lost. It lives like a charm and a spell, binding the heart of the native inhabitant to his country; it has become itself a part of the country.

The *Knickerbocker History* was revised and brought to completion beneath the darkest shadow that ever obscured Irving's sky. Matilda Hoffman, to whom he **Death of Miss Hoffman.** was engaged to be married, died after a brief illness in her eighteenth year. Her memory always lingered in his mind, ready to be called forth by the slightest occasion. He never again thought of marriage, and never accustomed himself to speak Miss Hoffman's name. There was something of fine chivalry in him that held him true even to a memory, and to the end he always kept before him the image of his early love in her first youth and beauty.

The next few years after the appearance of the *Knickerbocker History* saw nothing new from Irving's pen. His natural indolence must explain this, for his law practice made slight enough demands upon his time. In 1810 he was made a silent partner in a hardware business which was conducted by his brothers. This connection, though first the cause of much anxiety to him, was finally the making of his literary career. For, the business affairs of the firm having become embarrassed, in 1815 Irving was sent to a branch house in Liverpool for the purpose of putting things in order. For three years he labored over the uncongenial details of business. But the affairs of the firm passed from bad to worse, and, despite the brothers' best efforts, in 1818 they were finally driven to bankruptcy. In this apparent misfortune, however, there lay a blessing for Irving; his undisciplined nature always needed a strong incentive to work, and in the necessity of making a living he found this incentive. Leaving Liverpool, he went up to London, with no other defense against the hostility of fortune than his pen; and the rest of Irving's life is the story of the way in which, with that single weapon, he not only won wealth abundant but an enduring fame and honor better than all wealth.

The first fruit of Irving's activity in London was his most famous book—the *Sketch Book*. The story of the way this book was written shows clearly the difficulties under which Irving at the time labored. He was far from home, with no helpful friend to turn to for advice or comfort, and with no prospect of any certain income; worst of all, however, was his home friends' lack of faith in him. To them it seemed madness when Irving refused an unimportant government position at Washington which would have given him an assured income but would have shut the way entirely to any further literary advance. In the face of these difficulties Irving went bravely to work upon the project of the *Sketch Book*. His plan was to issue the book in numbers, in America only, under the name of Geoffrey Crayon. In the prospectus prefixed to the first number, he announced the plan of his work in a very tentative and hesitating manner, showing clearly how unsure he was of himself:

"The following writings are published on experiment; should they please, they may be followed by others. The writer will have to contend with some disadvantages. He is unsettled in his abode, subject to interruptions, and has his share of cares and vicissitudes. He cannot, therefore, promise a regular plan, nor regular periods of publication."

The first number appeared in May, 1819, and contained *The Author's Account of Himself, The Voyage, Roscoe, The Wife,* and *Rip Van Winkle.* The second number appeared several months later and contained four essays—*English Writers on America, Rural Life in England, The Broken Heart,* and *The Art of Book-making.* A third number appeared in September of the same year and was followed at irregular intervals by four more numbers, the last number appearing in September, 1820.

The success of the *Sketch Book* was immediate and general. The pen-name Geoffrey Crayon could not hide the fact that **Its success.** the *Knickerbocker History of New York* and the *Legend of Sleepy Hollow* were written by the same hand, and to the liking for the sketches themselves was added all Irving's earlier popularity. The books sold well and relieved their author of the worry and trouble of immediate need. But better than this, their success restored to him some of the confidence in himself which the anxieties of the past few years had robbed him of. Sir Walter Scott offered him the editorship of a new periodical publication about to be established in Edinburgh; and Irving, though he declined the offer because he felt himself unfit for the regular routine of such an occupation, was very much gratified at this renewed expression of good will on the part of the great author. The kind words of his intimate friends and the generous appreciation of many of the best critics in America revived him and gave him incentive to renewed effort. His fine sensitiveness to praise and blame shows clearly in the way in which he took the news of his success. The following extract is from a letter written to a friend in New York after the appearance of several numbers of the work:

"The manner in which the work has been received, and the eulogiums that have been passed upon it in the American papers and periodical works, have completely overwhelmed me. They go far, *far* beyond my most sanguine expectations; and, indeed, are expressed with such peculiar warmth and kindness, as to affect me in the tenderest manner. The receipt of your letter, and the reading of some of the criticisms this morning, have rendered me nervous for the whole day. I feel almost appalled by such success, and fearful that it cannot be real, or that it is not fully merited, or that I shall not act up to the expectations that may be formed. We are whimsically constituted beings. I had got out of conceit of all that I had written, and considered it very questionable stuff, and now that it is so extravagantly be-praised, I begin to feel that I shall not do as well again. However we shall see as we get on. As yet I am extremely irregular and precarious in my fits of composition. The least thing puts me out of the vein, and even applause flurries me, and prevents my writing; though, of course, it will ultimately be a stimulus.

"I hope you will not attribute all this sensibility to the kind reception I have met with to an author's vanity. I am sure it proceeds from very different sources. Vanity could not bring the tears into my eyes, as they have been brought by the kindness of my countrymen. I have felt cast down, blighted, and broken-spirited, and these sudden rays of sunshine agitate even more than they revive me."—*Life*, by P. M. Irving, Vol. I, pp. 330-31.

After the first six numbers of the *Sketch Book* had appeared in America, Irving was driven by the appearance of various unauthorized editions to publish them in England. The first attempt came to grief through the failure of his publisher; but finally, aided by the good words of Walter Scott, the book was accepted by Murray, the greatest of English publishers. Its success in England was as great as it was in America; **Publication in England.** perhaps the most evident mark of this is the fact that twice the publisher begged the author to accept a sum of one hundred guineas in addition to the terms agreed upon by them. We, as Americans, however, have special reason to feel gratified that the success of the *Sketch Book* was first won in America. In that day, American critical judgment depended only too often upon British example, and it is a pleasure to know that our first native writer of importance was accepted by us without waiting upon foreign opinion.

The next few years after the appearance of the *Sketch Book* were years of wandering. The autumn and winter of 1820–21 were spent on the continent, chiefly in Paris. Here Irving formed a firm friendship with Thomas Moore, the poet; and indeed we should expect sympathy of spirit between the man who wrote the *Broken Heart* and the author of the *Irish Melodies*. After his return to London, in January **Bracebridge Hall and Tales of a Traveller.** 1822, Irving published *Bracebridge Hall*, first in America, and in May of the same year in England. In method the book resembles the *Sketch Book;* it is a miscellaneous collection of essays and short stories suggested by the experiences of travel or elaborated from the outlines of things that had long been ripening in the author's memory. Though it did not have the charm of novelty, it was well received both in England and America. Again in 1822 Irving was on the continent, travelling through France and Germany. It was on this journey, while detained by illness at Mayence, that he wrote the introduction to a volume which takes its title from the circumstances of its composition—the *Tales of a Traveller*. The body of the book was written during the winter of 1823–24, in Paris, though the completed volume was not published until his return to England, in 1824. Despite Irving's own special liking for the *Tales of a Traveller* and despite the fact that it contains some of the author's best work, it was coolly received by the public. The reason for this is evident. The three books that he had so far published—the *Sketch Book*, *Bracebridge Hall*, and the *Tales of a Traveller*—were of a kind. They were all books made up of pleasant descriptive and reflective essays and humorous short stories; they all breathed the same quiet air of kindly though not very vigorous interest in the life of the world the author knew. Something of this was accepted eagerly and more was taken willingly; but Irving was guilty of the error of feeding to satiety the taste he had aroused, and his readers murmured at the same dish continually set before them.

Irving was not slow in seeing that the field he had hitherto been cultivating was worked out. He determined to place **Life in Spain.** himself in entirely new, fresh surroundings and to occupy himself with an entirely new sort of work. In 1826 he went to Spain, in which country he lived for three years. This period he spent in visiting the various famous places of the land and in much close reading of historical manuscripts in the chief Spanish libraries. The results of these historical studies appeared in the publication of his *Life of Columbus*, in 1828; of the *Conquest of Granada* in 1829; of the *Companions of Columbus* in 1831; and, as a final lighter postlude to these more serious works, of the *Alhambra* in 1832.

The year of the publication of the *Alhambra* closes a period in Irving's life. In that year, after an unbroken absence of seventeen years, he came home to New York. How eagerly he always looked forward to this return is made very evident in his letters to his friends throughout the whole of these seventeen years. He had never the slightest thought of a permanent residence abroad, and now that **The return home.** success had brought him an honorable name and an assured income, he rejoiced in them chiefly because they helped him to realize what had always been his first hope. After the disturbances of the home-coming were over and after several extensive trips through the South and the West, sections of the country which were almost unbroken wilderness when he left America but now were filled with cities and towns, he purchased the little Dutch cottage on the bank of the Hudson near Tarrytown, called by its former owner Wolfert's Roost, that is in English, Wolfert's Rest, but known to us better by the name which Irving gave it,— Sunnyside. Here he passed the rest of his life with the exception of four years, from 1842–46, during which time he served as minister to Spain.

During Irving's residence at Madrid, no diplomatic complications which might have tested his political wisdom arose. The distractions of his position were sufficient, however, to prevent him from carrying out any of his literary plans, and at the close of his four years he was glad to return to his home on the banks of the Hudson. These years at Sunnyside were serene and happy ones. Irving was the foremost man of letters in America, and his home became the natural center

of all the literary life of the country. He was looked upon as both the founder and the patriarch of American letters. He was not, however, content to rest in honor, and as a result of these last labors he published in 1849 *Oliver Goldsmith, a Biography* and a *Life of Mahomet.* His last work was a *Life of Washington.* He had been engaged upon
Last works and death. this task for many years, and he intended that it should stand as the most lasting monument to his memory. The first volume was published in 1855; ill-health delayed the completion of the second volume, and it was not until 1859 that it was ready for publication. It came as a fitting close to a life of unceasing industry. After a long and trying sickness, borne with great equanimity of spirit, Irving died in November of the same year.

As a man, perhaps kindliness was Irving's main characteristic. There was nothing of self-assertion in him or of contempt for the wishes or the weaknesses of
Irving's disposition. his fellow-men. This side of his character is well illustrated by an action of his later years. After his return to America he was engaged upon a work which was to treat of the Spanish invasion of Mexico. He had gathered his material and had already begun the actual composition of the book when his attention was called to the fact that a young man hitherto unknown to him, named Prescott, was engaged upon the same subject. After determining the seriousness of his rival and his ability to accomplish the task he had chosen, Irving generously relinquished the subject to him. As a result we gained Prescott's *Conquest of Mexico,* though we missed from Irving the story of a period that he was peculiarly fitted to treat. We cannot but feel, however, that one such action is worth more than a whole row of volumes. Throughout Irving's long and varied life, we do not know that he ever cherished a single enmity or that

he was ever mixed up in any of the petty quarrels such as spot
the lives of so many men of letters.   Yet his amiability was
due to no weakness of character or want of fixed opinions.
The sure judgment of his own powers maintained in the face
of a disheartening opposition, the uninterrupted faithfulness
to his country during a long residence abroad in which he
had every encouragement to forget that country, and finally
the depth and sincerity of the attachment of his half-dozen
personal friends to him—these are sufficient indications of
strength and individuality of character.

The second main characteristic of the man was delicacy
and refinement of feeling.   Perhaps his was not a very pro-
His delicacy found or strenuous nature.   He never cared to
and refinement mix in politics or in the daily concerns of a
of feeling. business life; his sense of personal repugnance
towards sordid details was stronger than his sense of the good
to be accomplished through the use of such tools.   This attitude towards the things of daily life is not, to be sure, very
unusual, nor is it generally to be commended.   The justification of it in Irving is to be found in a real and not an affected
delicacy of nature.   Irving's temperament was that of a poet
—a poet of a tender and somewhat sentimental cast of imagination.   The characteristic of his work is always beauty
rather than power.   However much he may have felt in his
heart the deeper mysteries of existence, in open life he preferred the play of gentler feelings and emotions.

As a corrective to what might otherwise have proved a
cloying sweetness of nature, Irving was possessed of a third
                    main characteristic—an unfailing sense of the
His sense humorous and whimsical in life.   The world
of humor. was not tragic to him; neither was it entirely
happy.   It was a place of mixed good and evil where one
could rejoice at the good, sorrow at the evil, it is true, but

forget it chiefly, in the distractions which a kind fate has put at our disposal.

II. IRVING'S LIFE OF GOLDSMITH

The life of Goldsmith was the most rapidly composed of all Irving's writings. It was written during the summer months of the year 1849, at the time when Irving was occupied with seeing through the press the first collected edition of his works. Happening to be one day in his publisher's office, when the latter was looking over Forster's life of Goldsmith with the intention of reprinting it, Irving remarked that the subject was a favorite one with him, and that he had often thought of extending a sketch made some years before into a volume. At the solicitation of the publisher, Irving took up the task in earnest, and within two months the first sheets of the *Biography* were in the hands of the printers.

Date of the Biography.

Of the various methods which a biographer may follow in the treatment of his subject, Irving chose one of the simplest. He did not attempt to reconstruct for us the whole life of the period of which Goldsmith was a part, to show the special conditions of race and environment which might explain the character of Goldsmith and his writings. This would be the method of the scientific or philosophic biographer. Neither is his method that of the scholarly biographer who devotes himself to the collection and orderly classification of all documents and traditions that may help to illuminate his subject. The lives of Goldsmith by Prior and Forster are written after this method, and upon them Irving depended almost entirely for his material. When asked whether he had introduced any anecdotes into his *Biography* which were not found in the above lives, he answered, No—he could not invent any new ones;

The method of the Biography.

but that he had made more of the Jessamy Bride than the earlier biographers.

It was thus neither as the exact analyst of character nor as the special student that Irving set to work on his life of Goldsmith. His endeavor was a simpler one—merely to present a picture of the character of Goldsmith as that character appealed to his sympathies. He selected his details entirely from this point of view, and what seemed to him not significant or expressive of some trait of character in his subject, he omitted. There are consequently few dates in the book, few records of fact, and practically no discussion of Goldsmith's writings considered apart from the life of their author; nor is there any attempt to estimate the value of these writings or to fix Goldsmith's place in the history of literature. The work, indeed, may be described as Irving's personal estimate of the character of Goldsmith.

It is as an attempt at sympathetic character delineation, therefore, that the book should be considered, first of all. It gives us a distinct and expressive portrait, unobscured by the confusion which results from a too great abundance of detail. The result is especially successful because the subject was one that Irving was admirably fitted to treat. Goldsmith's temper was one that Irving was heartily in sympathy with; this sympathy he has recorded in the verses from Dante which conclude the preface to the *Biography*, though, even if we did not have these verses to guide us, Goldsmith's literary influence might be readily seen all through his work. They were indeed spiritual brothers; there is in both the same whimsical humor and kindly, gentle satire, the same poetic feeling always tinged with a shade of half-hidden pathos.

The personal point of view, however, which Irving takes in his treatment of Goldsmith gives the work somewhat the character of a special plea; he rises to defend Goldsmith, to give the apology for his life. The necessity and point of such a defense is evident from the quoted criticisms of Boswell.[1] But one naturally seeks to know what conclusions other students of Goldsmith's life have arrived at, to measure Irving's estimate by comparing it with the judgment of others. To assist the student in this attempt, a number of representative estimates of Goldsmith from the pen of competent critics have been collected and are presented in an appendix. After reading Irving's *Biography* the student is advised to take up this section of the book and see how far the opinions there expressed contradict, how far they bear out, Irving's treatment of the subject.

Second after the study of the *Biography* as an effort at character appreciation, the story there presented may best be studied as that of a representative man of letters of the period. For this purpose the *Biography* offers plenty of material, concerning both Goldsmith and his contemporary fellow-craftsman, Johnson. A few words, however, of general character, may be of assistance to the student in determining the wider significance of the specific events there recorded.

Goldsmith as a representative man of letters of the eighteenth century.

First of all, it should be kept in mind that the pursuit of letters is as definitely a profession as medicine or the law and that the study of the life of an author, aside, of course, from the critical examination of his works, is largely taken up with the study of the relations that exist between him and the public that he endeavors to reach. Goldsmith's relations with his fellow-men were almost entirely literary; for, though his early years were spent in the study of medicine, of which study his doctor's title seems to be a sort of recognition by courtesy, it was only as a man of

---

[1] See below, Chapter XXXIX.

letters that he was of consequence in his own period, or is of interest to us to-day. The life of a man of letters in Goldsmith's period is of special interest to the student of literary history, for the period was a transitional one, and an understanding of the position of the author in the social and intellectual life of that day will help largely to an understanding of the whole history of the profession.

Literature as a profession, a means of livelihood, has existed from the earliest times, from the time when the wandering minstrel sang the heroic deeds of his nation or tribe and received as reward meat and drink and the protection of some powerful chief, with occasionally, perhaps, a share in the plunder of the warriors. In later times, since literature has been recorded in writing and printing, the methods by which an author gained his living from his pen may be considered in three periods. The first of these we may call the period of patronage; the second, Goldsmith's period, the period of the publishers or the booksellers; and the third, the period of modern publishing, may be best described as a system of profit sharing. According to the modern method an author does not usually sell his book outright to the publisher, but receives his pay in the form of a fixed percentage on each copy sold. This is manifestly the fairest arrangement for all concerned; the ill-success of a book is visited equally upon the publisher and the author, just as unlooked-for good fortune is shared by them in proportion. It has taken, however, many generations of books and book-makers to arrive at this practical and equitable system of profit sharing, and Goldsmith's period is interesting as marking one of the chief steps in this evolution. Before describing, however, the methods of Goldsmith's day, it will be necessary to say a word concerning the period of patronage.

Literature as a profession.

The term patronage itself describes the system. The author attached himself immediately and personally to some **Patronage.** distinguished man who had patronage to dispense, and depended for his recompense, not on the sale of his manuscripts or of his books, but on the munificence of his patron. Thus, in his early youth Chaucer attached himself to the retinue of Lionel, Duke of Clarence, and later considered himself a member of the household of John of Gaunt, Duke of Lancaster. In return for his services to his patrons, services which consisted probably largely of clerical duties, attendance on embassies, and similar tasks, he received several pensions, and, besides the pensions, appointments to offices which brought some addition to his income. His literary works themselves were never sold, and it was thus only indirectly that he gained his living from his writing. His relations towards his patrons, however, were perfectly honorable ones and implied no sense of inferiority or servility on the part of the poet. In a somewhat similar way Shakspere chose two noble patrons, the Earl of Southampton and Sir William Herbert; but we have no record of gifts from these patrons to the dramatist, and it is not probable that he was dependent upon them for his support as Chaucer was upon the Dukes of Clarence and Lancaster. In a still later time, in the early part of the eighteenth century, during the days of Addison and his contemporaries, the system of literary patronage reached its greatest development and passed into its decline. At this period also a new element entered into the system, the element of politics and adherence to political parties. In the days of Chaucer and Shakspere adherence to a patron was largely personal; whatever return the patron received from his dependent consisted in personal services or in the distinction which accrued to the patron and his family from having the poet or historian in his retinue. Tributes of respect were purely voluntary, as when, at the death of Blanche, first wife of John of Gaunt, Chaucer wrote his poem the *Boke of the Duchesse* in her memory as testimony of his allegiance to the family. In Addison's day, however, patronage was bestowed in return for political services. The author was expected to support with his pen the special tenets and principles of the party or the politician he attached himself to, and in turn he received his reward in the shape of gifts of money or of salaried offices. Thus Addison himself supported the principles of the Whig party and rose finally to the appointment of Secretary of State. Swift, Dryden, Steele, and practically all men of letters of the period, held more or less important positions under the government.

Political patronage was, on the whole, the worst development of the system of patronage, and its excesses carried with them the seeds of the destruction of the system. **Evil results of patronage.** Writers were compelled to spend much of their time and energy in the discussion of questions which could not be of more than occasional and ephemeral interest. A much greater evil, however, lay in the complete lack of independence and sincerity in which the system resulted. Men even of the highest ability came to look upon the pen merely as a tool which was rightfully at the service of the party that could pay the highest price. Then it was, as De Quincey has said, that from the noblest of professions literature became a trade. We see writers of the period changing parties and principles with an ease and, what is as remarkable, with a lack of evil consequences to themselves, that, according to our present standards, is quite inconsistent with moral and intellectual honesty. In the more private relations also of the author towards his patron, there was at this time, an utter lack of dignity and self-respect.

The author found it necessary to gain the good-will of his leaders, and this he endeavored to do by the most humiliating obsequiousness and servility. The dedications of their books were commonly used by authors to call themselves to the attention of the patrons. This practice, already familiar in the seventeenth century, "received a sudden expansion in the reign of Queen Anne, when Lord Halifax made the customary twenty guineas almost mechanical. We are told by Tickell and others that no one who dedicated a poem to Halifax came empty away; and in several cases, most notably that of Congreve, he used his great position as Chancellor of the Exchequer and afterwards First Lord of the Treasury to find for meritorious poets lucrative sinecures in the public service."[1] These dedications are frequently replete with fulsome flattery, and betray the utmost meanness of spirit. Thomson, author of the *Seasons*, in his dedication of *Summer*, in 1727, says that the character of his patron, "in which the Virtues, the Graces, and the Muses join their influence, as much exceeds the expression of the most elegant and judicious pen as the finished beauty does the representation of the pencil." We may explain away some of the extravagance of such dedications by supposing that they were looked upon as mere formalities or conventions, and were not to be understood literally any more than are the polite formalities of greeting and leave-taking in ordinary daily life. But the dedications were more than mere polite formulas; they were often in deadly earnest, and meant to the author his very daily bread.

It is to the lasting credit of Goldsmith and the men of his period that they once and for all broke away from the system of patronage and placed the profession of letters on

---

[1] "The Patron in the Eighteenth Century," *Harper's Magazine*, June, 1903. In this essay Mr. Gosse endeavors to say a good word for the patron.

a more dignified and self-respecting basis than it had ever
before occupied. This reform was not, indeed, entirely
voluntary on the part of the men of letters, for on the formation of the ministry of Sir Robert Walpole in 1721, the
system of patronage was almost entirely given up by the
political leaders. It is said that only one pension was granted
to a man of letters during the ministry of Walpole. George
II., also, who succeeded to the throne in 1727, was no patron
of letters or of art, and as he did not seek for popularity among
his people, he felt himself under no necessity of gaining the
good will of the authors, who largely form and express
the feeling of the people. On the other hand, much of the
reform was due to the sturdy honesty and independence of
such men as Pope, Johnson, and Goldsmith. The significance of Goldsmith's action in refusing the patronage of
the Earl of Northumberland, Lord Lieutenant of Ireland,
and of his declaration that he depended on the booksellers,
who were his best friends, is apparent; it was not, as it has
been called, the action of an "idiot in the affairs of the
world trifling with his fortunes," but rather the action of a
man who realized the true worth of his independence and his
own self-respect. And by the side of the servile dedications
mentioned above, should be placed the following famous
letter of Johnson's, called by Carlyle the death-knell of
patronage, in which he refuses the once-offered but long-
delayed patronage of the Earl of Chesterfield:

To the Right Honourable[1] the Earl of Chesterfield.
February 7, 1755.

My Lord,—I have been lately informed, by the proprietor of the World, that two papers in which my Dictionary
is recommended to the publick, were written by your Lord-

---

[1] The original spellings have been retained.

ship. To be so distinguished, is an honour, which being very little accustomed to favours from the great, I know not well how to receive, or in what terms to acknowledge.

When, upon some slight encouragement, I first visited your Lordship, I was overpowered, like the rest of mankind, by the enchantment of your address; and could not forbear to wish that I might boast myself *Le vainquer du vainquer de la terre;*[1]—that I might obtain that regard for which I saw the world contending; but I found my attendance so little encouraged, that neither pride nor modesty would suffer me to continue it. When I had once addressed your Lordship in publick, I had exhausted all the art of pleasing which a retired and uncourtly scholar can possess. I had done all that I could; and no man is well pleased to have his all neglected, be it ever so little.

Seven years, my Lord, have now past, since I waited in your outward rooms, or was repulsed from your door; during which time I have been pushing on my work through difficulties, of which it is useless to complain, and have brought it, at last, to the verge of publication, without one act of assistance, one word of encouragement, or one smile of favour. Such treatment I did not expect, for I never had a Patron before.

The shepherd in Virgil grew at last acquainted with Love and found him a native of the rocks.

Is not a Patron, my Lord, one who looks with unconcern on a man struggling for life in the water, and, when he has reached ground, encumbers him with help? The notice which you have been pleased to take of my labours, had it been early, had been kind; but it has been delayed until I am indifferent and cannot enjoy it; till I am solitary and cannot impart it; till I am known, and do not want it. I hope it is no very cynical asperity not to confess obligations where no benefit has been received, or to be unwilling that the publick should consider me as owing that to a Patron, which Providence has enabled me to do for myself.

Having carried on my work thus far with so little obligation to any favourer of learning, I shall not be disappointed

---

[1] The conqueror of the conqueror of the earth.

though I should conclude it, if less be possible, with less; for
I have been long wakened from that dream of hope, in which
I once boasted myself with so much exultation,

My Lord,

Your Lordship's most humble,

Most obedient servant,

SAM. JOHNSON.

It has been said that on the withdrawal of patronage the
author fell from the company of courtiers to the gutter, and
The period the phrase is hardly an extravagant expression
of the of the hardships that the average author of the
booksellers. middle and the second half of the eighteenth
century was compelled to undergo.[1] The old manner of
support was withdrawn before a new one was evolved, and
it took some time before a new and just economic equilib-
rium could be established. In the meantime, in this period
of transition, the author was the chief sufferer. Literature
was passing from the protection of patrons to that of the
public, and the necessary medium through which it must
reach the public was the bookseller. But the bookseller
was naturally at first the stronger member in the new part-
nership. He was the man of business experience who knew
how to drive sharp bargains in purchasing his wares, and
as his wants were not so pressing as those of the beggar
author, his bargains were not conditioned by his necessities.
The prices paid for literary work were consequently extremely low, besides being irregular and uncertain. This
uncertainty as to his income naturally begot in the author a
careless and extravagant habit of life. He passed from the
extremes of starvation to the extremes of dissipation; Macaulay says: "If a sum was bestowed on the wretched adventurer, such as, properly husbanded, might have supplied him

---

[1] See below, p. 129.

for six months, it was instantly spent in strange freaks of
sensuality, and, before forty-eight hours had elapsed, the
poet was again pestering all his acquaintance for twopence
to get a plate of shin of beef at a subterraneous cook-shop."
In a passage preceding the one just quoted, Macaulay gives
a vivid summary of the characteristics of this transitional
period:

"A writer had little to hope from the patronage of powerful individuals. The patronage of the public did not yet
furnish the means of comfortable subsistence. The prices
paid by booksellers to authors were so low that a man of
considerable talents and unremitting industry could do little
more than provide for the day which was passing over him.
The lean kine had eaten up the fat kine. The thin and
withered ears had devoured the good ears. The season of
rich harvest was over and the period of famine had begun.
All that is squalid and miserable might now be summed up
in the word Poet. That word denoted a creature dressed
like a scare-crow, familiar with compters and sponging-
houses, and perfectly qualified to decide on the comparative
merits of the Common Side in the King's Bench prison and
of Mount Scoundrel in the Fleet. Even the poorest pitied
him; and they well might pity him. For if their condition
was equally abject, their aspirings were not equally high nor
their sense of insult equally acute. To lodge in a garret up
four pair of stairs, to dine in a cellar among footmen out of
place, to translate ten hours a day for the wages of a ditcher,
to be hunted by bailiffs from one haunt of beggary and pes-
tilence to another, from Grub Street to St. George's Fields,
and from St. George's Fields to the alleys behind St. Mar-
tin's Church, to sleep on a bulk in June, and amidst the
ashes of a glass-house in December, to die in an hospital
and to be buried in a parish-vault, was the fate of more than
one writer who, if he had lived thirty years earlier, would
have been admitted to the sittings of the Kit-cat or the Scrib-
lerus club, would have sat in Parliament, and would have
been entrusted with embassies to the High Allies; who, if
he had lived in our time, would have found encouragement

scarcely less munificent in Albemarle Street or in Paternoster Row."—*Essay on Croker's Edition of Boswell's Life of Johnson.*

But this is plainly the dark side of the picture. Macaulay is speaking here specifically of Johnson's early years in London when, possibly, the fortunes of authors were at a lower ebb than when Goldsmith began his literary career some ten or fifteen years later. In the *Citizen of the World* (Letter 84) Goldsmith himself says "a writer of real merit now may easily be rich, if his heart be set only on fortune: and for those who have no merit, it is but fit that such should remain in merited obscurity." And after his first few years of struggling his own income was more than sufficient to satisfy the needs of moderate living.

Of this income, with Goldsmith as with the other writers of his period, the greater part was derived from that occupation known as hack-writing, or in Goldsmith's own phrase, book-building. In this business of **Hack-writing.** book-building Goldsmith was always deeply involved; at least one half of all his published writings might fairly come under this head. And that Goldsmith was no exception is evident from the frequent allusions to the hack-writer in the literature of the period. He was a familiar type and the object of much satire. Naturally the typical figure in these satirical pictures is not the man who ground out books on subjects that he was capable of treating, but the one who attempted subjects of which he was ignorant. Goldsmith himself was not entirely free of this fault, as we learn from Irving's account of his *Animated Nature.* He might, indeed, have been in Smollett's mind when the latter wrote his amusing description of a dinner-party of hack-writers in his novel *Humphrey Clinker.* The guests at this party were accustomed to meet together on

Sunday, as that was the only day on which they were safe from arrest for debt. They were all men who had translated, compiled, or abridged from the works of others, and their usual fate had been to write on those subjects about which they knew least. There was a Scotchman who gave lectures on the pronunciation of the English language, and the author of a book of travels through Europe and Asia, who had never been outside of London; a third "who labored under the αγροφοβια, or *horror of green fields*, had just finished a treatise on practical agriculture, though, in fact, he had never seen corn growing in his life, and was so ignorant of grain that our entertainer, in the face of the whole company, made him own, that a plate of hominy was the best rice-pudding he had ever ate." Books written with such equipment might well be not only as interesting as a Persian tale, as Johnson predicted that Goldsmith's *Natural History* would be, but also quite as wonderful. On another occasion Johnson said, concerning Goldsmith's venture, "Goldsmith, sir, will give us a very fine book upon the subject, but if he can distinguish a cow from a horse that, I believe, may be the extent of his knowledge of natural history."

The whole tribe of hack-writers was dependent on the bookseller. He was their Maecenas and their task-master in one. In the life of Goldsmith, we have much to do with one who may stand as a typical representative of the class, Mr. John Newbery, publisher and general promoter of profitable industries. This worthy, born in 1713, the son of a small farmer, began life as an apprentice to a newspaper printer in Reading. On the death of his master, he thriftily paid addresses to the widow, and having won her, thus became proprietor of the business. Besides the publication of his newspaper, which was of course a much simpler undertaking

A bookseller of the eighteenth century.

at that time than at present, he carried on a general publishing business and a miscellaneous traffic in cutlery, haberdashery, and medicines of various kinds. In 1744 he shifted the center of his activities to London, still continuing his trade in books and patent medicines. Of the latter, his most famous product was a composition known as Dr. James's Fever Powders, just at that time a fashionable and popular remedy. The story of the Fever Powders is not only illustrative of Mr. Newbery's business ventures, but as well of the state of eighteenth century medical practice. The powders were the discovery of a Dr. James, a physician of respectable standing, and were supposed to be a cure for all ills that flesh is heir to. They were used in tremendous quantities, Dr. James and Newbery, his partner, both becoming rich men from their sale. It is not necessary to suppose that they were an entire fraud, though the indiscriminate use of them must often have resulted in much injury, as we know happened in the case of Goldsmith.[1] It was a period however, when quackery flourished and, in the end, one nostrum was as bad as another. Fleet Street was the favorite haunt of the quacks, and the signs in front of their shops lured the unwary by their splendid promises. The notable thing is not that such wares were offered for sale and bought in large quantities, but that they should have numbered among their victims the most intelligent members of the community. A most remarkable and, on the part of the originator, honest delusion, was that concerning the tarwater remedy exploited by Bishop Berkeley, a name frequently occurring in the pages of Irving's *Biography.* A distinguished writer and a profound thinker on philosophical subjects, Berkeley published in 1744 a work entitled *Siris,* which is primarily an argument for the medicinal

[1] See below, p. 325.

virtues of tar-water. Straightway, Sir Walter Besant tells us,[1] all the world was using tar-water for everything, and there was not a corner of the land where it was not found for sale. With these successes of quackery in mind, we have reason to feel grateful that Goldsmith was not successful in the practice of medicine.

Another business venture of Mr. Newbery's was the publication of children's books. They were not, on the whole, bad children's books; *Goody Two Shoes*, which seems pretty certainly to have been the work of Goldsmith,[2] is still occasionally reprinted for the modern reader. But to speak of Mr. Newbery as "the philanthropic publisher of St. Paul's Churchyard," as Goldsmith is supposed to do in his *Vicar of Wakefield*, is generously to place stress on a motive that probably very slightly moved him. The children's books were frankly a business venture, as the patent medicines were, and in some of the books the two interests were ludicrously combined. Thus, in *Goody Two Shoes*, we are told that the little heroine's father was "seized with a violent fever in a place where Dr. James's Fever Powder was not to be had, and where he died miserably." Similar examples of "puffing" are to be found in this as well as in other of Mr. Newbery's children's books. Yet withal, such offences must be counted as rather against good taste than honesty, and good taste was probably not a quality to which Mr. Newbery made any pretensions. The worthy publisher was evidently an efficient business man, a man of many affairs, industrious, shrewd, and ingenious, though truly not burdened with much understanding of literature or much sense of its dignity. The sensitive author might flinch at the necessity of bringing forth his creations

---

[1] *London in the Eighteenth Century*, p. 369 ff.
[2] See below, p. 204.

under such patronage, at having them ranked lower
than the Fever Powders because less profitable, but he
always had the compensation of knowing that he was
the victim of ignorance and stupidity, that his money
was honestly earned, and that he got less than he
deserved.

There is still one other of the many sides of interest of
the *Biography* to which the attention of the reader should
perhaps be drawn, and that is its interest and value as giving
us glimpses of the life of eighteenth century London.
Goldsmith's London represents a picturesque and interesting phase in the ever-changing history of
Goldsmith's the great city. The city was then not so
London. large or its interests so many and diverse
but that it still retained somewhat the character of a
town. There were, of course, groups and classes of people,
ranging from the business world, called technically the
City, with no interests beyond business, up to the great
world of exclusive fashion. But bewteen the two there
remained a homogeneous body of citizens, men of like
interests who lived in the same community, not in
scattered suburbs, that might be denominated the Town.
To be well known was to be known of practically all
the people of the Town—to meet them in the coffee-
houses or at the play-house, to be able to gossip about
and be interested in the trivial affairs of their every-day
life. In this community conversation, the most rational
of social pleasures, flourished, encouraged as it was by
the frequent gatherings in the clubs and coffee-houses.
The last poem or pamphlet or witty saying, was amply
discussed and the appropriate amount of praise or
blame was bestowed upon its author. It was preëmi-
nently a social period, and to live in it must have been

the keenest pleasure to a man of Goldsmith's social temper.

The life of the Town in the eighteenth century centered in Fleet Street and the adjoining streets. The chief shops, inns, and coffee-houses were in this neighborhood.

London streets. Here also was the habitat of authors; Dr. Johnson declared that between the hours of twelve and four every sixth man who passed under Temple Bar was an author. Fleet Street is still the home of the London newspapers and magazines and the eighteenth century author probably lived there because he was near to the booksellers and printing-offices. It was Dr. Johnson's favorite street, and Goldsmith's years in London were passed in regions just off Fleet Street. At the western end of Fleet Street stood Temple Bar, separating Fleet Street from its extension, the Strand; near Temple Bar were the entrances to the Temple Gardens and buildings, where Goldsmith's last years were passed. A short distance up the Strand was and is Charing Cross, at which place Dr. Johnson once remarked there "flowed the full tide of human existence."

Animated this region may have been, but it can hardly have been an attractive dwelling-place. The Fleet must have been a narrow, crowded, jostling, noisy, dirty street, smoke and fog begrimed in the day-time and almost without lighting at night. Though probably the most frequented street of the city, it was often dangerous to be abroad upon it at night unprotected. In the summer time the watch was not set until ten o'clock, in the winter until nine; and often, before the watch was set, and afterwards in spite of the watch, roving bands of rowdies took possession of the street. The probable appearance of the street may be learned from the following description by Sir Walter Besant of a typical eighteenth century street:

"There were no kerbs; in the middle of the street ran a gutter, sometimes foul, sometimes a succession of noisome puddles, sometimes a rapid stream, the splashing from which, when a cart or carriage passed along, was fatal to white silk stockings and neatly brushed shoes. At intervals there were causeways by which the street could be crossed; these consisted of broader stones than those which composed the rudimentary paving. The less important streets had no posts [to protect people on the pathway or sidewalk], and in such cases there was danger of being run over by a cart. . . . The dangers of the streets were many and various, though by bringing them all together we may present a greatly exaggerated picture. One was not always thrust out into the kennel by swaggering bullies; the cart did not always have an opportunity of splashing the passengers; the tiles did not always drop on the heads of the people; nor were they always struck by falling fragments of masonry; nor did the oil of the street lamp always drop on the heads of those who walked below."—*London in the Eighteenth Century*, p. 89.

Green Arbor Court, at which place Goldsmith took up his residence in 1758, was but a minute's distance from Fleet

Green Arbor Court.

Street. It was not a cheerful neighborhood. Near by was the Old Bailey Sessions House where all prisoners taken within twelve miles of London were tried, and, when condemned, were executed within free gaze of an admiring public. In a period when a man might be hanged for stealing a pocket-handkerchief, the number of executions was appallingly large. In the immediate vicinity was also Newgate Prison, famous in the annals of British crime. The Court itself has been vividly described by Irving,[1] and its appearance in Goldsmith's day doubtless differed little from its appearance at the time of Irving's visit. A less appropriate name than Green Arbor for this miserable little square could hardly be imagined.

---

[1] See below, p. 152.

It is pleasant to know that Goldsmith's last years were spent in the comparative peace of the Temple. This ancient **The Temple.** foundation, originally the residence of the crusading Knights Templars in the twelfth century, passed in the fourteenth century into the hands of the students of the law, and since that time it has occupied a memorable position in the history of English scholarship and letters. The buildings, with their gardens and courts, still stand just without the noise and bustle of Fleet Street; and with Irving's description of Green Arbor Court we may well contrast this description of the Temple, taken from his essay, *London Antiques*, in the *Sketch Book:*

"I had been buffeting for some time against the current of population setting through Fleet Street. The warm weather had unstrung my nerves, and made me sensitive to every jar and jostle and discordant sound. The flesh was weary, the spirit faint, and I was getting out of humor with the bustling, busy throng through which I had to struggle, when in a fit of desperation I tore my way through the crowd, plunged into a bye-lane, and after passing through several obscure nooks and angles, emerged into a quaint and quiet court with a grass plot in the center, overhung by elms and kept perpetually fresh and green by a fountain with its sparkling jet of water. A student with book in hand was seated on a stone bench, partly reading, partly meditating on the movements of two or three trim nursery maids with their infant charges.

"I was like an Arab who had suddenly come upon an oasis amid the panting sterility of the desert. By degrees the quiet and coolness of the place soothed my nerves and refreshed my spirit. I pursued my walk and came, hard by, to a very ancient chapel, with a low-browed Saxon portal of massive and rich architecture. The interior was circular and lofty and lighted from above. Around were monumental tombs of ancient date, on which were extended the marble effigies of warriors in armor. Some had the hands devoutly crossed upon the breast; others grasped the pommel of the sword, menacing hostility even in the tomb!—while the crossed legs of several indicated soldiers of the Faith who had been on crusades to the Holy Land.

"I was, in fact, in the chapel of the Knights Templars, strangely situated in the very center of sordid traffic and I do not know a more impressive lesson for the man of the world than thus suddenly to turn aside from the highway of busy, money-seeking life, and sit down among these shadowy sepulchres, where all is twilight, dust, and forgetfulness."

Such are a few of the conditions under which Goldsmith lived and wrote. It may seem that, in the foregoing paragraphs, the unpleasant sides of the life of an eighteenth century man of letters have been unduly emphasized. But in truth the picture we get of the literary life of that day, as it is presented for example in the biography of Goldsmith, is not one to arouse our envy. There was much in the life that was sordid, much that was painful and hard to bear. It was not the period when the graceful dilettante flourished. Only a serious and deep sense of the necessity of writing could give a man courage to face the hardships that confronted the professional writer of the period. And indeed the attitude of such men as Johnson and Goldsmith towards literature is above all manly and vigorous; there is no sentimentalizing on their part, no ascribing of false values to the offspring of their pens. Their writings are characterized by a directness and truth which is born of the hard reality of the experiences through which it was their fate to pass. These writings, it should never be forgotten, are after all our object of chief concern, and no student will stop short of them. The best complement to the life of Goldsmith is the writings of Goldsmith, to which as corollary may be added the writings of Johnson; and the student who wishes to understand Goldsmith and his period cannot do better than devote his time to the works of these two authors.

III. BIBLIOGRAPHY

Irving's works are published in several standard editions by G. P. Putnam's Sons, New York City.

The Life and Letters of Washington Irving, by his nephew, Pierre M. Irving, was published in four volumes, New York, 1862–64. A new edition, revised and condensed into three volumes, was published by the Putnams in 1895. This *Life* is of special value because it is the only place in which Irving's letters and travelling journal are accessible. A shorter life is Charles Dudley Warner's *Washington Irving,* Boston, 1881, in the American Men of Letters series. Mr. Warner also has a briefer sketch prefixed to the Geoffrey Crayon edition of Irving's works, and a short study in a separate volume, *Work of Washington Irving,* published by Harpers. There are few critical works of importance. Besides the several studies by Warner given above and the standard histories of American literature, the following may be mentioned: George William Curtis, in *Literary and Social Essays;* Edwin W. Morse, in *Historians and Essayists* the Warner Classics (Doubleday and McClure Company), pp. 143–168; and for a discussion of the national element in Irving, Lodge, *Studies in History,* pp. 344–46.

Besides the lives of Goldsmith by Prior (1837), Forster (1848), and Dobson (1888), may be mentioned one by William Black (1878) in the English Men of Letters series. To the essays on Goldsmith by Carlyle, Macaulay, Thackeray, and De Quincey mentioned in the appendix (p. 408) may be added one by Leigh Hunt in his *Classic Tales.* For the general life of the period Boswell's *Life of Johnson* (best edition by G. B. Hill), Dobson's *Eighteenth Century Vignettes,* and Besant's recent book, *London in the Eighteenth Century,* may be consulted.

CHRONOLOGICAL TABLE

LIFE AND WORKS OF GOLDSMITH.	GENERAL ENGLISH LITERATURE.	GENERAL HISTORY AND FOREIGN LITERATURE.
1728. Nov. 10, Goldsmith born.	1631-1700. John Dryden.	1697-1764. Hogarth.
1749. Feb. 27, takes his B. A. degree.	1667. *Paradise Lost.*	1714-1727. George I.
1753-1756. Travels and studies on the Continent.	1672-1719. Joseph Addison.	1716-1779. David Garrick.
1759. *Enquiry into the Present State of Polite Learning in Europe.*	1671-1729. Sir Richard Steele.	1723-1792. Sir Joshua Reynolds.
The Bee.	1688-1744. Alexander Pope.	1727-1760. George II.
Makes the acquaintance of Johnson.	1751. *Elegy in a Country Churchyard.*	1746. Princeton College founded.
1762. *Citizen of the World.*	1764. Horace Walpole, *The Castle of Otranto.*	Battle of Culloden.
1764. *History of England in a Series of Letters.*	1771. *Encyclopædia Britannica.* 1st edition, 3 volumes.	1750. Black Hole of Calcutta.
Becomes a member of the Literary Club.	1772. *Letters of Junius* (collected edition).	1757. Voltaire, *Candide.*
The Traveller.	1774. Earl of Chesterfield. *Letters to His Son.*	1760-1820. George III.
1765. *Essays* (a collection of previously published essays).	1775. Sheridan, *The Rivals.*	1762. Rousseau, *Contrat Social.*
1766. *Vicar of Wakefield* (probably written in 1762).	1777. Sheridan, *The School for Scandal.*	1765. Stamp Act.
History of Little Goody Two Shoes (attributed to Goldsmith).	1776-88. Gibbon, *The History of the Decline and Fall of the Roman Empire.*	1768. Royal Academy founded.
The Good-Natur'd Man.	1777. Publication of the collected works of Thomas Chatterton.	1769. Napoleon born.
1768. *Roman History.*	1785. Cowper, *The Task.*	1773. Goethe, *Götz von Berlichingen.*
1769. Elected professor of History to the Royal Academy.	1791. Boswell, *Life of Dr Johnson.*	1775. Beginning of the war of American Independence.
1770. *The Deserted Village.*	1796. Death of Robert Burns.	1778. Death of Voltaire.
Makes a visit to Paris.	1770-1850. William Wordsworth.	Death of Rousseau.
1771. *History of England.*	1771-1832. Sir Walter Scott.	1782. Independence of the United States acknowledged.
1773. *She Stoops to Conquer.*	1775-1834. Charles Lamb.	1789. Storming of the Bastille.
1774. April 4, death of Goldsmith.	1729-1797. Edmund Burke.	
April 19, *Retaliation.*		
June, *History of the Earth and Animated Nature.*		
1776. *The Haunch of Venison.*		

PREFACE

In the course of a revised edition of my works I have come to a biographical sketch of Goldsmith, published several years since. It was written hastily, as introductory to a selection from his writings; and, though the facts contained in it were collected from various sources, I was chiefly indebted for them to the voluminous work of Mr. James Prior, who had collected and collated the most minute particulars of the poet's history with unwearied research and scrupulous fidelity; but had rendered them, as I thought, in a form too cumbrous and overlaid with details and disquisitions, and matters uninteresting to the general reader.   .

When I was about of late to revise my biographical sketch, preparatory to republication, a volume was put into my hands, recently given to the public by Mr. John Forster, of the Inner Temple, who, likewise availing himself of the labors of the indefatigable Prior, and of a few new lights since evolved, has produced a biography of the poet, executed with a spirit, a feeling, a grace, and an eloquence, that leave nothing to be desired.   Indeed it would have been presumption in me to undertake the subject after it had been thus felicitously treated, did I not stand committed by my previous sketch. That sketch now appeared too meagre and insufficient to satisfy public demand; yet it had to take its place in the revised series of my works unless something more satisfactory could be substituted.   Under these circumstances I have again taken up the subject, and gone into it with more fulness than formerly, omitting none of the facts which I considered illustrative of the life and character of the poet, and giving them in as graphic a style as I could command. Still the hurried manner in which I have had to do this amidst the pressure of other claims on my attention, and with the press dogging at my heels, has prevented me from giving some parts of the subject the thorough handling I could have wished. Those who would like to see it treated still more at large, with the addition of critical disquisitions and the advantage of collateral facts, would do well to refer themselves to Mr. Prior's circumstantial volumes, or to the elegant and discursive pages of Mr. Forster.

For my own part, I can only regret my shortcomings in what to me is a labor of love; for it is a tribute of gratitude to the memory of an author whose writings were the delight of my childhood, and have been a source of enjoyment to me throughout life; and to whom, of all others, I may address the beautiful apostrophe of Dante to Virgil,—

> Tu se' lo mio maestro, e 'l mio autore:
> Tu se' solo colui, da cu' io tolsi
> Lo bello stile, che m' ha fatto onore.[1]

W. I.

Sunnyside, Aug. 1, 1849.

---

[1] Thou art my master and my author; thou alone art he from whom I took the fair style that hath done me honor.—Dante, *Divine Comedy*, tr. by C. E. Norton, Vol. I, p. 4.

OLIVER GOLDSMITH

CHAPTER I

BIRTH AND PARENTAGE — CHARACTERISTICS OF THE GOLDSMITH
RACE — POETICAL BIRTHPLACE — GOBLIN HOUSE — SCENES OF
BOYHOOD—LISSOY—PICTURE OF A COUNTRY PARSON — GOLD-
SMITH'S SCHOOLMISTRESS — BYRNE, THE VILLAGE SCHOOL-
MASTER — GOLDSMITH'S HORNPIPE AND EPIGRAM — UNCLE
CONTARINE — SCHOOL STUDIES AND SCHOOL SPORTS — MIS-
TAKES OF A NIGHT.

There are few writers for whom the reader feels such
personal kindness as for Oliver Goldsmith, for few have so
eminently possessed the magic gift of identifying themselves
with their writings. We read his character in every page,
and grow into familiar intimacy with him as we read. The
artless benevolence that beams throughout his works; the
whimsical, yet amiable views of human life and human nature;
the unforced humor, blending so happily with good feeling
and good sense, and singularly dashed at times with a pleasing melancholy; even the very nature of his mellow, and
flowing, and softly-tinted style,—all seem to bespeak his
moral as well as his intellectual qualities, and make us love
the man at the same time that we admire the author. While
the productions of writers of loftier pretension and more
sounding names are suffered to moulder on our shelves,
those of Goldsmith are cherished and laid in our bosoms.
We do not quote them with ostentation, but they mingle

with our minds, sweeten our tempers, and harmonize our thoughts; they put us in good-humor with ourselves and with the world, and in so doing they make us happier and better men.

An acquaintance with the private biography of Goldsmith lets us into the secret of his gifted pages. We there discover them to be little more than transcripts of his own heart and picturings of his fortunes. There he shows himself the same kind, artless, good-humored, excursive, sensible, whimsical, intelligent being that he appears in his writings. Scarcely an adventure or character is given in his works that may not be traced to his own parti-colored story. Many of his most ludicrous scenes and ridiculous incidents have been drawn from his own blunders and mischances, and he seems really to have been buffeted into almost every maxim imparted by him for the instruction of his reader.

Oliver Goldsmith was born on the 10th of November, 1728, at the hamlet of Pallas, or Pallasmore, county of Longford, in Ireland. He sprang from a respectable, but by no means a thrifty stock.[1] Some families seem to inherit kindliness and incompetency, and to hand down virtue and poverty from generation to generation. Such was the case with the Goldsmiths. "They were always," according to their own accounts, "a strange family; they rarely acted like other people; their hearts were in the right place, but their heads seemed to be doing anything but what they ought."—"They were remarkable," says another statement, "for their worth, but of no cleverness in the ways of the world." Oliver Goldsmith will be found faithfully to inherit the virtues and weaknesses of his race.

---

[1] "If the researches of the first biographers of Oliver Goldsmith are to be relied upon, the Goldsmith family was of English origin, the Irish branch having migrated from this country [England] to Ireland somewhere about the sixteenth century."—DOBSON, *Life*, p. 11.

His father, the Rev. Charles Goldsmith, with hereditary improvidence, married when very young and very poor, and starved along for several years on a small country curacy and the assistance of his wife's friends. His whole income, eked out by the produce of some fields which he farmed, and of some occasional duties performed for his wife's uncle, the rector of an adjoining parish, did not exceed forty pounds.

"And passing rich with forty pounds a year."[1]

He inhabited an old, half rustic mansion, that stood on a rising ground in a rough, lonely part of the country, over-looking a low tract occasionally flooded by the river Inny. In this house Goldsmith was born, and it was a birthplace worthy of a poet; for, by all accounts, it was haunted ground. A tradition handed down among the neighboring peasantry states that, in after-years, the house, remaining for some time untenanted, went to decay, the roof fell in, and it became so lonely and forlorn as to be a resort for the "good people" or fairies, who in Ireland are supposed to delight in old, crazy, deserted mansions for their midnight revels. All attempts to repair it were in vain; the fairies battled stoutly to main-tain possession. A huge misshapen hobgoblin used to bestride the house every evening with an immense pair of jackboots, which, in his efforts at hard riding, he would thrust through the roof, kicking to pieces all the work of the preceding day. The house was therefore left to its fate, and went to ruin.

Such is the popular tradition about Goldsmith's birth-place. About two years after his birth a change came over the circumstances of his father. By the death of his wife's uncle he succeeded to the rectory of Kilkenny West; and, abandoning the old goblin mansion, he removed to Lissoy,

---

[1] *Deserted Village*, l. 142.

in the county of Westmeath, where he occupied a farm of seventy acres, situated on the skirts of that pretty little village.

This was the scene of Goldsmith's boyhood, the little world whence he drew many of those pictures, rural and domestic, whimsical and touching, which abound throughout his works, and which appeal so eloquently both to the fancy and the heart. Lissoy is confidently cited as the original of his "Auburn" in the "Deserted Village"; his father's establishment, a mixture of farm and parsonage, furnished hints, it is said, for the rural economy of the "Vicar of Wakefield"; and his father himself, with his learned simplicity, his guileless wisdom, his amiable piety, and utter ignorance of the world, has been exquisitely portrayed in the worthy Dr. Primrose. Let us pause for a moment, and draw from Goldsmith's writings one or two of those pictures which, under feigned names, represent his father and his family, and the happy fireside of his childish days.

"My father," says the "Man in Black," who, in some respects, is a counterpart of Goldsmith himself,—"my father, the younger son of a good family, was possessed of a small living in the church. His education was above his fortune, and his generosity greater than his education. Poor as he was, he had his flatterers poorer than himself: for every dinner he gave them, they returned him an equivalent in praise; and this was all he wanted. The same ambition that actuates a monarch at the head of his army, influenced my father at the head of his table; he told the story of the ivy-tree, and that was laughed at; he repeated the jest of the two scholars and one pair of breeches, and the company laughed at that; but the story of Taffy in the sedan-chair was sure to set the table in a roar. Thus his pleasure increased in proportion to the pleasure he gave; he loved all the world, and he fancied all the world loved him.

"As his fortune was but small, he lived up to the very extent of it: he had no intention of leaving his children money, for that was dross; he resolved they should have learning, for learning, he used to observe, was better than silver or gold. For this purpose he undertook to instruct us himself, and took as much care to form our morals as to improve our understanding. We were told that universal benevolence was what first cemented society: we were taught to consider all the wants of mankind as our own; to regard the *human face divine* with affection and esteem; he wound us up to be mere machines of pity, and rendered us incapable of withstanding the slightest impulse made either by real or fictitious distress. In a word, we were perfectly instructed in the art of giving away thousands before we were taught the necessary qualifications of getting a farthing."[1]

In the "Deserted Village" we have another picture of his father and his father's fireside:—

"His house was known to all the vagrant train,
He chid their wanderings, but relieved their pain;
The long-remembered beggar was his guest,
Whose beard, descending, swept his aged breast;
The ruin'd spendthrift, now no longer proud,
Claim'd kindred there, and had his claims allow'd;
The broken soldier, kindly bade to stay,
Sat by his fire, and talked the night away;
Wept o'er his wounds, or tales of sorrow done,
Shoulder'd his crutch, and show'd how fields were won.
Pleased with his guests, the good man learned to glow,
And quite forgot their vices in their woe;
Careless their merits or their faults to scan,
His pity gave ere charity began."

---

[1] *Citizen of the World*, Letter XXVII. This and the preceding Letter, XXVI, though purporting to be a description of the "Man in Black," are manifestly largely autobiographical.

The family of the worthy pastor consisted of five sons and three daughters. Henry, the eldest, was the good man's pride and hope, and he tasked his slender means to the utmost in educating him for a learned and distinguished career. Oliver was the second son, and seven years younger than Henry, who was the guide and protector of his childhood, and to whom he was most tenderly attached throughout life.

Oliver's education began when he was about three years old; that is to say, he was gathered under the wings of one of those good old motherly dames, found in every village, who cluck together the whole callow brood of the neighborhood, to teach them their letters and keep them out of harm's way. Mistress Elizabeth Delap, for that was her name, flourished in this capacity for upward of fifty years, and it was the pride and boast of her declining days, when nearly ninety years of age, that she was the first that had put a book (doubtless a hornbook[1]) into Goldsmith's hands. Apparently he did not much profit by it, for she confessed he was one of the dullest boys she had ever dealt with, insomuch that she had sometimes doubted whether it was possible to make anything of him: a common case with imaginative children, who are apt to be beguiled from the dry abstractions of elementary study by the picturings of the fancy.

At six years of age he passed into the hands of the village schoolmaster, one Thomas (or, as he was commonly and irreverently named, Paddy) Byrne, a capital tutor for a poet. He had been educated for a pedagogue, but had enlisted in

---

[1] "It [a hornbook] consisted of a small sheet of paper, generally about 4 in. by 3 in. or so —sometimes smaller—on which was printed the alphabet, both in capitals and small text, the vowels and a few simple combinations such as ab, eb, ob, ub—ba, be, bi, bo, bu, etc., and the Lord's Prayer. This was laid on a flat piece of board with a roughly shaped handle, and covered with a thin plate of horn, fastened to the board by copper tacks driven through an edging of thin copper."—WELSH, *A Book-seller of the Last Century*, p. 91.

the army, served abroad during the wars of Queen Anne's time, and risen to the rank of quartermaster of a regiment in Spain. At the return of peace, having no longer exercise for the sword, he resumed the ferule, and drilled the urchin populace of Lissoy. Goldsmith is supposed to have had him and his school in view in the following sketch in his "Deserted Village":—

"Beside yon straggling fence that skirts the way,
With blossom'd furze unprofitably gay,
There, in his noisy mansion, skill'd to rule,
The village master taught his little school;
A man severe he was, and stern to view,
I knew him well, and every truant knew:
Well had the boding tremblers learn'd to trace
The day's disasters in his morning face;
Full well they laugh'd with counterfeited glee
At all his jokes, for many a joke had he;
Full well the busy whisper circling round,
Convey'd the dismal tidings when he frown'd:
Yet he was kind, or, if severe in aught,
The love he bore to learning was in fault;
The village all declared how much he knew,
'T was certain he could write, and cipher too;
Lands he could measure, terms and tides presage,
And e'en the story ran that he could gauge:
In arguing, too, the parson own'd his skill,
For, e'en though vanquished, he could argue still;
While words of learned length and thund'ring sound
Amazed the gazing rustics, ranged around,—
And still they gazed, and still the wonder grew,
That one small head could carry all he knew."

There are certain whimsical traits in the character of Byrne, not given in the foregoing sketch. He was fond of talking of his vagabond wanderings in foreign lands, and had brought with him from the wars a world of campaigning stories, of which he was generally the hero, and which

he would deal forth to his wondering scholars when he ought
to have been teaching them their lessons. These travellers'
tales had a powerful effect upon the vivid imagination of
Goldsmith, and awakened an unconquerable passion for
wandering and seeking adventure.

Byrne was, moreover, of a romantic vein, and exceedingly
superstitious. He was deeply versed in the fairy supersti-
tions which abound in Ireland, all which he professed
implicitly to believe. Under his tuition Goldsmith soon
became almost as great a proficient in fairy lore. From
this branch of good-for-nothing knowledge his studies, by
an easy transition, extended to the histories of robbers,
pirates, smugglers, and the whole race of Irish rogues and
rapparees. Everything, in short, that savored of romance,
fable, and adventure, was congenial to his poetic mind, and
took instant root there; but the slow plants of useful knowledge were apt to be overrun, if not choked, by the weeds of
his quick imagination.

Another trait of his motley preceptor, Byrne, was a disposition to dabble in poetry, and this likewise was caught
by his pupil. Before he was eight years old, Goldsmith had
contracted a habit of scribbling verses on small scraps of
paper, which, in a little while, he would throw into the fire.
A few of these sibylline leaves, however, were rescued from
the flames and conveyed to his mother. The good woman
read them with a mother's delight, and saw at once that her
son was a genius and a poet. From that time she beset her
husband with solicitations to give the boy an education suitable to his talents. The worthy man was already straitened
by the costs of instruction of his eldest son Henry, and had intended to bring his second son up to a trade; but the mother
would listen to no such thing; as usual, her influence
prevailed, and Oliver, instead of being instructed in some

humble, but cheerful and gainful handicraft, was devoted to poverty and the Muse.

A severe attack of the small-pox caused him to be taken from under the care of his story-telling preceptor, Byrne. His malady had nearly proved fatal, and his face remained pitted through life. On his recovery he was placed under the charge of the Rev. Mr. Griffin, schoolmaster of Elphin, in Roscommon, and became an inmate in the house of his uncle, John Goldsmith, Esq., of Ballyoughter, in that vicinity. He now entered upon studies of a higher order, but without making any uncommon progress. Still a careless easy facility of disposition, an amusing eccentricity of manners, and a vein of quiet and peculiar humor, rendered him a general favorite, and a trifling incident soon induced his uncle's family to concur in his mother's opinion of his genius.

A number of young folks had assembled at his uncle's to dance. One of the company, named Cummings, played on the violin. In the course of the evening Oliver undertook a hornpipe. His short and clumsy figure, and his face pitted and discolored with the small-pox, rendered him a ludicrous figure in the eyes of the musician, who made merry at his expense, dubbing him his little Æsop. Goldsmith was nettled by the jest, and, stopping short in the hornpipe, exclaimed,—

> "Our herald hath proclaimed this saying,
> See Æsop dancing, and his monkey playing."

The repartee was thought wonderful for a boy of nine years old, and Oliver became forthwith the wit and the bright genius of the family. It was thought a pity he should not receive the same advantages with his elder brother Henry, who had been sent to the University; and, as his father's circumstances would not afford it, several of his relatives, spurred on by the representations of his mother,

agreed to contribute towards the expense. The greater part,
however, was borne by his uncle, the Rev. Thomas Contarine. This worthy man had been the college companion
of Bishop Berkeley [1] and was possessed of moderate means,
holding the living of Carrick-on-Shannon. He had married
the sister of Goldsmith's father, but was now a widower,
with an only child a daughter, named Jane. Contarine
was a kind-hearted man, with a generosity beyond his means.
He took Goldsmith into favor from his infancy; his house was
open to him during the holidays; his daughter Jane, two years
older than the poet, was his early playmate; and uncle Contarine continued to the last one of his most active, unwavering, and generous friends.

Fitted out in a great measure by this considerate relative,
Oliver was now transferred to schools of a higher order, to
prepare him for the University; first to one at Athlone, kept
by the Rev. Mr. Campbell, and, at the end of two years, to
one at Edgeworthstown, under the superintendence of the
Rev. Patrick Hughes.

Even at these schools his proficiency does not appear to
have been brilliant. He was indolent and careless, however,
rather than dull, and, on the whole, appears to have been
well thought of by his teachers. In his studies he inclined
towards the Latin poets and historians; relished Ovid and
Horace, and delighted in Livy. He exercised himself with
pleasure in reading and translating Tacitus, and was brought
to pay attention to style in his compositions by a reproof
from his brother Henry, to whom he had written brief and
confused letters, and who told him in reply, that, if he had
but little to say, to endeavor to say that little well.

The career of his brother Henry at the University was

---

[1] George Berkeley (1685-1753), bishop of Cloyne, a writer on philosophical
subjects; see Introduction p. 45.

enough to stimulate him to exertion. He seemed to be real-
izing all his father's hopes, and was winning collegiate
honors that the good man considered indicative of his future
success in life.

In the meanwhile, Oliver, if not distinguished among his
teachers, was popular among his schoolmates. He had a
thoughtless generosity extremely captivating to young hearts:
his temper was quick and sensitive, and easily offended;
but his anger was momentary, and it was impossible for him
to harbor resentment. He was the leader of all boyish
sports, and athletic amusements, especially ball-playing, and
he was foremost in all mischievous pranks. Many years
afterward, an old man, Jack Fitzsimmons, one of the direc-
tors of the sports, and keeper of the ball-court at Ballymahon,
used to boast of having been schoolmate of "Noll Goldsmith,"
as he called him, and would dwell with vainglory on one of
their exploits, in robbing the orchard of Tirlicken, an old
family residence of Lord Annaly. The exploit, however,
had nearly involved disastrous consequences; for the crew
of juvenile depredators were captured, like Shakspere and
his deer-stealing colleagues; and nothing but the respecta-
bility of Goldsmith's connections saved him from the punishment that would have awaited more plebeian delinquents.

An amusing incident is related as occurring in Goldsmith's
last journey homeward from Edgeworthstown. His father's
house was about twenty miles distant; the road lay through
a rough country, impassable for carriages. Goldsmith procured a horse for the journey, and a friend furnished him
with a guinea for travelling expenses. He was but a stripling
of sixteen,[1] and being thus suddenly mounted on horseback,
with money in his pocket, it is no wonder that his head was

---

[1] According to Dobson, *Life*, p. 17, Goldsmith was between fourteen and
fifteen years of age at the time of this adventure.

turned. He determined to play the man, and to spend his money in independent traveller's style. Accordingly, instead of pushing directly for home, he halted for the night at the little town of Ardagh, and, accosting the first person he met, inquired, with somewhat of a consequential air, for the best house in the place. Unluckily, the person he had accosted was one Kelly, a notorious wag, who was quartered in the family of one Mr. Featherstone, a gentleman of fortune. Amused with the self-consequence of the stripling, and willing to play off a practical joke at his expense, he directed him to what was literally "the best house in the place," namely, the family mansion of Mr. Featherstone. Goldsmith accordingly rode up to what he supposed to be an inn, ordered his horse to be taken to the stable, walked into the parlor, seated himself by the fire, and demanded what he could have for supper. On ordinary occasions he was diffident and even awkward in his manners, but here he was "at ease in his inn," [1] and felt called upon to show his manhood and enact the experienced traveller. His person was by no means calculated to play off his pretensions, for he was short and thick, with a pock-marked face, and an air and carriage by no means of a distinguished cast. The owner of the house, however, soon discovered his whimsical mistake, and, being a man of humor, determined to indulge it, especially as he accidentally learned that this intruding guest was the son of an old acquaintance.

Accordingly, Goldsmith was "fooled to the top of his bent," [2] and permitted to have full sway throughout the evening. Never was schoolboy more elated. When supper was served, he most condescendingly insisted that the landlord, his wife and daughter should partake, and ordered a

---

[1] *I. Henry IV*, III, iii, 93.
[2] *Hamlet*, III, ii, 401.

bottle of wine to crown the repast and benefit the house. His last flourish was on going to bed, when he gave special orders to have a hot cake at breakfast. His confusion and dismay, on discovering the next morning that he had been swaggering in this free and easy way in the house of a private gentleman, may be readily conceived. True to his habit of turning the events of his life to literary account, we find this chapter of ludicrous blunders and cross-purposes dramatized many years afterward in his admirable comedy of "She Stoops to Conquer, or the Mistakes of a Night."

CHAPTER II

While Oliver was making his way somewhat negligently
through the schools, his elder brother Henry was rejoicing
his father's heart by his career at the University. He soon
distinguished himself at the examinations, and obtained a
scholarship in 1743. This is a collegiate distinction which
serves as a stepping stone in any of the learned professions,
and which leads to advancement in the University should the
individual choose to remain there. His father now trusted
that he would push forward for that comfortable provision,
a fellowship, and thence to higher dignities and emoluments.
Henry, however, had the improvidence, or the "unworldli-
ness" of his race: returning to the country during the succeeding vacation, he married for love, relinquished, of
course, all his collegiate prospects and advantages, set up a
school in his father's neighborhood, and buried his talents
and acquirements for the remainder of his life in a curacy
of forty pounds a year.

Another matrimonial event occurred not long afterward
in the Goldsmith family, to disturb the equanimity of its
worthy head. This was the clandestine marriage of his
daughter Catherine with a young gentleman of the name of
Hodson, who had been confided to the care of her brother
Henry to complete his studies. As the youth was of wealthy
parentage, it was thought a lucky match for the Goldsmith

family; but the tidings of the event stung the bride's father to the soul. Proud of his integrity, and jealous of that good name which was his chief possession, he saw himself and his family subjected to the degrading suspicion of having abused a trust reposed in them to promote a mercenary match. In the first transports of his feelings, he is said to have uttered a wish that his daughter might never have a child to bring like shame and sorrow on her head. The hasty wish, so contrary to the usual benignity of the man, was recalled and repented of almost as soon as uttered; but it was considered baleful in its effects by the superstitious neighborhood; for, though his daughter bore three children, they all died befo... her.

A more effectual measure was taken by Mr. Goldsmith to ward off the apprehended imputation, but one which imposed a heavy burden on his family. This was to furnish a marriage portion of four hundred pounds, that his daughter might not be said to have entered her husband's family empty-handed. To raise the sum in cash was impossible; but he assigned to Mr. Hodson his little farm and the income of his tithes until the marriage portion should be paid. In the meantime, as his living did not amount to £200 per annum he had to practice the strictest economy to pay off gradually this heavy tax incurred by his nice sense of honor.

The first of his family to feel the effects of this economy was Oliver. The time had now arrived for him to be sent to the University; and, accordingly, on the 11th June, 1745,[1] when seventeen years of age, he entered Trinity College, Dublin; but his father was no longer able to place him there as a pensioner, as he had done his eldest son Henry; he was

---

[1] The right date is June 11, 1744. " In the lives of Forster and Prior [which Irving follows], the year of admission is given as 1745, but this has been shown by Dr. J. F. Waller to be an error."—DOBSON, *Life*, p. 20.

obliged, therefore, to enter him as a sizer, or "poor scholar."
He was lodged in one of the top rooms adjoining the library
of the building, numbered 35, where it is said his name may
still be seen, scratched by himself upon a window-frame.[1]

A student of this class is taught and boarded gratuitously,
and has to pay but a small sum for his room. It is expected,
in return for these advantages, that he will be a diligent
student, and render himself useful in a variety of ways. In
Trinity College, at the time of Goldsmith's admission, several derogatory, and, indeed, menial offices were exacted
from the sizer, as if the college sought to indemnify itself for
conferring benefits by inflicting indignities. He was obliged
to sweep part of the courts in the morning; to carry up the
dishes from the kitchen to the fellows' table, and to wait in
the hall until that body had dined. His very dress marked
the inferiority of the "poor student" to his happier class-
mates. It was a black gown of coarse stuff without sleeves,
and a plain black cloth cap without a tassel. We can conceive nothing more odious and ill-judged than these distinctions, which attached the idea of degradation to poverty,
and placed the indigent youth of merit below the worthless
minion of fortune. They were calculated to wound and
irritate the noble mind, and to render the base mind baser.

Indeed, the galling effect of these servile tasks upon
youths of proud spirits and quick sensibilities became at
length too notorious to be disregarded. About fifty years
since, on a Trinity Sunday, a number of persons were assembled to witness the college ceremonies; and as a sizer was

---

[1] "The glass on which the name is written has, as we are informed by
a writer in *Notes and Queries* (2d Series IX, p. 91), been inclosed in a frame
and deposited in the Manuscript Room of the College Library, where it is
still to be seen."—MACAULAY, *Essay on Goldsmith* (1856). Thackeray per-
tinently asks how the poverty-stricken Goldsmith came by the diamond
with which the writing was done.

carrying up a dish of meat to the fellows' table, a burly citizen in the crowd made some sneering observation on the servility of his office. Stung to the quick, the high-spirited youth instantly flung the dish and its contents at the head of the sneerer. The sizer was sharply reprimanded for this outbreak of wounded pride, but the degrading task was from that day forward very properly consigned to menial hands.

It was with the utmost repugnance that Goldsmith entered college in this capacity. His shy and sensitive nature was affected by the inferior station he was doomed to hold among his gay and opulent fellow-students, and he became, at times, moody and despondent. A recollection of these early mortifications induced him, in after-years, most strongly to dissuade his brother Henry, the clergyman, from sending a son to college on a like footing. "If he has ambition, strong passions, and an exquisite sensibility of contempt, do not send him there, unless you have no other trade for him except your own."[1]

To add to his annoyances, the fellow of the college who had the peculiar control of his studies, the Rev. Theaker Wilder, was a man of violent and capricious temper, and of diametrically opposite tastes. The tutor was devoted to the exact sciences; Goldsmith was for the classics. Wilder endeavored to force his favorite studies upon the student by harsh means, suggested by his own coarse and savage nature. He abused him in presence of the class as ignorant and stupid; ridiculed him as awkward and ugly, and at times in the transports of his temper indulged in personal violence. The effect was to aggravate a passive distaste into a positive aversion. Goldsmith was loud in expressing his contempt for mathematics and his dislike of ethics and logic; and the prejudices thus imbibed continued through life. Mathe-

---

[1] For the whole letter from which this passage is taken, see below, p. 153 ff.

matics he always pronounced a science to which the meanest
intellects were competent.

A truer cause of this distaste for the severer studies may
probably be found in his natural indolence and his love of
.convivial pleasures. "I was a lover of mirth, good-humor,
and even sometimes of fun," said he, "from my childhood."
He sang a good song, was a boon companion, and could not
resist any temptation to social enjoyment. He endeavored
to persuade himself that learning and dulness went hand in
hand, and that genius was not to be put in harness. Even
in riper years, when the consciousness of his own deficiencies
ought to have convinced him of the importance of early
study, he speaks slightingly of college honors.

"A lad," says he, "whose passions are not strong enough
in youth to mislead him from that path of science which his
tutors, and not his inclination, have chalked out, by four or
five years' perseverance will probably obtain every advantage and honor his college can bestow. I would compare
the man whose youth has been thus passed in the tranquillity
of dispassionate prudence, to liquors that never ferment, and
consequently, continue always muddy."[1]

The death of his worthy father, which took place early
in 1747, rendered Goldsmith's situation at college extremely
irksome. His mother was left with little more than the
means of providing for the wants of her household, and was
unable to furnish him any remittances. He would have
been compelled, therefore, to leave college, had it not been
for the occasional contributions of friends, the foremost
among whom was his generous and warm-hearted uncle
Contarine. Still these supplies were so scanty and precarious, that in the intervals between them he was put to great
straits. He had two college associates from whom he would

---

[1] *Inquiry into the State of Polite Learning in Europe*, Chap. IX.

occasionally borrow small sums; one was an early school-
mate, by the name of Beatty; the other a cousin, and the
chosen companion of his frolics, Robert (or rather Bob)
Bryanton, of Ballymulvey House, near Ballymahon. When
these casual supplies failed him, he was more than once
obliged to raise funds for his immediate wants by pawning
his books. At times he sank into despondency, but he had
what he termed "a knack at hoping," which soon buoyed
him up again. He began now to resort to his poetical vein
as a source of profit, scribbling street-ballads, which he
privately sold for five shillings each at a shop which dealt
in such small wares of literature. He felt an author's affection for these unowned bantlings, and we are told would
stroll privately through the streets at night to hear them
sung, listening to the comments and criticisms of by-standers,
and observing the degree of applause which each received.

Edmund Burke was a fellow-student with Goldsmith at
the college. Neither the statesman nor the poet gave promise of their future celebrity, though Burke certainly sur-
passed his contemporary in industry and application, and
evinced more disposition for self-improvement, associating
himself with a number of his fellow-students in a debating
club, in which they discussed literary topics, and exercised
themselves in composition.

Goldsmith may likewise have belonged to this association, but his propensity was rather to mingle with the gay
and thoughtless. On one occasion we find him implicated
in an affair that came nigh producing his expulsion. A report
was brought to college that a scholar was in the hands of the
bailiffs. This was an insult in which every gownsman felt
himself involved. A number of the scholars flew to arms,
and sallied forth to battle, headed by a hair-brained fellow
nicknamed Gallows Walsh, noted for his aptness at mischief

and fondness for riot. The stronghold of the bailiff was carried by storm, the scholar set at liberty, and the delinquent catch-pole borne off captive to the college, where, having no pump to put him under, they satisfied the demands of collegiate law by ducking him in an old cistern.

Flushed with this signal victory, Gallows Walsh now harangued his followers, and proposed to break open Newgate, or the Black Dog, as the prison was called, and effect a general jail-delivery. He was answered by shouts of concurrence, and away went the throng of madcap youngsters, fully bent upon putting an end to the tyranny of law. They were joined by the mob of the city, and made an attack upon the prison with true Irish precipitation and thoughtlessness, never having provided themselves with cannon to batter its stone walls. A few shots from the prison brought them to their senses, and they beat a hasty retreat, two of the townsmen being killed, and several wounded.

A severe scrutiny of this affair took place at the University. Four students, who had been ringleaders, were expelled; four others, who had been prominent in the affray, were publicly admonished; among the latter was the unlucky Goldsmith.

To make up for this disgrace, he gained, within a month afterward, one of the minor prizes of the college. It is true it was one of the very smallest, amounting in pecuniary value to but thirty shillings, but it was the first distinction he had gained in his whole collegiate career. This turn of success and sudden influx of wealth proved too much for the head of our poor student. He forthwith gave a supper and dance at his chamber to a number of young persons of both sexes from the city, in direct violation of college rules. The unwonted sound of the fiddle reached the ears of the implacable Wilder. He rushed to the scene of unhallowed festivity, inflicted corporal punishment on the "father of the feast," and turned his astonished guests neck and heels out-of-doors. This filled the measure of poor Goldsmith's humiliations; he felt degraded both within college and without. He dreaded the ridicule of his fellow-students for the ludicrous termination of his orgie, and he was ashamed to meet his city acquaintances after the degrading chastisement received in their presence, and after their own ignominious expulsion. Above all, he felt it impossible to submit any longer to the insulting tyranny of Wilder: he determined, therefore, to leave, not merely the college, but also his native land, and to bury what he conceived to be his irretrievable disgrace in some distant country. He accordingly sold his books and clothes, and sallied forth from the college walls the very next day, intending to embark at Cork for—he scarce knew where —America, or any other part beyond sea. With his usual heedless imprudence, however, he loitered about Dublin until his finances were reduced to a shilling; with this amount of specie he set out on his journey.

For three whole days he subsisted on his shilling; when that was spent, he parted with some of the clothes from his back, until, reduced almost to nakedness, he was four-and-twenty hours without food, insomuch that he declared a handful of gray peas, given to him by a girl at a wake, was one of the most delicious repasts he had ever tasted. Hunger, fatigue, and destitution brought down his spirit and calmed his anger. Fain would he have retraced his steps, could he have done so with any salve for the lingerings of his pride. In his extremity he conveyed to his brother Henry information of his distress, and of the rash project on which he had set out. His affectionate brother hastened to his relief; furnished him with money and clothes; soothed his feelings with gentle counsel; prevailed upon him to return to college, and effected an indifferent reconciliation between him and Wilder.

After this irregular sally upon life he remained nearly two years longer at the University, giving proofs of talent in occasional translations from the classics, for one of which he received a premium, awarded only to those who are the first in literary merit. Still he never made much figure at college, his natural disinclination to study being increased by the harsh treatment he continued to experience from his tutor.

Among the anecdotes told of him while at college, is one indicative of that prompt but thoughtless and often whimsical benevolence which throughout life formed one of the most eccentric, yet endearing points of his character. He was engaged to breakfast one day with a college intimate, but failed to make his appearance. His friend repaired to his room, knocked at the door and was bidden to enter. To his surprise, he found Goldsmith in his bed, immersed to his chin in feathers. A serio-comic story explained the circumstance. In the course of the preceding evening's stroll he had met with a woman with five children, who implored his charity. Her husband was in the hospital; she was just from the country, a stranger, and destitute, without food or shelter for her helpless offspring. This was too much for the kind heart of Goldsmith. He was almost as poor as herself, it is true, and had no money in his pocket; but he brought her to the college-gate, gave her the blankets from his bed to cover her little brood, and part of his clothes for her to sell and purchase food; and, finding himself cold during the night, had cut open his bed and buried himself among the feathers.

At length, on the 27th of February, 1749, O. S.,[1] he was

---

admitted to the degree of Bachelor of Arts, and took his final leave of the University. He was freed from college rule, that emancipation so ardently coveted by the thoughtless student, and which too generally launches him amid the cares, the hardships, and vicissitudes of life. He was freed, too, from the brutal tyranny of Wilder. If his kind and placable nature could retain any resentment for past injuries, it might have been gratified by learning subsequently that the passionate career of Wilder was terminated by a violent death in the course of a dissolute brawl; but Goldsmith took no delight in the misfortunes even of his enemies.

He now returned to his friends, no longer the student to sport away the happy interval of vacation, but the anxious man, who is henceforth to shift for himself and make his way through the world. In fact, he had no legitimate home to return to. At the death of his father, the paternal house at Lissoy, in which Goldsmith had passed his childhood, had been taken by Mr. Hodson, who had married his sister Catherine. His mother had removed to Ballymahon, where she occupied a small house, and had to practise the severest frugality. His elder brother Henry served the curacy and taught the school of his late father's parish, and lived in narrow circumstances at Goldsmith's birthplace, the old goblin-house at Pallas.

None of his relatives were in circumstances to aid him with anything more than a temporary home, and the aspect of every one seemed somewhat changed. In fact, his career at college had disappointed his friends, and they began to doubt his being the great genius they had fancied him. He whimsically alludes to this circumstance in that piece of autobiography, "The Man in Black," in the "Citizen of the World."

"The first opportunity my father had of finding his expectations disappointed was in the middling figure I made at the University: he had flattered himself that he should soon see me rising into the foremost rank in literary reputation, but was mortified to find me utterly unnoticed and unknown. His disappointment might have been partly ascribed to his having overrated my talents, and partly to my dislike of mathematical reasonings at a time when my imagination and memory, yet unsatisfied, were more eager after new objects than desirous of reasoning upon those I knew. This, however, did not please my tutors, who observed, indeed, that I was a little dull, but at the same time allowed that I seemed to be very good-natured, and had no harm in me."*

The only one of his relatives who did not appear to lose faith in him was his uncle Contarine. This kind and considerate man, it is said, saw in him a warmth of heart requiring some skill to direct, and a latent genius that wanted time to mature; and these impressions none of his subsequent follies and irregularities wholly obliterated. His purse and affection, therefore, as well as his house, were now open to him, and he became his chief counsellor and director after his father's death. He urged him to prepare for holy orders; and others of his relatives concurred in the advice. Goldsmith had a settled repugnance to a clerical life. This has been ascribed by some to conscientious scruples, not considering himself of a temper and frame of mind for such a sacred office; others attributed it to his roving propensities, and his desire to visit foreign countries; he himself gives a whimsical objection in his biography of the "Man in Black":—"To be obliged to wear a long wig when I liked a short one, or a black coat when I generally dressed in brown, I thought such a restraint upon my liberty that I absolutely rejected the proposal."

---

* *Citizen of the World*, Letter XVII.

In effect, however, his scruples were overruled, and he agreed to qualify himself for the office. He was now only twenty-one, and must pass two years of probation. They were two years of rather loitering, unsettled life. Sometimes he was at Lissoy, participating with thoughtless enjoyment in the rural sports and occupations of his brother-in-law, Mr. Hodson; sometimes he was with his brother Henry, at the old goblin mansion at Pallas, assisting him occasionally in his school. The early marriage and unambitious retirement of Henry, though so subversive of the fond plans of his father had proved happy in their results. He was already surrounded by a blooming family; he was contented with his lot, beloved by his parishioners, and lived in the daily practice of all the amiable virtues, and the immediate enjoyment of their reward. Of the tender affection inspired in the breast of Goldsmith by the constant kindness of this excellent brother, and of the longing recollection with which, in the lonely wanderings of after-years, he looked back upon this scene of domestic felicity, we have a touching instance in the well-known opening to his poem of "The Traveller":—

"Remote, unfriended, melancholy, slow,
Or by the lazy Scheld or wandering Po;

.   .   .   .

Where'er I roam, whatever realms to see,
My heart untravell'd fondly turns to thee;
Still to my brother turns with ceaseless pain,
And drags at each remove a lengthening chain.

Eternal blessings crown my earliest friend,
And round his dwelling guardian saints attend;
Bless'd be that spot, where cheerful guests retire
To pause from toil, and trim their evening fire;
Bless'd that abode, where want and pain repair,
And every stranger finds a ready chair:

> Bless'd be those feasts with simple plenty crown'd
> Where all the ruddy family around
> Laugh at the jests or pranks that never fail,
> Or sigh with pity at some mournful tale;
> Or press the bashful stranger to his food,
> And learn the luxury of doing good."

During this loitering life Goldsmith pursued no study, but rather amused himself with miscellaneous reading; such as biography, travels, poetry, novels, plays—everything, in short, that administered to the imagination. Sometimes he strolled along the banks of the river Inny; where, in after years, when he had become famous, his favorite seats and haunts used to be pointed out. Often he joined in the rustic sports of the villagers, and became adroit at throwing the sledge, a favorite feat of activity and strength in Ireland. Recollections of these "healthful sports" we find in his "Deserted Village":—

> "How often have I bless'd the coming day,
> When toil remitting lent its turn to play,
> And all the village train, from labor free,
> Led up their sports beneath the spreading tree:
> And many a gambol frolicked o'er the ground,
> And sleights of art and feats of strength went round."

A boon companion in all his rural amusements was his cousin and college crony, Robert Bryanton, with whom he sojourned occasionally at Ballymulvey House in the neighborhood. They used to make excursions about the country on foot, sometimes fishing, sometimes hunting otter in the Inny. They got up a country club at the little inn of Ballymahon, of which Goldsmith soon became the oracle and prime wit; astonishing his unlettered associates by his learning, and being considered capital at a song and a story. From the rustic conviviality of the inn at Ballymahon, and the company which used to assemble there, it is surmised that he took some hints in after-life for his picturing of Tony Lumpkin[1] and his associates: "Dick Muggins, the exciseman; Jack Slang, the horse-doctor; little Aminidab, that grinds the music-box, and Tom Twist, that spins the pewter platter." Nay, it is thought that Tony's drinking-song at the "Three Jolly Pigeons" was but a revival of one of the convivial catches at Ballymahon:—

"Then come put the jorum about,
  And let us be merry and clever,
Our hearts and our liquors are stout,
  Here's the Three Jolly Pigeons forever.
Let some cry of woodcock or hare,
  Your bustards, your ducks, and your widgeons;
But of all the gay birds in the air,
  Here's a health to the Three Jolly Pigeons.
        Toroddle, toroddle, toroll."

Notwithstanding all these accomplishments and this rural popularity, his friends began to shake their heads and shrug their shoulders when they spoke of him; and his brother Henry noted with anything but satisfaction his frequent visits to the club at Ballymahon. He emerged, however, unscathed from this dangerous ordeal, more fortunate in this respect than his comrade Bryanton; but he retained throughout life a fondness for clubs: often, too, in the course of his checkered career, he looked back to this period of rural sports and careless enjoyments as one of the few sunny spots of his cloudy life; and though he ultimately rose to associate with birds of a finer feather, his heart would still yearn in secret after the "THREE JOLLY PIGEONS."

---

[1] In *She Stoops to Conquer*. The other allusions are to the same play.

CHAPTER III

The time had now arrived for Goldsmith to apply for
orders, and he presented himself accordingly before the bishop
of Elphin for ordination. We have stated his great objection to clerical life, the obligation to wear a black coat; and,
whimsical as it may appear, dress seems in fact to have
formed an obstacle to his entrance into the church. He had
ever a passion for clothing his sturdy but awkward little
person in gay colors; and on this solemn occasion, when it
was to be supposed his garb would be of suitable gravity,
he appeared luminously arrayed in scarlet breeches! He
was rejected by the bishop: some say for want of sufficient
studious preparation; his rambles and frolics with Bob Bryanton, and his revels with the club at Ballymahon, having been
much in the way of his theological studies; others attribute
his rejection to reports of his college irregularities, which
the bishop had received from his old tyrant Wilder; but
those who look into the matter with more knowing eyes, pronounce the scarlet breeches to have been the fundamental
objection. "My friends," says Goldsmith, speaking through
his humorous representative, the "Man in Black,"—"my
friends were now perfectly satisfied I was undone; and yet
they thought it a pity for one that had not the least harm in
him, and was so very good-natured."[1] His uncle Contarine,

---

[1] See above, p. 61, note.

however, still remained unwavering in his kindness, though much less sanguine in his expectations. He now looked round for a humbler sphere of action, and through his influence and exertions Oliver was received as tutor in the family of a Mr. Flinn, a gentleman of the neighborhood. The situation was apparently respectable; he had his seat at the table; and joined the family in their domestic recreations and their evening game at cards. There was a servility, however, in his position, which was not to his taste; nor did his deference for the family increase upon familiar intercourse. He charged a member of it with unfair play at cards. A violent altercation ensued, which ended in his throwing up his situation as tutor. On being paid off he found himself in possession of an unheard-of amount of money. His wandering propensity and his desire to see the world were instantly in the ascendency. Without communicating his plans or intentions to his friends, he procured a good horse, and, with thirty pounds in his pocket, made his second sally forth into the world.

The worthy niece and housekeeper of the hero of La Mancha[1] could not have been more surprised and dismayed at one of the Don's clandestine expeditions than were the mother and friends of Goldsmith, when they heard of his mysterious departure. Weeks elapsed, and nothing was seen or heard of him. It was feared that he had left the country on one of his wandering freaks, and his poor mother was reduced almost to despair, when one day he arrived at her door almost as forlorn in plight as the prodigal son. Of his thirty pounds not a shilling was left; and instead of the goodly steed on which he had issued forth on his errantry, he was

---

[1] In Cervantes' *Don Quixote*. The hero is under the delusion that he is a knight of chivalry, and escapes the watchful care of his household to wander off in search of adventures. See below, p. 103.

mounted on a sorry little pony, which he had nicknamed Fiddle-back. As soon as his mother was well assured of his safety, she rated him soundly for his inconsiderate conduct. His brothers and sisters, who were tenderly attached to him, interfered, and succeeded in mollifying her ire; and whatever lurking anger the good dame might have, was no doubt effectually vanquished by the following whimsical narrative which he drew up at his brother's house, and dispatched to her:—

"My dear mother, if you will sit down and calmly listen to what I say, you shall be fully resolved in every one of those many questions you have asked me. I went to Cork and converted my horse, which you prize so much higher than Fiddle-back, into cash, took my passage in a ship bound for America, and at the same time, paid the captain for my freight and all the other expenses of my voyage. But it so happened that the wind did not answer for three weeks; and you know, mother, that I could not command the elements. My misfortune was, that, when the wind served, I happened to be with a party in the country, and my friend, the captain, never inquired after me, but set sail with as much indifference as if I had been on board. The remainder of my time I employed in the city and its environs, viewing everything curious, and you know no one can starve while he has money in his pocket.

"Reduced, however, to my last two guineas, I began to think of my dear mother and friends whom I had left behind me, and so bought that generous beast, Fiddle-back, and bade adieu to Cork with only five shillings in my pocket. This, to be sure, was but a scanty allowance for man and horse towards a journey of above a hundred miles; but I did not despair, for I knew I must find friends on the road.

"I recollected particularly an old and faithful acquain-

tance I made at college, who had often and earnestly pressed
me to spend a summer with him, and he lived but eight
miles from Cork. This circumstance of vicinity he would
expatiate on to me with peculiar emphasis. 'We shall,'
says he, ' enjoy the delights of both city and country, and you
shall command my stable and my purse.'

"However, upon the way I met a poor woman all in
tears, who told me her husband had been arrested for a debt
he was not able to pay, and that his eight'children must now
starve, bereaved as they were of his industry, which had been
their only support. I thought myself at home, being not
far from my good friend's house, and therefore parted with
a moiety of all my store; and pray, mother, ought I not have
given her the other half-crown, for what she got would be
of little use to her? However, I soon arrived at the mansion
of my affectionate friend, guarded by the vigilance of a huge
mastiff, who flew at me and would have torn me to pieces
but for the assistance of a woman, whose countenance was
not less grim than that of the dog; yet she with great humanity relieved me from the jaws of this Cerberus, and was prevailed on to carry up my name to her master.

"Without suffering me to wait long, my old friend, who
was then recovering from a severe fit of sickness, came down
in his nightcap, nightgown, and slippers, and embraced me
with the most cordial welcome, showed me in, and, after
giving me a history of his indisposition, assured me that he
considered himself peculiarly fortunate in having under his
roof the man he most loved on earth, and whose stay with
him must, above all things, contribute to perfect his recovery.
I now repented sorely I had not given the poor woman the
other half-crown, as I thought all my bills of humanity
would be punctually answered by this worthy man. I revealed
to him my whole soul; I opened to him all my distresses;

and freely owned that I had but one half-crown in my pocket; but that now, like a ship after weathering out the storm, I considered myself secure in a safe and hospitable harbor. He made no answer, but walked about the room, rubbing his hands as one in deep study. This I imputed to the sympathetic feelings of a tender heart, which increased my esteem for him, and, as that increased, I gave the most favorable interpretation to his silence. I construed it into delicacy of sentiment, as if he dreaded to wound my pride by expressing his commiseration in words, leaving his generous conduct to speak for itself.

"It now approached six o'clock in the evening; and as I had eaten no breakfast, and as my spirits were raised, my appetite for dinner grew uncommonly keen. At length the old woman came into the room with two plates, one spoon, and a dirty cloth, which she laid upon the table. This appearance, without increasing my spirits, did not diminish my appetite. My protectress soon returned with a small bowl of sago, a small porringer of sour milk, a loaf of stale brown bread, and the heel of an old cheese all over crawling with mites. My friend apologized that his illness obliged him to live on slops, and that better fare was not in the house; observing, at the same time, that a milk diet was certainly the most healthful; and at eight o'clock he again recommended a regular life, declaring that for his part he would *lie down with the lamb and rise with the lark*. My hunger was at this time so exceedingly sharp that I wished for another slice of the loaf, but was obliged to go to bed without even that refreshment.

" This lenten entertainment I had received made me resolve to depart as soon as possible; accordingly, next morning, when I spoke of going, he did not oppose my resolution, he rather commended my design, adding some very sage counsel upon the occasion. 'To be sure,' said he, 'the longer you stay away from your mother, the more you will grieve her and your other friends; and possibly they are already afflicted at hearing of this foolish expedition you have made.' Notwithstanding all this, and without any hope of softening such a sordid heart, I again renewed the tale of my distress, and asking 'how he thought I could travel above a hundred miles upon one half-crown?' I begged to borrow a single guinea, which I assured him should be repaid with thanks. 'And you know, sir,' said I, 'it is no more than I have done for you.' To which he firmly answered, 'Why look you, Mr. Goldsmith, that is neither here nor there. I have paid you all you ever lent me, and this sickness of mine has left me bare of cash. But I have bethought myself of a conveyance for you; sell your horse, and I will furnish you a much better one to ride on.' I readily grasped at his proposal, and begged to see the nag; on which he led me to his bed-chamber, and from under the bed he pulled out a stout oak stick. 'Here he is,' said he; 'take this in your hand, and it will carry you to your mother's with more safety than such a horse as you ride.' I was in doubt, when I got it into my hand, whether I should not, in the first place, apply it to his pate; but a rap at the street-door made the wretch fly to it, and when I returned to the parlor he introduced me, as if nothing of the kind had happened, to the gentleman who entered, as Mr. Goldsmith, his most ingenious and worthy friend, of whom he had so often heard him speak with rapture. I could scarcely compose myself; and must have betrayed indignation in my mien to the stranger, who was a counsellor-at-law in the neighborhood, a man of engaging aspect and polite address.

"After spending an hour, he asked my friend and me to dine with him at his house. This I declined at first, as I wished to have no farther communication with my hospitable friend; but at the solicitation of both I at last consented, determined as I was by two motives: one, that I was prejudiced in favor of the looks and manner of the counsellor; and the other, that I stood in need of a comfortable dinner. And there, indeed, I found everything that I could wish, abundance without profusion, and elegance without affectation. In the evening, when my old friend, who had eaten very plentifully at his neighbor's table, but talked again of lying down with the lamb, made a motion to me for retiring, our generous host requested I should take a bed with him, upon which I plainly told my old friend that he might go home and take care of the horse he had given me, but that I should never reënter his doors. He went away with a laugh, leaving me to add this to the other little things the counsellor already knew of his plausible neighbor.

"And now, my dear mother, I found sufficient to reconcile me to all my follies; for here I spent three whole days. The counsellor had two sweet girls to his daughters, who played enchantingly on the harpsichord; and yet it was but a melancholy pleasure I felt the first time I heard them; for that being the first time also that either of them had touched the instrument since their mother's death, I saw the tears in silence trickle down their father's cheeks. I every day endeavored to go away, but every day was pressed and obliged to stay. On my going, the counsellor offered me his purse, with a horse and servant to convey me home; but the latter I declined, and only took a guinea to bear my necessary expenses on the road.

OLIVER GOLDSMITH.

"To Mrs. Anne Goldsmith, Ballymahon."

Such is the story given by the poet-errant of this his second sally in quest of adventures. We cannot but think it was here and there touched up a little with the fanciful pen of the future essayist, with a view to amuse his mother and soften her vexation; but even in these respects it is valuable as showing the early play of his humor, and his happy knack of extracting sweets from that worldly experience which to others yields nothing but bitterness.

CHAPTER IV

A new consultation was held among Goldsmith's friends
as to his future course, and it was determined he should try
the law. His uncle Contarine agreed to advance the necessary funds, and actually furnished him with fifty pounds,
with which he set off for London, to enter on his studies at
the Temple. Unfortunately, he fell in company at Dublin
with a Roscommon acquaintance, one whose wits had been
sharpened about town, who beguiled him into a gambling-
house, and soon left him as penniless as when he bestrode
the redoubtable Fiddle-back.

He was so ashamed of this fresh instance of gross heedlessness and imprudence, that he remained some time in
Dublin without communicating to his friends his destitute
condition. They heard of it, however, and he was invited
back to the country, and indulgently forgiven by his generous uncle, but less readily by his mother, who was mortified
and disheartened at seeing all her early hopes of him so
repeatedly blighted. His brother Henry, too, began to lose
patience at these successive failures, resulting from thoughtless indiscretion; and a quarrel took place, which for some
time interrupted their usually affectionate intercourse.

The only home where poor erring Goldsmith still received
a welcome, was the parsonage of his affectionate forgiving

92

uncle. Here he used to talk of literature with the good simple-hearted man, and delight him and his daughter with his verses. Jane, his early playmate, was now the woman grown; their intercourse was of a more intellectual kind than formerly; they discoursed of poetry and music; she played on the harpsichord, and he accompanied her with his flute. The music may not have been very artistic, as he never performed but by ear; it had probably as much merit as the poetry, which, if we may judge by the following specimen, was as yet but juvenile:—

TO A YOUNG LADY ON VALENTINE'S DAY

WITH THE DRAWING OF A HEART

With submission at your shrine,
Comes a heart your Valentine;
From the side where once it grew,
See it panting flies to you.
Take it, fair one, to your breast,
Soothe the fluttering thing to rest;
Let the gentle, spotless toy
Be your sweetest, greatest joy;
Every night when wrapp'd in sleep,
Next your heart the conquest keep;
Or if dreams your fancy move,
Here it whisper me and love;
Then in pity to the swain,
Who must heartless else remain,
Soft as gentle dewy show'rs,
Slow descend on April flow'rs;
Soft as gentle riv'lets glide,
Steal unnoticed to my side;
If the gem you have to spare,
Take your own and place it there.

If this Valentine was intended for the fair Jane, and expressive of a tender sentiment indulged by the stripling poet, it was unavailing; as not long afterwards she was married to a Mr. Lawder. We trust, however, it was but a poetical passion of that transient kind which grows up in idleness and exhales itself in rhyme. While Oliver was thus piping and poetizing at the parsonage, his uncle Contarine received a visit from Dean Goldsmith of Cloyne,—a kind of magnate in the wide but improvident family connection, throughout which his word was law and almost gospel. This august dignitary was pleased to discover signs of talent in Oliver, and suggested that, as he had attempted divinity and law without success, he should now try physic. The advice came from too important a source to be disregarded, and it was determined to send him to Edinburgh to commence his studies. The Dean having given the advice, added to it, we trust, his blessing, but no money; that was furnished from the scantier purses of Goldsmith's brother, his sister (Mrs. Hodson), and his ever-ready uncle, Contarine.

It was in the autumn of 1752 that Goldsmith arrived in Edinburgh. His outset in that city came near adding to the list of his indiscretions and disasters. Having taken lodgings at haphazard, he left his trunk there, containing all his worldly effects, and sallied forth to see the town. After sauntering about the streets until a late hour, he thought of returning home, when, to his confusion, he found he had not acquainted himself with the name either of his landlady or of the street in which she lived. Fortunately, in the height of his whimsical perplexity, he met the cawdy or porter who had carried his trunk, and who now served him as a guide.

He did not remain long in the lodgings in which he had put up. The hostess was too adroit at that hocus-pocus of the table which often is practised in cheap boarding-houses. No one could conjure a single joint through a greater variety of forms. A loin of mutton, according to Goldsmith's account, would serve him and two fellow-students a whole week. "A brandered chop was served up one day, a fried steak another, collops with onion-sauce a third, and so on until the fleshy parts were quite consumed, when finally a dish of broth was manufactured from the bones on the seventh day, and the landlady rested from her labors." Goldsmith had a good-humored mode of taking things, and for a short time amused himself with the shifts and expedients of his landlady, which struck him in a ludicrous manner; he soon, however, fell in with fellow-students from his own country, whom he joined at more eligible quarters.

He now attended medical lectures, and attached himself to an association of students called the Medical Society. He set out, as usual, with the best intentions, but, as usual, soon fell into idle, convivial, thoughtless habits. Edinburgh was indeed a place of sore trial for one of his temperament. Convivial meetings were all the vogue, and the tavern was the universal rallying-place of good-fellowship. And then Goldsmith's intimacies lay chiefly among the Irish students, who were always ready for a wild freak and frolic. Among them he was a prime favorite and somewhat of a leader, from his exuberance of spirits, his vein of humor, and his talent at singing an Irish song and telling an Irish story.

His usual carelessness in money matters attended him. Though his supplies from home were scanty and irregular, he never could bring himself into habits of prudence and economy; often he was stripped of all his present finances at play; often he lavished them away in fits of unguarded charity or generosity. Sometimes among his boon companions he assumed a ludicrous swagger in money-matters, which no one afterward was more ready than himself to laugh at. At a convivial meeting with a number of his fellow-students he suddenly proposed to draw lots with any one present which of the two should treat the whole party to the play.

The moment the proposition had bolted from his lips, his heart was in his throat. "To my great though secret joy," said he, "they all declined the challenge. Had it been accepted, and had I proved the loser, a part of my wardrobe must have been pledged in order to raise the money."

At another of these meetings there was an earnest dispute on the question of ghosts, some being firm believers in the possibility of departed spirits returning to visit their friends and familiar haunts. One of the disputants set sail the next day for London, but the vessel put back through stress of weather. His return was unknown except to one of the believers in ghosts, who concerted with him a trick to be played off on the opposite party. In the evening, at a meeting of the students, the discussion was renewed; and one of the most strenuous opposers of ghosts was asked whether he considered himself proof against ocular demonstration. He persisted in his scoffing. Some solemn process of conjuration was performed, and the comrade supposed to be on his way to London made his appearance. The effect was fatal. The unbeliever fainted at the sight, and ultimately went mad. We have no account of what share Goldsmith took in this transaction, at which he was present.

The following letter to his friend Bryanton contains some of Goldsmith's impressions concerning Scotland and its inhabitants, and gives indications of that humor which characterized some of his later writings.

"*Robert Bryanton, at Ballymahon, Ireland.*

"Edinburgh, September 26th, 1753.
"My dear Bob,—

"How many good excuses (and you know I was ever good at an excuse) might I call up to vindicate my past shameful silence. I might tell how I wrote a long letter on

my first coming hither, and seem vastly angry at my not
receiving an answer; I might allege that business (with business you know I was always pestered) had never given me
time to finger a pen. But I suppress those and twenty more
as plausible, and as easily invented, since they might be
attended with a slight inconvenience of being known to be
lies. Let me then speak truth. An hereditary indolence
(I have it from the mother's side) has hitherto prevented my
writing to you, and still prevents my writing at least twenty-
five letters more, due to my friends in Ireland. No turnspit
dog[1] gets up into his wheel with more reluctance than I sit
down to write; yet no dog ever loved the roast meat he turns
better than I do him I now address.

"Yet what shall I say now I am entered? Shall I tire
you with a description of this unfruitful country; where I
must lead you over their hills all brown with heath, or their
valleys scarcely able to feed a rabbit? Man alone seems to
be the only creature who has arrived to the natural size in
this poor soil. Every part of the country presents the same
dismal landscape. No grove, nor brook, lend their music
to cheer the stranger, or make the inhabitants forget their
poverty. Yet with all these disadvantages to call him down
to humility, a Scotchman is one of the proudest things alive.
The poor have pride ever ready to relieve them. If mankind should happen to despise them, they are masters of
their own admiration; and that they can plentifully bestow
upon themselves.

"From their pride and poverty, as I take it, results one
advantage this country enjoys; namely, the gentlemen here
are much better bred than among us. No such character

---

[1] "A kind of dog of small size, long-bodied and short-legged, formerly
used to work a kind of tread-mill wheel by means of which a spit was
turned."—*Standard Dictionary*.

here as our fox-hunters; and they have expressed great surprise when I informed them that some men in Ireland of one thousand pounds a year, spend their whole lives in running after a hare, and drinking to be drunk. Truly, if such a being, equipped in his hunting-dress, came among a circle of Scotch gentry, they would behold him with the same astonishment that a countryman does King George on horseback.

"The men here have generally high cheek bones, and are lean and swarthy, fond of action, dancing in particular. Now that I have mentioned dancing, let me say something of their balls, which are very frequent here. When a stranger enters the dancing-hall, he sees one end of the room taken up by the ladies, who sit dismally in a group by themselves;— in the other end stand their pensive partners that are to be;— but no more intercourse between the sexes than there is between two countries at war. The ladies indeed may ogle, and the gentlemen sigh; but an embargo is laid on any closer commerce. At length, to interrupt hostilities, the lady directress, or intendant, or what you will, pitches upon a lady and gentleman to walk a minuet; which they perform with a formality that approaches to despondence. After five or six couple have thus walked the gauntlet, all stand up to country dances; each gentleman furnished with a partner from the aforesaid lady directress; so they dance much, say nothing, and thus concludes our assembly. I told a Scotch gentleman that such profound silence resembled the ancient procession of the Roman matrons in honor of Ceres; and the Scotch gentleman told me (and faith I believe he was right) that I was a very great pedant for my pains.

"Now I am come to the ladies; and to show that I love Scotland, and everything that belongs to so charming a country, I insist on it, and will give him leave to break my

head that denies it—that the Scotch ladies are ten
thousand times finer and handsomer than the Irish. To
be sure, now, I see your sisters Betty and Peggy vastly surprised at my partiality,—but tell them flatly, I don't value
them—or their fine skins, or eyes, or good sense, or——, a
potato;—for I say, and will maintain it; and as a convincing
proof (I am in a great passion) of what I assert, the Scotch
ladies say it themselves. But to be less serious; where will
you find a language so prettily become a pretty mouth as the
broad Scotch? And the women here speak it in its highest
purity; for instance, teach one of your young ladies at home
to pronounce the "Whoar wull I gong?" with a becoming
widening of mouth, and I'll lay my life they'll wound every
hearer.

"We have no such character here as a coquette, but alas!
how many envious prudes! Some days ago I walked into
my Lord Kilcoubry's (don't be surprised, my lord is but a
glover*), when the Duchess of Hamilton (that fair who sacri-
ficed her beauty to her ambition, and her inward peace to a
title and gilt equipage) passed by in her chariot; her battered
husband, or more properly the guardian of her charms, sat
by her side. Straight envy began, in the shape of no less
than three ladies who sat with me, to find faults in her
faultless form.—'For my part,' says the first, 'I think what I
always thought, that the Duchess has too much of the red
in her complexion.' 'Madam, I am of your opinion,' says
the second; 'I think her face has a palish cast too much on
the delicate order.' 'And, let me tell you,' added the third
lady, whose mouth was puckered up to the size of an issue,
'that the Duchess has fine lips, but she wants a mouth.'—

---

*William Maclellan, who claimed the title, and whose son succeeded
in establishing the claim in 1773. The father is said to have voted at the
election of the sixteen Peers for Scotland, and to have sold gloves in the
lobby at this and other public assemblages.

At this every lady drew up her mouth as if going to pronounce the letter P.

"But how ill, my Bob, does it become me to ridicule women with whom I have scarcely any correspondence! There are, 'tis certain, handsome women here; and 'tis certain they have handsome men to keep them company. An ugly and poor man is society only for himself; and such society the world lets me enjoy in great abundance. Fortune has given you circumstances, and Nature a person to look charming in the eyes of the fair. Nor do I envy my dear Bob such blessings, while I may sit down and laugh at the world and at myself—the most ridiculous object in it. But you see I am grown downright splenetic, and perhaps the fit may continue till I receive an answer to this. I know you cannot send me much news from Ballymahon, but such as it is, send it all; everything you send will be agreeable to me.

"Has George Conway put up a sign yet; or John Binley left off drinking drams; or Tom Allen got a new wig? But I leave you to your own choice what to write. While I live, know you have a true friend in yours, &c., &c., &c.

OLIVER GOLDSMITH.

"P. S.—Give my sincere respects (not compliments, do you mind) to your agreeable family, and give my service to my mother, if you see her; for, as you express it in Ireland, I have a sneaking kindness for her still. Direct to me, ———, Student in Physic, in Edinburgh."

Nothing worthy of preservation appeared from his pen during his residence in Edinburgh; and indeed his poetical powers, highly as they had been estimated by his friends, had not as yet produced anything of superior merit. He made on one occasion a month's excursion to the Highlands. "I set out the first day on foot," says he, in a letter to his uncle Contarine, "but an ill-natured corn I have on my toe has for the future prevented that cheap mode of travelling; so the second day I hired a horse, about the size of a ram, and he walked away (trot he could not) as pensive as his master."

During his residence in Scotland his convivial talents gained him at one time attentions in a high quarter, which, however, he had the good sense to appreciate correctly. "I have spent," says he, in one of his letters, "more than a fortnight every second day at the Duke of Hamilton's; but it seems they like me more as a jester than as a companion, so I disdained so servile an employment as unworthy my calling as a physician." Here we again find the origin of another passage in his autobiography, under the character of the "Man in Black," wherein that worthy figures as a flatterer to a great man. "At first," says he, "I was surprised that the situation of a flatterer at a great man's table could be thought disagreeable; there was no great trouble in listening attentively when his lordship spoke, and laughing when he looked round for applause. This, even good manners might have obliged me to perform. I found, however, too soon, his lordship was a greater dunce than myself, and from that moment flattery was at an end. I now rather aimed at setting him right than at receiving his absurdities with submission: to flatter those we do not know is an easy task; but to flatter our intimate acquaintances, all whose foibles are strongly in our eyes, is drudgery insupportable. Every time I now opened my lips in praise, my falsehood went to my conscience; his lordship soon perceived me to be very unfit for his service: I was therefore discharged; my patron at the same time being graciously pleased to observe that he believed I was tolerably good-natured and had not the least harm in me." [1]

After spending two winters at Edinburgh, Goldsmith prepared to finish his medical studies on the Continent, for which his uncle Contarine agreed to furnish the funds. "I intend," said he, in a letter to his uncle, "to visit Paris, where the great Farheim, Petit, and Du Hamel de Monceau instruct their pupils in all the branches of medicine. They speak French,[2] and consequently I shall have much the advantage of most of my countrymen, as I am perfectly acquainted with that language, and few who leave Ireland are so. I shall spend the spring and summer in Paris, and the beginning of next winter go to Leyden. The great Albinus is still alive there, and 't will be proper to go, though only to have it said that we have studied in so famous a university.

"As I shall not have another opportunity of receiving money from your bounty till my return to Ireland, so I have drawn for the last sum that I hope I shall ever trouble you for; 'tis £20. And now, dear sir, let me here acknowledge the humility of the station in which you found me; let me tell how I was despised by most, and hateful to myself. Poverty, hopeless poverty, was my lot, and Melancholy was beginning to make me her own, when you—— But I stop here, to inquire how your health goes on? How does my cousin Jenny, and has she recovered her late complaint? How does my poor Jack Goldsmith? I fear his disorder is of such a nature as he won't easily recover. I wish, my dear sir, you would make me happy by another letter before I go abroad, for there I shall hardly hear from you. . . Give my—how shall I express it?—give my earnest love to Mr. and Mrs. Lawder."

[1] See above, p. 61, note.
[2] University lectures were usually given in Latin at this time; this was a survival from the medieval period when they were always so given.

Mrs. Lawder was Jane, his early playmate—the object of his valentine—his first poetical inspiration. She had been for some time married.

Medical instruction, it will be perceived, was the ostensible motive for this visit to the Continent, but the real one, in all probability, was his long-cherished desire to see foreign parts. This, however, he would not acknowledge even to himself, but sought to reconcile his roving propensities with some grand moral purpose. "I esteem the traveller who instructs the heart," says he, in one of his subsequent writings, "but I despise him who only indulges the imagination. A man who leaves home to mend himself and others, is a philosopher; but he who goes from country to country, guided by the blind impulse of curiosity, is only a vagabond."[1] He, of course, was to travel as a philosopher, and in truth his outfits for a Continental tour were in character. "I shall carry just £33 to France," said he, "with good store of clothes, shirts, &c., and that with economy will suffice." He forgot to make mention of his flute, which it will be found had occasionally to come in play when economy could not replenish his purse, nor philosophy find him a supper. Thus slenderly provided with money, prudence or experience, and almost as slightly guarded against "hard knocks" as the hero of La Mancha, whose head-piece was half iron, half pasteboard, he made his final sally forth upon the world; hoping all things; believing all things:[2] little anticipating the checkered ills in store for him; little thinking when he penned his valedictory letter to his good uncle Contarine, that he was never to see him more; never to return after all his wandering to the friend of his infancy: never to revisit his early and fondly remembered haunts at "sweet Lissoy" and Ballymahon.

---

[1] *Citizen of the World*, Letter VII.   [2] See 1 Cor. 18:7.

CHAPTER V

His usual indiscretion attended Goldsmith at the very
outset of his foreign enterprise. He had intended to take
shipping at Leith for Holland; but on arriving at that port,
he found a ship about to sail for Bordeaux, with six agreeable
passengers, whose acquaintance he had probably made at
the inn. He was not a man to resist a sudden impulse; so,
instead of embarking for Holland, he found himself plough-
ing the seas on his way to the other side of the continent.
Scarcely had the ship been two days at sea, when she was
driven by stress of weather to Newcastle-upon-Tyne. Here
"of course" Goldsmith and his agreeable fellow-passengers
found it expedient to go on shore and refresh themselves
after the fatigues of the voyage." "Of course" they frolicked
and made merry until a late hour in the evening, when, in
the midst of their hilarity, the door was burst open, and a
sergeant and twelve grenadiers entered with fixed bayonets,
and took the whole convivial party prisoners.

It seems that the agreeable companions with whom our
greenhorn had struck up such a sudden intimacy, were
Scotchmen in the French service, who had been in Scotland
enlisting recruits for the French army.

In vain Goldsmith protested his innocence; he was
marched off with his fellow-travellers to prison, whence he

with difficulty obtained his release at the end of a fortnight.
With his customary facility, however, at palliating his mis-
adventures, he found everything turn out for the best. His
imprisonment saved his life, for during his detention the ship
proceeded on her voyage, but was wrecked at the mouth of
the Garonne, and all on board perished.

Goldsmith's second embarkation was for Holland direct,
and in nine days he arrived at Rotterdam, whence he proceeded, without any more deviations, to Leyden. He gives
a whimsical picture, in one of his letters, of the appearance
of the Hollanders.   "The modern Dutchman is quite a
different creature from him of former times: he in everything imitates a Frenchman but in his easy, disengaged air.
He is vastly ceremonious, and is, perhaps, exactly what a
Frenchman might have been in the reign of Louis XIV.
Such are the better bred.   But the downright Hollander is
one of the oddest figures in nature.   Upon a lank head of
hair he wears a half-cocked narrow hat, laced with black
ribband; no coat, but seven waistcoats and nine pair of
breeches, so that his hips reach up almost to his armpits.
This well-clothed vegetable is now fit to see company or
make love.   But what a pleasing creature is the object of
his appetite! why, she wears a large fur cap, with a deal of
Flanders lace; and for every pair of breeches he carries, she
puts on two petticoats.

"A Dutch lady burns nothing about her phlegmatic admirer
but his tobacco. You must know, sir, every woman carries
in her hand a stove of coals, which, when she sits, she snugs
under her petticoats, and at this chimney, dozing Strephon
lights his pipe."

In the same letter he contrasts Scotland and Holland.
"There, hills and rocks intercept every prospect; here, it is
all a continued plain. There you might see a well-dressed

Duchess issuing from a dirty close, and here a dirty Dutchman inhabiting a palace. The Scotch may be compared to
a tulip, planted in dung; but I can never see a Dutchman
in his own house, but I think of a magnificent Egyptian
temple dedicated to an ox."

The country itself awakened his admiration. "Nothing,"
said he, "can equal its beauty; wherever I turn my eyes, fine
houses, elegant gardens, statues, grottos, vistas, present themselves; but when you enter their towns, you are charmed
beyond description. No misery is to be seen here, every one
is usefully employed." And again, in his noble description
in "The Traveller":

> "To men of other minds my fancy flies,
> Imbosom'd in the deep where Holland lies.
> Methinks her patient sons before me stand,
> Where the broad ocean leans against the land,
> And, sedulous to stop the coming tide,
> Lifts the tall rampire's artificial pride.
> Onward, methinks, and diligently slow,
> The firm connected bulwark seems to grow;
> Spreads its long arms amid the watery roar,
> Scoops out an empire, and usurps the shore,
> While the pent ocean, rising o'er the pile
> Sees an amphibious world before him smile:
> The slow canal, the yellow blossom'd vale,
> The willow tufted bank, the gliding sail,
> The crowded mart, the cultivated plain,
> A new creation rescued from his reign."

He remained about a year at Leyden, attending the lectures of Gaubius on chemistry and Albinus on anatomy;
though his studies are said to have been miscellaneous, and
directed to literature rather than science. The thirty-three
pounds with which he had set out on his travels were soon
consumed, and he was put to many a shift to meet his
expenses until his precarious remittances should arrive. He

had a good friend on these occasions in a fellow-student and countryman, named Ellis, who afterwards rose to eminence as a physician. He used frequently to loan small sums to Goldsmith, which were always scrupulously paid. Ellis discovered the innate merits of the poor awkward student, and used to declare in after-life that "it was a common remark in Leyden, that in all the peculiarities of Goldsmith, an elevation of mind was to be noted; a philosophical tone and manner; the feelings of a gentleman, and the language and information of a scholar."

Sometimes, in his emergencies, Goldsmith undertook to teach the English language. It is true he was ignorant of the Dutch, but he had a smattering of the French, picked up among the Irish priests at Ballymahon. He depicts his whimsical embarrassment in this respect, in his account in the "Vicar of Wakefield" of the *philosophical vagabond*,[1] who went to Holland to teach the natives English, without knowing a word of their own language. Sometimes, when sorely pinched, and sometimes, perhaps, when flush, he resorted to the gambling-tables, which in those days abounded in Holland. His good friend Ellis repeatedly warned him against this unfortunate propensity, but in vain. It brought its own cure, or rather its own punishment, by stripping him of every shilling.

Ellis once more stepped in to his relief with a true Irishman's generosity, but with more considerateness than generally characterizes an Irishman, for he only granted pecuniary aid on condition of his quitting the sphere of danger. Goldsmith gladly consented to leave Holland, being anxious to visit other parts. He intended to proceed to Paris and pursue his studies there, and was furnished by his friend with money for the journey.

[1] *Vicar of Wakefield*, Chap. XX.

Unluckily, he rambled into the garden of a florist just before quitting Leyden. The tulip-mania was still prevalent in Holland, and some species of that splendid flower brought immense prices. In wandering through the garden, Goldsmith recollected that his uncle Contarine was a tulip-fancier. The thought suddenly struck him that here was an opportunity of testifying, in a delicate manner, his sense of that generous uncle's past kindnesses. In an instant his hand was in his pocket; a number of choice and costly tulip-roots were purchased and packed up for Mr. Contarine; and it was not until he had paid for them that he bethought himself that he had spent all the money borrowed for his travelling expenses. Too proud, however, to give up his journey, and too shame-faced to make another appeal to his friend's liberality, he determined to travel on foot, and depend upon chance and good luck for the means of getting forward; and it is said that he actually set off on a tour of the Continent, in February, 1755, with but one spare shirt, a flute, and a single guinea.

"Blessed," says one of his biographers, "with a good constitution, an adventurous spirit, and with that thoughtless, or, perhaps, happy disposition which takes no care for to-morrow, he continued his travels for a long time in spite of innumerable privations." In his amusing narrative of the adventures of a "Philosophic Vagabond" in the "Vicar of Wakefield," we find shadowed out the expedients he pursued. "I had some knowledge of music, with a tolerable voice; I now turned what was once my amusement into a present means of subsistence. I passed among the harmless peasants of Flanders, and among such of the French as were poor enough to be very merry, for I ever found them sprightly in proportion to their wants. Whenever I approached a peasant's house towards nightfall, I played one of my merri-

est tunes, and that procured me not only a lodging, but subsistence for the next day; but in truth I must own, whenever
I attempted to entertain persons of a higher rank, they always
thought my performance odious, and never made me any
return for my endeavors to please them." [1]

At Paris he attended the chemical lectures of Rouelle, then
in great vogue, where he says he witnessed as bright a circle
of beauty as graced the court of Versailles. His love of theatricals also led him to attend the performances of the celebrated
actress Mademoiselle Clairon, with which he was greatly
delighted. He seems to have looked upon the state of
society with the eye of a philosopher, but to have read the
signs of the times with the prophetic eye of a poet. In his
rambles about the environs of Paris he was struck with the
immense quantities of game running about almost in a tame
state; and saw in those costly and rigid preserves for the
amusement and luxury of the privileged few, a sure "badge
of the slavery of the people." This slavery he predicted was
drawing towards a close. "When I consider that these par-
liaments, the members of which are all created by the court,
and the presidents of which can only act by immediate direction, presume even to mention privileges and freedom, who
till of late received directions from the throne with implicit
humility; when this is considered, I cannot help fancying that
the genius of Freedom has entered that kingdom in disguise.
If they have but three weak monarchs more successively on
the throne, the mask will be laid aside, and the country
will certainly once more be free." [2] Events have testified
to the sage forecast of the poet.

During a brief sojourn in Paris, he appears to have gained
access to valuable society, and to have had the honor and

---

[1] See above, p. 107, note.
[2] *Citizen of the World*, Letter LVI.

pleasure of making the acquaintance of Voltaire;[1] of whom, in after-years, he wrote a memoir. "As a companion," says he, "no man ever exceeded him when he pleased to lead the conversation; which, however, was not always the case. In company which he either disliked or despised, few could be more reserved than he; but when he was warmed in discourse, and got over a hesitating manner, which sometimes he was subject to, it was rapture to hear him. His meagre visage seemed insensibly to gather beauty: every muscle in it had meaning, and his eye beamed with unusual brightness. The person who writes this memoir," continues he, "remembers to have seen him in a select company of wits of both sexes at Paris, when the subject happened to turn upon English taste and learning. Fontenelle, (then nearly a hundred years old,) who was of the party, and who being unacquainted with the language or authors of the country he undertook to condemn, with a spirit truly vulgar began to revile both. Diderot, who liked the English, and knew something of their literary pretensions, attempted to vindicate their poetry and learning, but with unequal abilities. The company quickly perceived that Fontenelle was superior in the dispute, and were surprised at the silence which Voltaire had preserved all the former part of the night, particularly as the conversation happened to turn upon one of his favorite topics. Fontenelle continued his triumph until about twelve o'clock, when Voltaire appeared at last roused from his reverie. His whole frame seemed animated. He began his defence with the utmost defiance mixed with spirit, and now and then let fall the finest strokes of raillery upon his antagonist; and his harangue lasted till three in the morning. I must confess, that, whether from

---

[1] As Voltaire was not in Paris at the time of Goldsmith's sojourn there, Forster conjecturally places this episode at Geneva, where Voltaire had a house.

national partiality, or from the elegant sensibility of his manner, I never was so charmed, nor did I ever remember so
absolute a victory as he gained in this dispute." Goldsmith's
ramblings took him into Germany and Switzerland, from
which last-mentioned country he sent to his brother in Ireland the first brief sketch, afterwards amplified into his poem
of the "Traveller."

At Geneva he became travelling tutor to a mongrel young
gentleman, son of a London pawnbroker, who had been
suddenly elevated into fortune and absurdity by the death
of an uncle. The youth, before setting up for a gentleman,
had been an attorney's apprentice, and was an arrant pettifogger in money-matters. Never were two beings more illy
assorted than he and Goldsmith. We may form an idea of
the tutor and the pupil from the following extract from the
narrative of the "Philosophic Vagabond."

"I was to be the young gentleman's governor, but with a
proviso that he should always be permitted to govern himself.
My pupil, in fact, understood the art of guiding in money-
concerns much better than I. He was heir to a fortune of
about two hundred thousand pounds, left him by an uncle
in the West Indies; and his guardians, to qualify him for the
management of it, had bound him apprentice to an attorney.
Thus avarice was his prevailing passion; all his questions on
the road were, how money might be saved,—which was the
least expensive course of travel,—whether anything could be
bought that would turn to account when disposed of again
in London? Such curiosities on the way as could be seen
for nothing he was ready enough to look at; but if the sight
of them was to be paid for, he usually asserted that he had
been told that they were not worth seeing. He never paid
a bill that he would not observe how amazingly expensive
travelling was, and all this though not yet twenty-one."

In this sketch Goldsmith undoubtedly shadows forth his annoyances as travelling tutor to this concrete young gentleman, compounded of the pawnbroker, the pettifogger, and the West Indian heir, with an overlaying of the city miser. They had continual difficulties on all points of expense until they reached Marseilles, where both were glad to separate.

Once more on foot, but freed from the irksome duties of "bear-leader," and with some of his pay, as tutor, in his pocket, Goldsmith continued his half vagrant peregrinations through part of France and Piedmont and some of the Italian States. He had acquired, as has been shown, a habit of shifting along and living by expedients, and a new one presented itself in Italy. "My skill in music," says he, in the "Philosophic Vagabond," "could avail me nothing in a country where every peasant was a better musician than I; but by this time I had acquired another talent, which answered my purpose as well, and this was a skill in disputation. In all the foreign universities and convents there are, upon certain days, philosophical theses maintained against every adventitious disputant, for which, if the champion opposes with any dexterity, he can claim a gratuity in money, a dinner, and a bed for one night." Though a poor wandering scholar, his reception in these learned piles was as free from humiliation as in the cottages of the peasantry. "With the members of these establishments," said he, "I could converse on topics of literature, *and then I always forgot the meanness of my circumstances.*"

At Padua, where he remained some months, he is said to have taken his medical degree.[1] It is probable he was

---

[1] According to a correspondent of the *Athenæum* (July 21, 1894), who made inquiries of the officials of the University of Padua, there is no record in the university registers of Goldsmith's name among its graduates or alumni. It is not probable that the doctor's degree was ever officially conferred upon Goldsmith.

brought to a pause in this city by the illness of his uncle Contarine; who had hitherto assisted him in his wanderings by occasional, though, of course, slender remittances. Deprived of this source of supplies, he wrote to his friends in Ireland, and especially to his brother-in-law, Hodson, describing his destitute situation. His letters brought him neither money nor reply. It appears, from subsequent correspondence, that his brother-in-law actually exerted himself to raise a subscription for his assistance among his relatives, friends, and acquaintance, but without success. Their faith and hope in him were most probably at an end; as yet he had disappointed them at every point, he had given none of the anticipated proofs of talent, and they were too poor to support what they may have considered the wandering propensities of a heedless spendthrift.

Thus left to his own precarious resources, Goldsmith gave up all further wandering in Italy, without visiting the south, though Rome and Naples must have held out powerful attractions to one of his poetical cast. Once more resuming his pilgrim staff, he turned his face toward England, "walking along from city to city, examining mankind more nearly, and seeing both sides of the picture." In traversing France his flute—his magic flute!—was once more in requisition, as we may conclude by the following passage in his "Traveller":—

> "Gay, sprightly land of mirth and social ease,
> Pleased with thyself, whom all the world can please,
> How often have I led thy sportive choir
> With tuneless pipe beside the murmuring Loire!
> Where shading elms along the margin grew
> And freshened from the wave the zephyr flew;
> And haply though my harsh note falt'ring still,
> But mocked all tune, and marr'd the dancer's skill;

Yet would the village praise my wondrous power,
And dance forgetful of the noontide hour.
Alike all ages: Dames of ancient days
Have led their children through the mirthful maze,
And the gay grandsire, skill'd in gestic lore,
Has frisk'd beneath the burden of three-score."

CHAPTER VI

After two years spent in roving about the Continent,
"pursuing novelty," as he said, "and losing content," Goldsmith landed at Dover early in 1756. He appears to have
had no definite plan of action. The death of his uncle Contarine, and the neglect of his relatives and friends to reply
to his letters, seem to have produced in him a temporary
feeling of loneliness and destitution, and his only thought
was to get to London, and throw himself upon the world.
But how was he to get there? His purse was empty. England was to him as completely a foreign land as any part of
the Continent, and where on earth is a penniless stranger
more destitute? His flute and his philosophy were no longer
of any avail; the English boors cared nothing for music;
there were no convents; and as to the learned and the clergy,
not one of them would give a vagrant scholar a supper and
night's lodging for the best thesis that ever was argued. "You
may easily imagine," says he, in a subsequent letter to his
brother-in-law, "what difficulties I had to encounter, left as
I was without friends, recommendations, money, or impu-
dence, and that in a country where being born an Irishman
was sufficient to keep me unemployed. Many, in such circumstances, would have had recourse to the friar's cord or

115

the suicide's halter.　But, with all my follies, I had principle
to resist the one, and resolution to combat the other."

He applied at one place, we are told, for employment in
the shop of a country apothecary; but all his medical science
gathered in foreign universities could not gain him the management of a pestle and mortar.　He even resorted, it is said,
to the stage as a temporary expedient, and figured in low
comedy at a country town in Kent.　This accords with his
last shift of the Philosophic Vagabond, and with the knowledge of country theatricals displayed in his "Adventures of
a Strolling Player," or may be a story suggested by them.
All this part of his career, however, in which he must have
trod the lowest paths of humility, are only to be conjectured
from vague traditions, or scraps of autobiography gleaned
from his miscellaneous writings.

At length we find him launched on the great metropolis,
or rather drifting about its streets, at night, in the gloomy
month of February, with but a few half-pence in his pocket.
The Deserts of Arabia are not more dreary and inhospitable
than the streets of London at such a time, and to a stranger
in such a plight.　Do we want a picture as an illustration?
We have it in his own works, and furnished, doubtless, from
his own experience.

"The clock has just struck two; what a gloom hangs all
around!　no sound is heard but of the chiming clock, or the
distant watch-dog.　How few appear in those streets, which
but some few hours ago were crowded!　But who are those
who make the streets their couch, and find a short repose
from wretchedness at the doors of the opulent?　They are
strangers, wanderers, and orphans, whose circumstances are
too humble to expect redress, and whose distresses are too
great even for pity.　Some are without the covering even of
rags, and others emaciated with disease; the world has dis-

claimed them; society turns its back upon their distress, and has given them up to nakedness and hunger. *These poor shivering females have once seen happier days, and been flattered into beauty.* They are now turned out to meet the severity of winter. Perhaps now, lying at the doors of their betrayers, they sue to wretches whose hearts are insensible, or debauchees who may curse, but will not relieve them.

"Why, why was I born a man, and yet see the sufferings of wretches I cannot relieve! Poor houseless creatures! The world will give you reproaches, but will not give you relief." [1]

Poor houseless Goldsmith! we may here ejaculate—to what shifts he must have been driven to find shelter and sustenance for himself in this his first venture into London! Many years afterwards, in the days of his social elevation, he startled a polite circle at Sir Joshua Reynolds's by humorously dating an anecdote about the time he "lived among the beggars of Axe Lane." Such may have been the desolate quarters with which he was fain to content himself when thus adrift upon the town, with but a few half-pence in his pocket.

The first authentic trace we have of him in this new part of his career, is filling the situation of an usher to a school, and even this employ he obtained with some difficulty, after a reference for a character to his friends in the University of Dublin. In the "Vicar of Wakefield" he makes George Primrose undergo a whimsical catechism concerning the requisites for an usher. "Have you been bred apprentice to the business?" "No." "Then you won't do for a school. Can you dress the boys' hair?" "No." "Then you won't do for a school. Can you lie three in a bed?" "No." "Then you will never do for a school. Have you a good stomach?" "Yes." "Then you will by no means do for a school. I have

---

[1] *Citizen of the World*, Letter CXVII.

been an usher in a boarding-school myself, and may I die of
an anodyne necklace,[1] but I had rather be under-turnkey in
Newgate. I was up early and late: I was browbeat by the
master, hated for my ugly face by the mistress, worried by
the boys." [2]

Goldsmith remained but a short time in this situation, and
to the mortifications experienced there we doubtless owe the
picturings given in his writings of the hardships of an usher's
life. "He is generally," says he, "the laughing-stock of the
school. Every trick is played upon him; the oddity of his
manner, his dress, or his language, is a fund of eternal ridicule; the master himself now and then cannot avoid joining
in the laugh; and the poor wretch, eternally resenting this
ill-usage, lives in a state of war with all the family." . . . .
"He is obliged, perhaps, to sleep in the same bed with the
French teacher, who disturbs him for an hour every night in
papering and filleting his hair, and stinks worse than a car-
rion with his rancid pomatums, when he lays his head beside
him on the bolster." [3]

His next shift was as assistant in the laboratory of a
chemist near Fish-Street Hill. After remaining here a few
months, he heard that Dr. Sleigh, who had been his friend
and fellow-student at Edinburgh, was in London. Eager to
meet with a friendly face in this land of strangers, he immediately called on him; "but though it was Sunday, and it is
to be supposed I was in my best clothes, Sleigh scarcely knew
me—such is the tax the unfortunate pay to poverty. However, when he did recollect me, I found his heart as warm as
ever, and he shared his purse and friendship with me during his continuance in London."

---

[1] That is, the hangman's noose.
[2] *Vicar of Wakefield*, Chap. XX.
[3] *The Bee*, No. VI.

Through the advice and assistance of Dr. Sleigh, he now commenced the practice of medicine, but in a small way, in Bankside, Southwark, and chiefly among the poor; for he wanted the figure, address, polish, and management, to succeed among the rich. His old school-mate and college companion, Beatty, who used to aid him with his purse at the university, met him about this time, decked out in the tarnished finery of a second-hand suit of green and gold, with a shirt and neckcloth of a fortnight's wear.

Poor Goldsmith endeavored to assume a prosperous air in the eyes of his early associate. "He was practising physic," he said, "and *doing very well!*" At this moment poverty was pinching him to the bone in spite of his practice and his dirty finery. His fees were necessarily small and ill paid, and he was fain to seek some precarious assistance from his pen. Here his quondam fellow-student, Dr. Sleigh, was again of service, introducing him to some of the booksellers, who gave him occasional, though starveling, employment. According to tradition, however, his most efficient patron just now was a journeyman printer, one of his poor patients of Bankside, who had formed a good opinion of his talents, and perceived his poverty and his literary shifts. The printer was in the employ of Mr. Samuel Richardson, the author of "Pamela," "Clarissa," and "Sir Charles Grandison"; who combined the novelist and the publisher, and was in flourishing circumstances. Through the journeyman's intervention Goldsmith is said to have become acquainted with Richardson, who employed him as reader and corrector of the press, at his printing establishment in Salisbury Court,—an occupation which he alternated with his medical duties.

Being admitted occasionally to Richardson's parlor, he began to form literary acquaintances, among whom the most important was Dr. Young, the author of "Night Thoughts,"

a poem in the height of fashion. It is not probable, however,
that much familiarity took place at the time between the
literary lion of the day and the poor Æsculapius of Bankside,
the humble corrector of the press. Still the communion with
literary men had its effect to set his imagination teeming.
Dr. Farr, one of his Edinburgh fellow-students, who was at
London about this time, attending the hospitals and lectures,
gives us an amusing account of Goldsmith in his literary
character.

"Early in January he called upon me one morning before
I was up, and, on my entering the room, I recognized my
old acquaintance, dressed in a rusty, full-trimmed black suit,
with his pockets full of papers, which instantly reminded me
of the poet in Garrick's farce of 'Lethe.' After we had finished
our breakfast, he drew from his pocket part of a tragedy,
which he said he had brought for my correction. In vain I
pleaded inability, when he began to read; and every part on
which I expressed a doubt as to the propriety was immediately
blotted out. I then most earnestly pressed him not to trust
to my judgment, but to take the opinion of persons better
qualified to decide on dramatic compositions. He now told
me he had submitted his production, so far as he had written,
to Mr. Richardson, the author of 'Clarissa,' on which I per-
emptorily declined offering another criticism on the performance."

From the graphic description given of him by Dr. Farr,
it will be perceived that the tarnished finery of green and
gold had been succeeded by a professional suit of black, to
which, we are told, were added the wig and cane indispensa-
ble to medical doctors in those days. The coat was a second-
hand one, of rusty velvet, with a patch on the left breast,
which he adroitly covered with his three-cornered hat during
his medical visits; and we have an amusing anecdote of his

contest of courtesy with a patient who persisted in endeavoring to relieve him from the hat, which only made him press it more devoutly to his heart.

Nothing further has ever been heard of the tragedy mentioned by Dr. Farr; it was probably never completed. The same gentleman speaks of a strange Quixotic scheme which Goldsmith had in contemplation at the time, of going to decipher the inscriptions on the *written mountains*,[1] though he was altogether ignorant of Arabic, or the language in which they might be supposed to be written. "The salary of three hundred pounds," adds Dr. Farr, "which had been left for the purpose, was the temptation." This was probably one of the many dreamy projects with which his fervid brain was apt to teem. On such subjects he was prone to talk vaguely and magnificently, but inconsiderately, from a kindled imagination rather than a well-instructed judgment. He had always a great notion of expeditions to the East, and wonders to be seen and effected in the Oriental countries.

---

[1] The mountains are situated on the west side of the Sinaitic peninsula. The inscriptions, about which so much was said in Goldsmith's day, have turned out to be of very little importance.

CHAPTER VII

LIFE OF A PEDAGOGUE—KINDNESS TO SCHOOLBOYS—PERTNESS
IN RETURN—EXPENSIVE CHARITIES—THE GRIFFITHS AND THE
"MONTHLY REVIEW"—TOILS OF A LITERARY HACK—RUPTURE
WITH THE GRIFFITHS.

Among the most cordial of Goldsmith's intimates in London during this time of precarious struggle, were certain of his former fellow-students in Edinburgh. One of these was the son of a Dr. Milner, a dissenting minister, who kept a classical school of eminence at Peckham, in Surrey. Young Milner had a favorable opinion of Goldsmith's abilities and attainments, and cherished for him that goodwill which his genial nature seems ever to have inspired among his school and college associates. His father falling ill, the young man negotiated with Goldsmith to take temporary charge of the school. The latter readily consented; for he was discouraged by the slow growth of medical reputation and practice, and as yet had no confidence in the coy smiles of the Muse. Laying by his wig and cane, therefore, and once more wielding the ferule, he resumed the character of the pedagogue, and for some time reigned as vicegerent over the academy at Peckham. He appears to have been well treated by both Dr. Milner and his wife; and became a favorite with the scholars from his easy, indulgent good-nature. He mingled in their sports; told them droll stories; played on the flute for their amusement, and spent his money in treating them to sweetmeats and other schoolboy dainties. His familiarity was sometimes carried too far; he indulged in boyish pranks and practical jokes, and drew upon himself retorts in

122

kind, which, however, he bore with great good-humor. Once,
indeed, he was touched to the quick by a piece of schoolboy
pertness. After playing on the flute, he spoke with enthusiasm of music, as delightful in itself, and as a valuable accomplishment for a gentleman, whereupon a youngster, with a
glance at his ungainly person, wished to know if he considered himself a gentleman. Poor Goldsmith, feelingly alive
to the awkwardness of his appearance and the humility of his
situation, winced at this unthinking sneer, which long rankled
in his mind.

As usual, while in Dr. Milner's employ, his benevolent
feelings were a heavy tax upon his purse, for he never could
resist a tale of distress, and was apt to be fleeced by every
sturdy beggar; so that, between his charity and his munificence, he was generally in advance of his slender salary.
"You had better, Mr. Goldsmith, let me take care of your
money," said Mrs. Milner one day, "as I do for some of the
young gentlemen."   "In truth, madam, there is equal need!"
was the good-humored reply.

Dr. Milner was a man of some literary pretensions, and
wrote occasionally for the "Monthly Review," of which a
bookseller, by the name of Griffiths, was proprietor. This
work was an advocate for Whig principles, and had been in
prosperous existence for nearly eight years. Of late, however, periodicals had multiplied exceedingly, and a formidable
Tory rival had started up in the "*Critical Review,*" published
by Archibald Hamilton, a bookseller, and aided by the powerful and popular pen of Dr. Smollett.[1]   Griffiths was obliged
to recruit his forces. While so doing he met Goldsmith, a
humble occupant of a seat at Dr. Milner's table, and was
struck with remarks on men and books, which fell from him

---

[1] Tobias George Smollett (1721-1771) was a prolific novelist and writer on
miscellaneous literary and political questions.

in the course of conversation. He took occasion to sound him privately as to his inclination and capacity as a reviewer, and was furnished by him with specimens of his literary and critical talents. They proved satisfactory. The consequence was that Goldsmith once more changed his mode of life, and in April, 1757, became a contributor to the "Monthly Review," at a small fixed salary, with board and lodging; and accordingly took up his abode with Mr. Griffiths, at the sign of the Dunciad, Paternoster Row. As usual we trace this phase of his fortunes in his semi-fictitious writings; his sudden transmutation of the pedagogue into the author being humorously set forth in the case of "George Primrose" in the "Vicar of Wakefield." "Come," says George's adviser, "I see you are a lad of spirit and some learning; what do you think of commencing author like me? You have read in books, no doubt, of men of genius starving at the trade: at present I'll show you forty very dull fellows about town that live by it in opulence. All honest, jog-trot men, who go on smoothly and dully, and write history and politics, and are praised: men, sir, who, had they been bred cobblers, would all their lives only have mended shoes, but never made them." "Finding," (says George) "that there was no great degree of gentility affixed to the character of an usher, I resolved to accept his proposal; and, having the highest respect for literature, hailed the *antiqua mater*[1] of Grub Street[2] with reverence. I thought it my glory to pursue a track which Dryden and Otway trod before me."[3] Alas, Dryden struggled with indigence all his days; and Otway, it is said, fell a victim to famine

---

[1] Ancient mother.

[2] Grub Street is thus whimsically but adequately defined by Johnson in his *Dictionary:* "The name of a street in London, much inhabited by writers of small histories, dictionaries, and temporary poems; whence any mean production is called Grub Street."

[3] Dryden (1631-1700); Thomas Otway (1651-1685), a late Elizabethan dramatist. The passage is from the *Vicar of Wakefield*, Chap. XX.

in his thirty-fifth year, being strangled by a roll of bread, which he devoured with the voracity of a starving man.

In Goldsmith's experience the track soon proved a thorny one. Griffiths was a hard business-man, of shrewd, worldly good sense, but little refinement or cultivation. He meddled or rather muddled with literature, too, in a business way, altering and modifying occasionally the writings of his contributors, and in this he was aided by his wife, who, according to Smollett, was "an antiquated female critic and a dabbler in the 'Review.'" Such was the literary vassalage to which Goldsmith had unwarily subjected himself. A diurnal drudgery was imposed on him, irksome to his indolent habits, and attended by circumstances humiliating to his pride. He had to write daily from nine o'clock until two, and often throughout the day; whether in the vein or not and on subjects dictated by his task-master, however foreign to his taste; in a word, he was treated as a mere literary hack. But this was not the worst; it was the critical supervision of Griffiths and his wife, which grieved him; the "illiterate, bookselling Griffiths," as Smollett called them, "who presumed to revise, alter, and amend the articles contributed to their 'Review.' Thank Heaven," crowed Smollett, "the 'Critical Review' is not written under the restraint of a bookseller and his wife. Its principal writers are independent of each other, unconnected with booksellers, and unawed by old women!"

This literary vassalage, however, did not last long. The bookseller became more and more exacting. He accused his hack-writer of idleness; of abandoning his writing-desk and literary workshop at an early hour of the day; and of assuming a tone and manner *above his situation*. Goldsmith, in return, charged him with impertinence; his wife, with meanness and parsimony in her household treatment

of him, and both of literary meddling and marring. The
engagement was broken off at the end of five months, by
mutual consent, and without any violent rupture, as it will
be found they afterwards had occasional dealings with each
other.

Though Goldsmith was now nearly thirty years of age,
he had produced nothing to give him a decided reputation.
He was as yet a mere writer for bread. The articles he had
contributed to the "Review" were anonymous, and were
never avowed by him. They have since been, for the most
part, ascertained; and though thrown off hastily, often treating on subjects of temporary interest, and marred by the
Griffith interpolations, they are still characterized by his
sound, easy good sense, and the genial graces of his style.
Johnson observed that Goldsmith's genius flowered late; he
should have said it flowered early, but was late in bringing
its fruit to maturity.

CHAPTER VIII

NEWBERY, OF PICTURE-BOOK MEMORY—HOW TO KEEP UP AP-
PEARANCES—MISERIES OF AUTHORSHIP—A POOR RELATION—
LETTER TO HODSON.

Being now known in the publishing world, Goldsmith
began to find casual employment in various quarters; among
others he wrote occasionally for the "Literary Magazine,"
a production set on foot by Mr. John Newbery, bookseller,
St. Paul's Churchyard, renowned in nursery literature
throughout the latter half of the last century for his picture-
books for children. Newbery was a worthy, intelligent,
kind-hearted man, and a seasonable, though cautious friend
to authors, relieving them with small loans when in pecuniary difficulties, though always taking care to be well repaid
by the labor of their pens. Goldsmith introduces him in a
humorous yet friendly manner in his novel of the "Vicar of
Wakefield." "This person was no other than the philanthropic bookseller in St. Paul's Churchyard, who has written
so many little books for children; he called himself their
friend; but he was the friend of all mankind. He was no
sooner alighted but he was in haste to be gone; for he was
ever on business of importance, and was at that time actually
compiling materials for the history of one Mr. Thomas Trip.
I immediately recollected this good-natured man's red-pim-
pled face." [1]

Besides his literary job-work, Goldsmith also resumed his
medical practice, but with very trifling success. The scan-

---

[1] See Introduction, p. 44 ff. The passage is from the *Vicar of Wakefield*,
Chap. XVIII. Johnson humorously describes Newbery under the name
Jack Whirler in the *Idler*, No. 19 (Saturday, August 19, 1758).

tiness of his purse still obliged him to live in obscure lodgings somewhere in the vicinity of Salisbury Square, Fleet Street; but his extended acquaintance and rising importance caused him to consult appearances. He adopted an expedient, then very common, and still practised in London among those who have to tread the narrow path between pride and poverty: while he burrowed in lodgings suited to his means, he "hailed," as it is termed, from the Temple Exchange Coffee-House near Temple Bar. Here he received his medical calls; hence he dated his letters; and here he passed much of his leisure hours, conversing with the frequenters of the place. "Thirty pounds a year," said a poor Irish painter, who understood the art of shifting, "is enough to enable a man to live in London without being contemptible. Ten pounds will find him clothes and linen; he can live in a garret on eighteen pence a week; hail from a coffee-house, where, by occasionally spending three-pence, he may pass some hours each day in good company; he may breakfast on bread and milk for a penny; dine for sixpence; do without supper; and on *clean-shirt-day* he may go abroad and pay visits."

Goldsmith seems to have taken a leaf from this poor devil's manual in respect to the coffee-house at least. Indeed, coffee-houses in those days were the resorts of wits and *literati;* where the topics of the day were gossiped over, and the affairs of literature and the drama discussed and criticised. In this way he enlarged the circle of his intimacy, which now embraced several names of notoriety.

Do we want a picture of Goldsmith's experience in this part of his career? we have it in his observations on the life of an author in the *"Inquiry into the State of Polite Learning,"* published some years afterwards.

"The author, unpatronized by the great, has naturally recourse to the bookseller. There cannot, perhaps, be imagined a combination more prejudicial to taste than this. It is the interest of the one to allow as little for writing, and for the other to write as much as possible; accordingly, tedious compilations and periodical magazines are the result of their joint endeavors. In these circumstances the author bids adieu to fame; writes for bread; and for that only imagination is seldom called in. He sits down to address the venal Muse with the most phlegmatic apathy; and, as we are told of the Russian, courts his mistress by falling asleep in her lap."

Again. "Those who are unacquainted with the world are apt to fancy the man of wit as leading a very agreeable life. They conclude, perhaps, that he is attended with silent admiration, and dictates to the rest of mankind with all the eloquence of conscious superiority. Very different is his present situation. He is called an author, and all know that an author is a thing only to be laughed at. His person, not his jest, becomes the mirth of the company. At his approach the most fat, unthinking face brightens into malicious meaning. Even aldermen laugh, and avenge on him the ridicule which was lavished on their forefathers. . . . . The poet's poverty is a standing topic of contempt. His writing for bread is an unpardonable offence. Perhaps of all mankind, an author in these times is used most hardly. We keep him poor, and yet revile his poverty. We reproach him for living by his wit, and yet allow him no other means to live. His taking refuge in garrets and cellars has of late been violently objected to him, and that by men who, I have hope, are more apt to pity than insult his distress. Is poverty a careless fault? No doubt he knows how to prefer a bottle of champagne to the nectar of the neighboring ale-house, or a venison pasty to a plate of potatoes. Want of delicacy is not in him, but in those who deny him the opportunity of

making an elegant choice. Wit certainly is the property of
those who have it, nor should we be displeased if it is the only
property a man sometimes has. We must not underrate him
who uses it for subsistence, and flees from the ingratitude of
the age, even to a bookseller for redress." . . . .

"If the author be necessary among us, let us treat him
with proper consideration as a child of the public, not as a
rent-charge on the community. And indeed a child of the
public he is in all respects; for while so well able to direct
others, how incapable is he frequently found of guiding himself. His simplicity exposes him to all the insidious approaches of cunning: his sensibility, to the slightest invasions
of contempt. Though possessed of fortitude to stand un-
moved the expected bursts of an earthquake, yet of feelings
so exquisitely poignant, as to agonize under the slightest disappointment. Broken rest, tasteless meals, and causeless
anxieties shorten life and render it unfit for active employ-
ments; prolonged vigils and intense applications still farther
contract his span, and make his time glide insensibly away."[1]

While poor Goldsmith was thus struggling with the difficulties and discouragements which in those days beset the
path of an author, his friends in Ireland received accounts
of his literary success and of the distinguished acquaintances
he was making. This was enough to put the wise heads at
Lissoy and Ballymahon in a ferment of conjectures. With
the exaggerated notions of provincial relatives concerning
the family great man in the metropolis, some of Goldsmith's
poor kindred pictured him to themselves seated in high places,
clothed in purple and fine linen, and hand and glove with the
givers of gifts and dispensers of patronage. Accordingly,
he was one day surprised at the sudden apparition, in his
miserable lodging, of his younger brother Charles, a raw

---

[1] Cf. Introduction, p. 42.

youth of twenty-one, endowed with a double share of the family heedlessness, and who expected to be forthwith helped into some snug by-path to fortune by one or other of Oliver's great friends. Charles was sadly disconcerted on learning that, so far from being able to provide for others, his brother could scarcely take care of himself. He looked round with a rueful eye on the poet's quarters, and could not help expressing his surprise and disappointment at finding him no better off. "All in good time, my dear boy," replied poor Goldsmith, with infinite good humor; "I shall be richer by-and-by. Addison, let me tell you, wrote his poem of the 'Campaign'[1] in a garret in the Haymarket, three stories high, and you see I am not come to that yet, for I have only got to the second story."

Charles Goldsmith did not remain long to embarrass his brother in London. With the same roving disposition and inconsiderate temper of Oliver, he suddenly departed in an humble capacity to seek his fortune in the West Indies, and nothing was heard of him for above thirty years, when, after having been given up as dead by his friends, he made his reappearance in England.

Shortly after his departure, Goldsmith wrote a letter to his brother-in-law, Daniel Hodson, Esq., of which the following is an extract; it was partly intended, no doubt, to dissipate any further illusions concerning his fortunes which might float on the magnificent imagination of his friends in Bally-mahon.

"I suppose you desire to know my present situation. As there is nothing in it at which I should blush or which mankind could censure, I see no reason for making it a secret.

---

[1] Addison wrote his *Campaign* in 1704, after the battle of Blenheim. It is a panegyric of the Duke of Marlborough, the hero of Blenheim, and secured for Addison his first important appointment from the leaders of the Whig party.

In short, by very little practice as a physician, and a very
little reputation as a poet, I make a shift to live. Nothing is
more apt to introduce us to the gates of the Muses than poverty; but it were well if they only left us at the door. The
mischief is, they sometimes choose to give us their company
to the entertainment; and want, instead of being gentleman-
usher, often turns master of the ceremonies.

"Thus, upon learning I write, no doubt you imagine I
starve; and the name of an author naturally reminds you of
a garret. In this particular I do not think proper to unde-
ceive my friends. But, whether I eat or starve, live in a
first floor or four pairs of stairs high, I still remember them
with ardor; nay, my very country comes in for a share of my
affection. Unaccountable fondness for country, this *maladie
du pais*, as the French call it! Unaccountable that he should
still have an affection for a place, who never, when in it,
received above common civility; who never brought anything
out of it except his brogue and his blunders. Surely my
affection is equally ridiculous with the Scotchman's, who
refused to be cured of the itch because it made him unco'
thoughtful of his wife and bonny Inverary.

"But, now, to be serious: let me ask myself what gives
me a wish to see Ireland again. The country is a fine one,
perhaps? No. There are good company in Ireland? No.
The conversation there is generally made up of a smutty
toast or a bawdy song; the vivacity supported by some
humble cousin, who had just folly enough to earn his dinner.
Then, perhaps, there is more wit and learning among the
Irish? Oh, Lord, no! There has been more money spent
in the encouragement of the Padareen mare[1] there one season,
than given in rewards to learned men since the time of Usher.[2]

---

[1] That is, in horse-racing.
[2] James Usher (1580-1656), Archbishop of Armagh, in Ireland.

All their productions in learning amount to perhaps a translation, or a few tracts in divinity; and all their productions
in wit to just nothing at all. Why the plague, then, so fond
of Ireland? Then, all at once, because you, my dear friend,
and a few more who are exceptions to the general picture,
have a residence there. This it is that gives me all the pangs
I feel in separation. I confess I carry this spirit sometimes
to the souring the pleasures I at present possess. If I go to
the opera, where Signora Columba pours out all the mazes
of melody, I sit and sigh for Lissoy fireside, and Johnny
Armstrong's 'Last Good-night' from Peggy Golden. If I
climb Hampstead Hill, than where nature never exhibited
a more magnificent prospect, I confess it fine: but then I
had rather be placed on the little mount before Lissoy
gate, and there take in, to me, the most pleasing horizon in
nature.

"Before Charles came hither, my thoughts sometimes
found refuge from severer studies among my friends in Ireland. I fancied strange revolutions at home; but I find it
was the rapidity of my own motion that gave an imaginary
one to objects really at rest. No alterations there. Some
friends, he tells me, are still lean, but very rich; others very
fat, but still very poor. Nay, all the news I hear of you is,
that you sally out in visits among the neighbors, and sometimes make a migration from the blue bed to the brown. I
could from my heart wish that you and she (Mrs. Hodson),
and Lissoy and Ballymahon, and all of you, would fairly
make a migration into Middlesex; though, upon second
thoughts, this might be attended with a few inconveniences.
Therefore, as the mountain will not come to Mohammed,
why Mohammed shall go to the mountain; or, to speak plain
English, as you cannot conveniently pay me a visit, if next
summer I can contrive to be absent six weeks from London,

I shall spend three of them among my friends in Ireland. But first, believe me, my design is purely to visit, and neither to cut a figure nor levy contributions; neither to excite envy nor solicit favor; in fact, my circumstances are adapted to neither. I am too poor to be gazed at, and too rich to need assistance."

CHAPTER IX

For some time Goldsmith continued to write miscellane-
ously for reviews and other periodical publications, but
without making any decided hit, to use a technical term.
Indeed as yet he appeared destitute of the strong excitement
of literary ambition, and wrote only on the spur of necessity
and at the urgent importunity of his bookseller. His indolent and truant disposition, ever averse from labor and delighting in holiday, had to be scourged up to its task; still it
was this very truant disposition which threw an unconscious
charm over everything he wrote; bringing with it honeyed
thoughts and pictured images which had sprung up in his
mind in the sunny hours of idleness: these effusions, dashed
off on compulsion in the exigency of the moment, were published anonymously; so that they made no collective impression on the public, and reflected no fame on the name of
their author.

In an essay published some time subsequently in the
"Bee," Goldsmith adverts in his own humorous way to his
impatience at the tardiness with which his desultory and
unacknowledged essays crept into notice. "I was once
induced," says he, "to show my indignation against the
public by discontinuing my efforts to please; and was bravely

resolved, like Raleigh,[1] to vex them by burning my manuscripts in a passion. Upon reflection, however, I considered
what set or body of people would be displeased at my rash-
ness. The sun, after so sad an accident, might shine next
morning as bright as usual; men might laugh and sing the
next day, and transact business as before; and not a single
creature feel any regret but myself. Instead of having Apollo
in mourning or the Muses in a fit of the spleen; instead of
having the learned world apostrophizing at my untimely
decease; perhaps all Grub Street might laugh at my fate, and
self-approving dignity be unable to shield me from ridicule." [2]

Circumstances occurred about this time to give a new
direction to Goldsmith's hopes and schemes. Having resumed
for a brief period the superintendence of the Peckham school,
during a fit of illness of Dr. Milner, that gentleman, in requi-
tal for his timely services, promised to use his influence with
a friend, an East-India director, to procure him a medical
appointment in India.

There was every reason to believe that the influence of
Dr. Milner would be effectual; but how was Goldsmith to
find the ways and means of fitting himself out for a voyage
to the Indies? In this emergency he was driven to a more
extended exercise of the pen than he had yet attempted. His
skirmishing among books as a reviewer, and his disputatious
ramble among the schools and universities and *literati* of
the Continent, had filled his mind with facts and observations
which he now set about digesting into a treatise of some mag-
nitude, to be entitled "An Inquiry into the Present State of
Polite Learning in Europe." As the work grew on his hands,
his sanguine temper ran ahead of his labors. Feeling secure

---

[1] Sir Walter Raleigh, who in a fit of anger destroyed the second part of
his *History of the World* on the publisher's complaint of the slow sale of the
first part, published in 1614.

[2] *The Bee*, No. IV.

of success in England, he was anxious to forestall the piracy
of the Irish press; for as yet, the union not having taken place,[1]
the English law of copyright did not extend to the other side
of the Irish channel. He wrote, therefore, to his friends in
Ireland, urging them to circulate his proposals for his con-
templated work, and obtain subscriptions payable in advance;
the money to be transmitted to a Mr. Bradley, an eminent
bookseller in Dublin, who would give a receipt for it and be
accountable for the delivery of the books. The letters written by him on this occasion are worthy of copious citation
as being full of character and interest. One was to his
relative and college intimate, Edward Wells, who had studied
for the bar, but was now living at ease on his estate at Roscommon. "You have quitted," writes Goldsmith, "the plan
of life which you once intended to pursue, and given up ambition for domestic tranquillity. I cannot avoid feeling some
regret that one of my few friends has declined a pursuit in
which he had every reason to expect success. I have often
let my fancy loose when you were the subject, and have
imagined you gracing the bench, or thundering at the bar:
while I have taken no small pride to myself, and whispered
to all that I could come near, that this was my cousin. Instead of this, it seems, you are merely contented to be a happy
man; to be esteemed by your acquaintances; to cultivate your
paternal acres; to take unmolested a nap under one of your
own hawthorns, or in Mrs. Wells's bedchamber, which, even
a poet must confess, is rather the more comfortable place of
the two. But, however your resolutions may be altered with
regard to your situation in life, I persuade myself they are
unalterable with respect to your friends in it. I cannot
think the world has taken such entire possession of that heart
(once so susceptible of friendship) as not to have left a corner

---

[1] The act of union of Great Britain and Ireland was passed in 1800.

there for a friend or two, but I flatter myself that even I have a place among the number. This I have a claim to from the similitude of our dispositions; or setting that aside, I can demand it as a right by the most equitable law of nature: I mean that of retaliation; for indeed you have more than your share in mine. I am a man of few professions; and yet at this very instant I cannot avoid the painful apprehension that my present professions (which speak not half my feelings) should be considered only as a pretext to cover a request, as I have a request to make. No, my dear Ned, I know you are too generous to think so, and you know me too proud to stoop to unnecessary insincerity;—I have a request, it is true, to make; but as I know to whom I am a petitioner, I make it without diffidence or confusion. It is in short this: I am going to publish a book in London," &c. The residue of the letter specifies the nature of the request, which was merely to aid in circulating his proposals and obtaining subscriptions. The letter of the poor author, however, was unattended· to and unacknowledged by the prosperous Mr. Wells, of Roscommon, though in after-years he was proud to claim relationship to Dr. Goldsmith, when he had risen to celebrity.

Another of Goldsmith's letters was to Robert Bryantòn, with whom he had long ceased to be in correspondence. "I believe," writes he, "that they who are drunk, or out of their wits, fancy everybody else in the same condition. Mine is a friendship that neither distance nor time can efface, which is probably the reason that, for the soul of me, I can't avoid thinking yours of the same complexion; and yet I have many reasons for being of a contrary opinion, else why, in so long an absence, was I never made a partner in your concerns? To hear of your success would have given me the utmost pleasure; and a communication of your very disappointments would divide the uneasiness I too frequently feel for my own. Indeed, my dear Bob, you don't conceive how unkindly you have treated one whose circumstances afford him few prospects of pleasure, except those reflected from the happiness of his friends. However, since you have not let me hear from you, I have in some measure disappointed your neglect by frequently thinking of you. Every day or so I remember the calm anecdotes of your life, from the fireside to the easy chair; recall the various adventures that first cemented our friendship; the school, the college, or the tavern; preside in fancy over your cards; and am displeased at your bad play when the rubber goes against you, though not with all that agony of soul as when I was once your partner. Is it not strange that two of such like affections should be so much separated, and so differently employed as we are? You seem placed at the centre of fortune's wheel, and, let it revolve ever so fast, are insensible of the motion. I seem to have been tied to the circumference, and whirled disagreeably round, as if on a whirligig."

He then runs into a whimsical and extravagant tirade about his future prospects, the wonderful career of fame and fortune that awaits him, and after indulging in all kinds of humorous gasconades, concludes: "Let me, then, stop my fancy to take a view of my future self,—and, as the boys say, light down to see myself on horseback. Well, now that I am down, where the d—l *is I?* Oh gods! gods! here in a garret, writing for bread, and expecting to be dunned for a milk score!"

He would, on this occasion, have doubtless written to his uncle Contarine, but that generous friend was sunk into a helpless hopeless state from which death soon released him.

Cut off thus from the kind coöperation of his uncle, he addresses a letter to his daughter Jane, the companion of his

schoolboy and happy days, now the wife of Mr. Lawder.
The object was to secure her interest with her husband in
promoting the circulation of his proposals. The letter is
full of character.

"If you should ask," he begins, "why, in an interval of
so many years, you never heard from me, permit me, madam,
to ask the same question. I have the best excuse in recrim-
ination. I wrote to Kilmore from Leyden in Holland, from
Louvain in Flanders, and Rouen in France, but received no
answer. To what could I attribute this silence but to dis-
pleasure or forgetfulness? Whether I was right in my
conjecture I do not pretend to determine; but this I must
ingenuously own, that I have a thousand times in my turn
endeavored to forget *them*, whom I could not but look upon as
forgetting *me*. I have attempted to blot their names from my
memory, and, I confess it, spent whole days in efforts to tear
their image from my heart. Could I have succeeded, you had
not now been troubled with this renewal of a discontinued
correspondence; but, as every effort the restless make to procure sleep serves but to keep them waking, all my attempts
contributed to impress what I would forget deeper on my
imagination. But this subject I would willingly turn from,
and yet, 'for the soul of me,' I can't till I have said all. I was,
madam, when I discontinued writing to Kilmore, in such
circumstances, that all my endeavors to continue your regards
might be attributed to wrong motives. My letters might
be looked upon as the petitions of a beggar, and not
the offerings of a friend; while all my professions, instead of
being considered of the result of disinterested esteem, might
be ascribed to venal insincerity. I believe, indeed, you had ·
too much generosity to place them in such a light, but I could
not bear even the shadow of such a suspicion. The most
delicate friendships are always most sensible of the slightest

invasion, and the strongest jealousy is ever attendant on the warmest regard. I could not—I own I could not—continue a correspondence in which every acknowledgement for past favors might be considered as an indirect request for future ones; and where it might be thought I gave my heart from a motive of gratitude alone, when I was conscious of having bestowed it on much more disinterested principles. It is true, this conduct might have been simple enough; but yourself must confess it was in character. Those who know me at all, know that I have always been actuated by different principles from the rest of mankind: and while none regarded the interest of his friend more, no man on earth regarded his own less. I have often affected bluntness to avoid the imputation of flattery; have frequently seemed to overlook those merits too obvious to escape notice, and pretended disregard to those instances of good nature and good sense, which I could not fail tacitly to applaud; and all this lest I should be ranked among the grinning tribe, who say 'very true' to all that is said; who fill a vacant chair at a tea-table; whose narrow souls never moved in a wider circle than the circumference of a guinea; and who had rather be reckoning the money in your pocket than the virtue in your breast. All this, I say, I have done, and a thousand other very silly, though very disinterested, things in my time; and for all which no soul cares a farthing about me. . . . Is it to be wondered that he should once in his life forget you, who has been all his life forgetting himself? However, it is probable you may one of these days see me turned into a perfect hunks, and as dark and intricate as a mouse-hole. I have already given my landlady orders for an entire reform in the state of my finances. I declaim against hot suppers, drink less sugar in my tea, and check my grate with brickbats. Instead of hanging my room with pictures, I intend to adorn it with maxims of frugality. Those will make pretty furniture enough, and won't be a bit too expensive; for I will draw them all out with my own hands, and my landlady's daughter shall frame them with the parings of my black waistcoat. Each maxim is to be inscribed on a sheet of clean paper, and wrote with my best pen; of which the following will serve as a specimen. *Look sharp: Mind the main chance: Money is money now: If you have a thousand pounds you can put your hands by your sides, and say you are worth a thousand pounds every day of the year: Take a farthing from a hundred and it will be a hundred no longer.* Thus, which way soever I turn my eyes, they are sure to meet one of those friendly monitors; and as we are told of an actor who hung his room round with looking-glass to correct the defects of his person, my apartment shall be furnished in a peculiar manner, to correct the errors of my mind. Faith! madam, I heartily wish to be rich, if it were only for this reason, to say without a blush how much I esteem you. But, alas! I have many a fatigue to encounter before that happy time comes, when your poor old simple friend may again give a loose to the luxuriance of his nature; sitting by Kilmore fireside, recount the various adventures of a hard-fought life; laugh over the follies of the day; join his flute to your harpsichord; and forget that ever he starved in those streets where Butler[1] and Otway starved before him. And now I mention those great names—my Uncle! he is no more that soul of fire as when I once knew him. Newton and Swift[2] grew dim with age as well as he. But what shall I say? His mind was too active an inhabitant not to disorder the feeble mansion of its abode; for the richest jewels soonest wear their settings. Yet, who but the fool would lament his

---

[1] Samuel Butler (1612-1680), author of the satirical poem *Hudibras;* for Otway, see above, p. 124.

[2] Newton and Swift both lost control of their minds in their last years.

condition! He now forgets the calamities of life. Perhaps indulgent Heaven has given him a foretaste of that tranquillity here, which he so well deserves hereafter. But I must come to business; for business, as one of my maxims tells me, must be minded or lost. I am agoing to publish in London a book entitled '*The Present State of Taste and Literature in Europe.*' The booksellers in Ireland republish every performance there without making the author any consideration. I would, in this respect, disappoint their avarice, and have all the profits of my labor to myself. I must, therefore, request Mr. Lawder to circulate among his friends and acquaintances a hundred of my proposals, which I have given the book-seller, Mr. Bradley, in Dame Street, directions to send to him. If, in pursuance of such circulation, he should receive any subscriptions, I entreat, when collected, they may be sent to Mr. Bradley, as aforesaid, who will give a receipt, and be accountable for the work, or a return of the subscription. If this request (which, if it be complied with, will in some measure be an encouragement to a man of learning) should be disagreeable or troublesome, I would not press it; for I would be the last man on earth to have my labors go a-begging; but if I know Mr. Lawder (and sure I ought to know him), he will accept the employment with pleasure. All I can say—if he writes a book, I will get him two hundred subscribers, and those of the best wits in Europe. Whether this request is complied with or not, I shall not be uneasy; but there is one petition I must make to him and to you, which I solicit with the warmest ardor, and in which I cannot bear a refusal. I mean, dear madam, that I may be allowed to subscribe myself, your ever affectionate and obliged kins-man, OLIVER GOLDSMITH. Now see how I blot and blunder, when I am asking a favor."

CHAPTER X

While Goldsmith was yet laboring at his treatise, the
promise made him by Dr. Milner was carried into effect, and
he was actually appointed physician and surgeon to one of
the factories on the coast of Coromandel. His imagination
was immediately on fire with visions of Oriental wealth and
magnificence. It is true the salary did not exceed one hundred pounds, but then, as appointed physician, he would
have the exclusive practice of the place, amounting to one
thousand pounds per annum; with advantages to be derived
from trade and from the high interest of money—twenty per
cent.; in a word, for once in his life, the road to fortune lay
broad and straight before him.

Hitherto, in his correspondence with his friends, he had
said nothing of his India scheme; but now he imparted to
them his brilliant prospects, urging the importance of their
circulating his proposals and obtaining him subscriptions
and advances on his forthcoming work, to furnish funds for
his outfit.

In the meantime he had to task that poor drudge, his
Muse, for present exigencies. Ten pounds were demanded
for his appointment-warrant. Other expenses pressed hard
upon him. Fortunately, though as yet unknown to fame,
his literary capability was known to "the trade," and the

144

coinage of his brain passed current in Grub Street. Archibald Hamilton, proprietor of the "Critical Review," the rival to that of Griffiths, readily made him a small advance on receiving three articles for his periodical. His purse thus slenderly replenished, Goldsmith paid for his warrant; wiped off the score of his milkmaid; abandoned his garret, and moved into a shabby first floor in a forlorn court near the old Bailey; there to await the time of his migration to the magnificent coast of Coromandel.

Alas! poor Goldsmith! ever doomed to disappointment. Early in the gloomy month of November, that month of fog and despondency in London, he learnt the shipwreck of his hope. The great Coromandel enterprise fell through; or rather the post promised him was transferred to some other candidate. The cause of this disappointment it is now impossible to ascertain. The death of his *quasi* patron, Dr. Milner, which happened about this time, may have had some effect in producing it; or there may have been some heedlessness and blunder on his own part; or some obstacle arising from his insuperable indigence;—whatever may have been the cause, he never mentioned it, which gives some ground to surmise that he himself was to blame. His friends learnt with surprise that he had suddenly relinquished his appointment to India, about which he had raised such sanguine expectations: some accused him of fickleness and caprice; others supposed him unwilling to tear himself from the growing fascinations of the literary society of London.

In the meantime, cut down in his hopes, and humiliated in his pride by the failure of his Coromandel scheme, he sought, without consulting his friends, to be examined at the College of Physicians for the humble situation of hospital mate. Even here poverty stood in his way. It was necessary to appear in a decent garb before the examining committee; but how was he to do so? He was literally out at elbows as well as out of cash. Here again the Muse, so often jilted and neglected by him, came to his aid. In consideration of four articles furnished to the "Monthly Review," Griffiths, his old task-master, was to become his security to the tailor for a suit of clothes. Goldsmith said he wanted them but for a single occasion, upon which depended his appointment to a situation in the army; as soon as that temporary purpose was served they would either be returned or paid for. The books to be reviewed were accordingly lent to him; the Muse was again set to her compulsory drudgery; the articles were scribbled off and sent to the bookseller, and the clothes came in due time from the tailor.

From the records of the College of Surgeons, it appears that Goldsmith underwent his examination at Surgeons' Hall, on the 21st of December, 1758. Either from a confusion of mind incident to sensitive and imaginative persons on such occasions, or from a real want of surgical science, which last is extremely probable, he failed in his examination, and was rejected as unqualified. The effect of such a rejection was to disqualify him for every branch of public service, though he might have claimed a reëxamination, after the interval of a few months devoted to further study. Such a reëxamination he never attempted, nor did he ever communicate his discomfiture to any of his friends.

On Christmas-day, but four days after his rejection by the College of Surgeons, while he was suffering under the mortification of defeat and disappointment, and hard pressed for means of subsistence, he was surprised by the entrance into his room of the poor woman of whom he hired his wretched apartment, and to whom he owed some small arrears of rent. She had a piteous tale of distress, and was clamorous in her afflictions. Her husband had been arrested in the night for debt, and thrown into prison. This was too much for the quick feelings of Goldsmith; he was ready at any time to help the distressed, but in this instance he was himself in some measure a cause of the distress. What was to be done? He had no money, it is true; but there hung the new suit of clothes in which he had stood his unlucky examination at Surgeon's Hall. Without giving himself time for reflection, he sent it off to the pawnbroker's, and raised thereon a sufficient sum to pay off his own debt, and to release his landlord from prison.

Under the same pressure of penury and despondency, he borrowed from a neighbor a pittance to relieve his immediate wants, leaving as a security the books which he had recently reviewed. In the midst of these straits and harassments, he received a letter from Griffiths, demanding in peremptory terms, the return of the clothes and books, or immediate payment for the same. It appears that he had discovered the identical suit at the pawnbroker's. The reply of Goldsmith is not known; it was out of his power to furnish either the clothes or the money; but he probably offered once more to make the Muse stand his bail. His reply only increased the ire of the wealthy man of trade, and drew from him another letter still more harsh than the first; using the epithets of knave and sharper, and containing threats of prosecution and a prison.

The following letter from poor Goldsmith gives the most touching picture of an inconsiderate but sensitive man, harassed by care, stung by humiliations, and driven almost to despondency.

"SIR,—I know of no misery but a jail to which my own imprudences and your letter seem to point. I have seen it inevitable these three or four weeks, and, by heavens! request

it as a favor—as a favor that may prevent something more
fatal. I have been some years struggling with a wretched
being—with all that contempt that indigence brings with
it—with all those passions which make contempt insupportable. What, then, has a jail that is formidable? I shall at
least have the society of wretches, and such is to me true
society. I tell you, again and again, that I am neither able
nor willing to pay you a farthing, but I will be punctual to any
appointment you or the tailor shall make; thus far, at least,
I do not act the sharper, since, unable to pay my own debts
one way, I would generally give some security another. No,
sir; had I been a sharper—had I been possessed of less good
nature and native generosity, I might surely now have been in
better circumstances.

"I am guilty, I own, of meannesses which poverty unavoidably brings with it: my reflections are filled with repentance
for my imprudence, but not with any remorse for being a
villain: that may be a character you unjustly charge me with.
Your books, I can assure you, are neither pawned nor sold,
but in the custody of a friend, from whom my necessities
obliged me to borrow some money: whatever becomes of my
person, you shall have them in a month. It is very possible
both the reports you heard and your own suggestions may
have brought you false information with respect to my character; it is very possible that the man whom you now regard with
detestation may inwardly burn with grateful resentment. It
is very possible that, upon a second perusal of the letter I
sent you, you may see the workings of a mind strongly agitated with gratitude and jealousy. If such circumstances
should appear, at least spare invective till my book with
Mr. Dodsley shall be published, and then, perhaps, you may
see the bright side of a mind, when my professions shall not
appear the dictates of necessity, but of choice.

"You seem to think Dr. Milner knew me not. Perhaps so; but he was a man I shall ever honor; but I have friendships only with the dead! I ask pardon for taking up so much time; nor shall I add to it by any other professions than that I am, sir, your humble servant,

"OLIVER GOLDSMITH.

"P.S.—I shall expect impatiently the result of your resolutions."

The dispute between the poet and the publisher was afterward imperfectly adjusted, and it would appear that the clothes were paid for by a short compilation advertised by Griffiths in the course of the following month; but the parties were never really friends afterward and the writings of Goldsmith were harshly and unjustly treated in the "Monthly Review."

We have given the preceding anecdote in detail, as furnishing one of the many instances in which Goldsmith's prompt and benevolent impulses outran all prudent forecast, and involved him in difficulties and disgraces which a more selfish man would have avoided. The pawning of the clothes, charged upon him as a crime by the grinding bookseller, and apparently admitted by him as one of "the meannesses which poverty unavoidably brings with it," resulted, as we have shown, from a tenderness of heart and generosity of hand, in which another man would have gloried; but these were such natural elements with him, that he was unconscious of their merit. It is a pity that wealth does not oftener bring such "meannesses" in its train.

And now let us be indulged in a few particulars about these lodgings in which Goldsmith was guilty of this thoughtless act of benevolence. They were in a very shabby house, No. 12 Green Arbor Court, between the Old Bailey and

Fleet Market. An old woman was still living in 1820 who was a relative of the identical landlady whom Goldsmith relieved by the money received from the pawnbroker. She was a child about seven years of age at the time that the poet rented his apartment of her relative, and used frequently to be at the house in Green Arbor Court. She was drawn there, in a great measure, by the good-humored kindness of Goldsmith, who was always exceedingly fond of the society of children. He used to assemble those of the family in his room, give them cakes and sweetmeats, and set them dancing to the sound of his flute. He was very friendly to those around him, and cultivated a kind of intimacy with a watchmaker in the Court, who possessed much native wit and humor. He passed most of the day, however, in his room, and only went out in the evenings. His days were no doubt devoted to the drudgery of the pen, and it would appear that he occasionally found the booksellers urgent task-masters. On one occasion a visitor was shown up to his room, and immediately their voices were heard in high altercation, and the key was turned within the lock. The landlady, at first, was disposed to go to the assistance of her lodger; but a calm succeeding, she forebore to interfere.

Late in the evening the door was unlocked; a supper ordered by the visitor from a neighboring tavern, and Goldsmith and his intrusive guest finished the evening in great good-humor. It was probably his old task-master Griffiths, whose press might have been waiting, and who found no other mode of getting a stipulated task from Goldsmith than by locking him in, and staying by him until it was finished.

But we have a more particular account of these lodgings in Green Arbor Court from the Rev. Thomas Percy, afterward Bishop of Dromore, and celebrated for his relics of ancient poetry, his beautiful ballads, and other works. During an occasional visit to London, he was introduced to Goldsmith by Grainger, and ever after continued one of his most steadfast and valued friends. The following is his description of the poet's squalid apartment: "I called on Goldsmith at his lodgings in March, 1759, and found him writing his 'Inquiry,' in a miserable, dirty-looking room, in which there was but one chair; and when, from civility, he resigned it to me, he himself was obliged to sit in the window. While we were conversing together, some one tapped gently at the door, and, being desired to come in, a poor ragged little girl, of a very becoming demeanor, entered the room, and, dropping a courtesy, said, 'My mamma sends her compliments, and begs the favor of you to lend her a chamberpot full of coals.' "

We are reminded in this anecdote of Goldsmith's picture of the lodgings of Beau Tibbs, and of the peep into the secrets of a make-shift establishment given to a visitor by the blundering old Scotch woman.

"By this time we were arrived as high as the stairs would permit us to ascend, till we came to what he was facetiously pleased to call the first floor down the chimney; and, knocking at the door, a voice from within demanded 'Who's there?' My conductor answered that it was him. But this not satisfying the querist, the voice again repeated the demand, to which he answered louder than before; and now the door was opened by an old woman with cautious reluctance.

"When we got in, he welcomed me to his house with great ceremony; and, turning to the old woman, asked where was her lady. 'Good troth,' replied she, in a peculiar dialect, 'she's washing your twa shirts at the next door, because they have taken an oath against lending the tub any longer.' 'My

two shirts,' cried he, in a tone that faltered with confusion;
'what does the idiot mean?' 'I ken what I mean weel enough,'
replied the other; 'she's washing your twa shirts at the next
door, because'— 'Fire and fury! no more of thy stupid
explanations,' cried he; 'go and inform her we have company.
Were that Scotch hag to be for ever in my family, she would
never learn politeness, nor forget that absurd poisonous accent
of hers, or testify the smallest specimen of breeding or high
life; and yet it is very surprising too, as I had her from a Parliament man, a friend of mine from the Highlands, one of the
politest men in the world; but that's a secret.' " *

Let us linger a little in Green Arbor Court, a place con-
secrated by the genius and the poverty of Goldsmith, but
recently obliterated in the course of modern improvements.
The writer of this memoir visited it not many years since on
a literary pilgrimage, and may be excused for repeating a
description of it which he has heretofore inserted in another
publication. "It then existed in its pristine state, and was a
small square of tall and miserable houses, the very intestines
of which seemed turned inside out, to judge from the old
garments and frippery that fluttered from every window. It
appeared to be a region of washerwomen, and lines were
stretched about the little square, on which clothes were
dangling to dry.

"Just as we entered the square, a scuffle took place between
two viragoes about a disputed right to a wash-tub, and immediately the whole community was in a hubbub. Heads in
mob-caps popped out of every window, and such a clamor of
tongues ensued that I was fain to stop my ears. Every
amazon took part with one or other of the disputants, and
brandished her arms, dripping with soapsuds, and fired away
from her window as from the embrasure of a fortress; while

---

* *Citizen of the World*, Letter IV.

the screams of children nestled and cradled in every pro-
creant chamber of this hive, waking with the noise, set up
their shrill pipes to swell the general concert." *

While in these forlorn quarters, suffering under extreme
depression of spirits, caused by his failure at Surgeon's Hall,
the disappointment of his hopes, and his harsh collisions with
Griffiths, Goldsmith wrote the following letter to his brother
Henry, some parts of which are most touchingly mournful.

"DEAR SIR,—

"Your punctuality in answering a man whose trade is
writing, is more than I had reason to expect; and yet you see
me generally fill a whole sheet, which is all the recompense I
can make for being so frequently troublesome. The behavior
of Mr. Mills and Mr. Lawder is a little extraordinary. However, their answering neither you nor me is a sufficient indication of their disliking the employment which I assigned them.
As their conduct is different from what I had expected, so I
have made an alteration in mine. I shall, the beginning of
next month, send over two hundred and fifty books,† which
are all that I fancy can be well sold among you, and I would
have you make some distinction in the persons who have
subscribed. The money, which will amount to sixty pounds,
may be left with Mr. Bradley as soon as possible. I am not
certain but I shall quickly have occasion for it.

"I have met with no disappointment with respect to my
East India voyage, nor are my resolutions altered; though,
at the same time, I must confess, it gives me some pain to
think I am almost beginning the world at the age of thirty-one.
Though I never had a day's sickness since I saw you, yet I am

---

* *Tales of a Traveller*. [Club of Queer Fellows in "Buckthorne and his
Friends."]

† The "*Inquiry into Polite Literature*." His previous remarks apply to
the subscription.

not that strong, active man you once knew me. You scarcely
can conceive how much eight years of disappointment, anguish, and study have worn me down. If I remember right,
you are seven or eight years older than me, yet I dare venture
to say, that, if a stranger saw us both, he would pay me the
honors of seniority. Imagine to yourself a pale, melancholy
visage, with two great wrinkles between the eyebrows, with an
eye disgustingly severe, and a big wig, and you may have a
perfect picture of my present appearance. On the other hand,
I conceive you as perfectly sleek and healthy, passing many
a happy day among your own children, or those who knew
you a child.

"Since I knew what it was to be a man, this is a pleasure I
have not known. I have passed my days among a parcel of
cool, designing beings, and have contracted all their suspicious
manner in my own behavior. I should actually be as unfit
for the society of my friends at home, as I detest that which I
am obliged to partake of here. I can now neither partake of
the pleasure of a revel, nor contribute to raise its jollity. I can
neither laugh nor drink; have contracted a hesitating, disagreeable manner of speaking, and a visage that looks ill-nature
itself; in short, I have thought myself into a settled melancholy,
and an utter disgust of all that life brings with it. Whence this
romantic turn that all our family are possessed with? Whence
this love for every place and every country but that in which
we reside—for every occupation but our own? this desire of
fortune, and yet this eagerness to dissipate? I perceive, my
dear sir, that I am at intervals for indulging this splenetic manner, and following my own taste, regardless of yours.

"The reasons you have given me for breeding up your son
a scholar are judicious and convincing; I should, however, be
glad to know for what particular profession he is designed.
If he be assiduous and divested of strong passions (for passions

in youth always lead to pleasure), he may do very well in your college; for it must be owned that the industrious poor have good encouragement there, perhaps better than in any other in Europe. But if he has ambition, strong passions, and an exquisite sensibility of contempt, do not send him there, unless you have no other trade for him but your own. It is impossible to conceive how much may be done by proper education at home. A boy, for instance, who understands perfectly well Latin, French, arithmetic, and the principles of the civil law, and can write a fine hand, has an education that may qualify him for any undertaking; and these parts of learning should be carefully inculcated, let him be designed for whatever calling he will.

"Above all things, let him never touch a romance or novel: these paint beauty in colors more charming than nature, and describe happiness that man never tastes. How delusive, how destructive are those pictures of consummate bliss! They teach the youthful mind to sigh after beauty and happiness that never existed; to despise the little good which fortune has mixed in our cup, by expecting more than she ever gave; and, in general, take the word of a man who has seen the world, and who has studied human nature more by experience than precept; take my word for it, I say, that books teach us very little of the world. The greatest merit in a state of poverty would only serve to make the possessor ridiculous—may distress, but cannot relieve him. Frugality, and even avarice, in the lower orders of mankind, are true ambition. These afford the only ladder for the poor to rise to preferment. Teach then, my dear sir, to your son, thrift and economy. Let his poor wandering uncle's example be placed before his eyes. I had learned from books to be disinterested and generous, before I was taught from experience the necessity of being prudent. I had contracted the habits and notions of a philosopher, while I was exposing myself to the approaches of insidious cunning; and often by being, even with my narrow finances, charitable to excess, I forgot the rules of justice, and placed myself in the very situation of the wretch who thanked me for my bounty. When I am in the remotest part of the world, tell him this, and perhaps he may improve from my example. But I find myself again falling into my gloomy habits of thinking.

"My mother, I am informed, is almost blind; even though I had the utmost inclination to return home, under such circumstances I could not, for to behold her in distress without a capacity of relieving her from it, would add much to my splenetic habit. Your last letter was much too short; it should have answered some queries I had made in my former. Just sit down as I do, and write forward until you have filled all your paper. It requires no thought, at least from the ease with which my own sentiments rise when they are addressed to you. For, believe me, my head has no share in all I write; my heart dictates the whole. Pray give my love to Bob Bryanton, and entreat him from me not to drink. My dear sir, give me some account about poor Jenny.* Yet her husband loves her: if so, she cannot be unhappy.

"I know not whether I should tell you—yet why should I conceal these trifles, or, indeed, anything from you? There is a book of mine will be published in a few days; the life of a very extraordinary man; no less than the great Voltaire. You know already by the title that it is no more than a catchpenny. However, I spent but four weeks on the whole performance, for which I received twenty pounds. When published, I shall take some method of conveying it to you, unless you may think it dear of the postage, which may amount to four or five shil-

---

*His sister, Mrs. Johnston; her marriage, like that of Mrs. Hodson, was private, but in pecuniary matters much less fortunate.

lings. However, I fear you will not find an equivalent of amusement.

"Your last letter, I repeat it, was too short; you should have given me your opinion of the design of the heroi-comical poem which I sent you. You remember I intended to introduce the hero of the poem as lying in a paltry ale-house. You may take the following specimen of the manner, which I flatter myself is quite original. The room in which he lies may be described somewhat in this way:—

> " 'The window, patched with paper, lent a ray
> That feebly show'd the state in which he lay,
> The sanded floor that grits beneath the tread,
> The humid wall with paltry pictures spread;
> The game of goose was there exposed to view,
> And the twelve rules the royal martyr drew;
> The Seasons, framed with listing, found a place,
> And Prussia's monarch[1] show'd his lamp-black face.
> The morn was cold: he views with keen desire
> A rusty grate unconscious of a fire;
> An unpaid reckoning on the frieze was scored,
> And five crack'd tea-cups dress'd the chimney-board.'

"And now imagine, after his soliloquy the landlord to make his appearance in order to dun him for the reckoning:—

> " 'Not with that face, so servile and so gay,
> That welcomes every stranger that can pay:
> With sulky eye he smoked the patient man,
> Then pull'd his breeches tight, and thus began,' etc.*

---

[1] Frederick the Great; another version of the poem reads Prince William, that is William Augustus, Duke of Cumberland.

* The projected poem, of which the above were specimens, appears never to have been completed. [The fragment was first printed, according to Cunningham, *Complete Works of Goldsmith*, Vol. I, p. 112, in the *Citizen of the World*, Letter XXX; it was afterwards inserted with a few variations, in the *Deserted Village*. The "royal martyr" is Charles I., and his twelve rules are: 1. Urge no healths; 2. Profane no divine ordinances; 3. Touch no state matters; 4. Reveal no secrets; 5. Pick no quarrels; 6. Make no comparisons; 7. Maintain no ill opinions; 8. Keep no bad company; 9. Encourage no vice; 10. Make no long meals; 11. Repeat no grievances; 12. Lay no wagers.]

"All this is taken, you see, from nature. It is a good remark of Montaigne's,[1] that the wisest men often have friends with whom they do not care how much they play the fool. Take my present follies as instances of my regard. Poetry is a much easier and more agreeable species of composition than prose; and, could a man live by it, it were not unpleasant employment to be a poet. I am resolved to leave no space, though I should fill it up only by telling you, what you very well know already, I mean that I am your most affectionate friend and brother,   "OLIVER GOLDSMITH."

The "Life of Voltaire," alluded to in the latter part of the preceding letter, was the literary job undertaken to satisfy the demands of Griffiths. It was to have preceded a translation of the "Henriade,"[2] by Ned Purdon, Goldsmith's old schoolmate, now a Grub-Street writer, who starved rather than lived by the exercise of his pen, and often tasked Goldsmith's scanty means to relieve his hunger. His miserable career was summed up by our poet in the following lines written some years after the time we are treating of, on hearing that he had suddenly dropped dead in Smithfield:—

"Here lies poor Ned Purdon, from misery freed,
　Who long was a bookseller's hack:
He led such a damnable life in this world,
　I don't think he'll wish to come back."

The memoir and translation, though advertised to form a volume, were not published together, but appeared separately in a magazine.

As to the heroi-comical poem, also, cited in the foregoing letter, it appears to have perished in embryo. Had it been brought to maturity, we should have had further traits of auto-

---

[1] Montaigne (1533-1592), was a French essayist.
[2] An heroic poem by Voltaire, published in 1728, on Henry IV. of France.

biography; the room already described was probably his own squalid quarters in Green Arbor Court; and in a subsequent morsel of the poem we have the poet himself, under the euphonious name of Scroggin:—

> "Where the Red Lion peering o'er the way,
> Invites each passing stranger that can pay;
> Where Calvert's butt and Parson's black champagne[1]
> Regale the drabs and bloods of Drury Lane:
> There, in a lonely room, from bailiffs snug,
> The muse found Scroggin stretch'd beneath a rug;
> A nightcap deck'd his brows instead of bay,
> A cap by night, a stocking all the day!"

It is to be regretted that this poetical conception was not carried out; like the author's other writings, it might have abounded with pictures of life and touches of nature drawn from his own observation and experience, and mellowed by his own humane and tolerant spirit; and might have been a worthy companion or rather contrast to his "Traveller" and "Deserted Village," and have remained in the language a first-rate specimen of the mock heroic.

---

[1] The Calverts and Humphrey Parsons were noted brewers of "entire butt beer" or porter, also known familiarly as "British Burgundy" and "Black Champagne."—DOBSON, *Selected Poems of Goldsmith*, p. 167.

CHAPTER XI

Towards the end of March, 1759, the treatise on which Goldsmith had laid so much stress, on which he at one time had calculated to defray the expenses of his outfit to India, and to which he had adverted in his correspondence with Griffiths, made its appearance.[1] It was published by the Dodsleys, and entitled "An Inquiry into the Present State of Polite Learning in Europe."

In the present day, when the whole field of contemporary literature is so widely surveyed and amply discussed, and when the current productions of every country are constantly collated and ably criticised, a treatise like that of Goldsmith would be considered as extremely limited and unsatisfactory; but at that time it possessed novelty in its views and wideness in its scope, and being imbued with the peculiar charm of style inseparable from the author, it commanded public attention and a profitable sale. As it was the most important produc- tion that had yet come from Goldsmith's pen, he was anxious to have the credit of it; yet it appeared without his name on the title-page. The authorship, however, was well known throughout the world of letters, and the author had now grown into sufficient literary importance to become an object of hos- tility to the underlings of the press. One of the most virulent attacks upon him was in a criticism on this treatise, and ap-

---

[1] The *Inquiry*, according to Dobson, *Life*, p. 65, was published in April.

peared in the "Monthly Review" to which he himself had
been recently a contributor. It slandered him as a man while
it decried him as an author, and accused him, by innuendo,
of "laboring under the infamy of having, by the vilest and
meanest actions, forfeited all pretensions to honor and honesty,"
and of practising "those acts which bring the sharper to the
cart's tail or the pillory."

It will be remembered that the Review was owned by
Griffiths, the bookseller, with whom Goldsmith had recently
had a misunderstanding. The criticism, therefore, was no
doubt dictated by the lingerings of resentment, and the impu-
tations upon Goldsmith's character for honor and honesty,
and the vile and mean actions hinted at, could only allude to
the unfortunate pawning of the clothes. All this, too, was
after Griffiths had received the affecting letter from Goldsmith,
drawing a picture of his poverty and perplexities, and after
the latter had made him a literary compensation. Griffiths,
in fact, was sensible of the falsehood and extravagance of the
attack, and tried to exonerate himself by declaring that the
criticism was written by a person in his employ; but we see no
difference in atrocity between him who wields the knife and
him who hires the cut-throat. It may be well, however, in
passing, to bestow our mite of notoriety upon the miscreant
who launched the slander. He deserves it for a long course
of dastardly and venomous attacks, not merely upon Goldsmith,
but upon most of the successful authors of the day. His name
was Kenrick. He was originally a mechanic, but possessing
some degree of talent and industry, applied himself to literature as a profession. This he pursued for many years, and
tried his hand in every department of prose and poetry; he
wrote plays and satires, philosophical tracts, critical disserta-
tions, and works on philology; nothing from his pen ever rose
to first-rate excellence, or gained him a popular name, though

he received from some university the degree of Doctor of Laws. Dr. Johnson characterized his literary career in one short sentence. "Sir, he is one of the many who have made themselves *public* without making themselves *known*."

Soured by his own want of success, jealous of the success of others, his natural irritability of temper increased by habits of intemperance, he at length abandoned himself to the practice of reviewing, and became one of the Ishmaelites of the press. In this his malignant bitterness soon gave him a notoriety which his talents had never been able to attain. We shall dismiss him for the present with the following sketch of him by the hand of one of his contemporaries:—

> "Dreaming of genius which he never had,
> Half wit, half fool, half critic, and half mad;
> Seizing, like Shirley, on the poet's lyre,
> With all his rage, but not one spark of fire;
> Eager for slaughter, and resolved to tear
> From other's brows that wreath he must not wear—
> Next Kenrick came: all furious and replete
> With brandy, malice, pertness, and conceit;
> Unskill'd in classic lore, through envy blind
> To all that's beauteous, learned, or refined:
> For faults alone behold the savage prowl,
> With reason's offal glut his ravening soul;
> Pleased with his prey, its inmost blood he drinks,
> And mumbles, paws, and turns it—till it stinks." [1]

The British press about this time was extravagantly fruitful of periodical publications. That "oldest inhabitant," the "Gentleman's Magazine," almost coeval with St. John's gate which graced its title-page, had long been elbowed by magazines and reviews of all kinds: Johnson's "Rambler" had introduced the fashion of periodical essays,[2] which he had

---

[1] From *The Race*, by Cuthbert Shaw (Semple, *Life of Goldsmith*, p. 284).
[2] Johnson's *Rambler* (1750-1752), was rather a revival of an old fashion, the periodical essay having been first introduced by Addison and Steele in the *Tatler* (1709-11), and the *Spectator* (1711-14).

followed up in his "Adventurer" and "Idler." Imitations had sprung up on every side, under every variety of name; until British literature was entirely overrun by a weedy and transient efflorescence. Many of these rival periodicals choked each other almost at the outset, and few of them have escaped oblivion.

Goldsmith wrote for some of the most successful, such as the "Bee," the "Busy-body," and the "Lady's Magazine." His essays, though characterized by his delightful style, his pure, benevolent morality, and his mellow, unobtrusive humor, did not produce equal effect at first with more garish writings of infinitely less value; they did not "strike," as it is termed; but they had that rare and enduring merit which rises in estimation on every perusal. They gradually stole upon the heart of the public, were copied into numerous contemporary publications, and now they are garnered up among the choice productions of British literature.

In his "Inquiry into the State of Polite Learning," Goldsmith had given offense to David Garrick, at that time autocrat of the Drama, and was doomed to experience its effect. A clamor had been raised against Garrick for exercising a despotism over the stage, and bringing forward nothing but old plays to the exclusion of original productions. Walpole[1] joined in this charge. "Garrick," said he, "is treating the town as it deserves and likes to be treated,—with scenes, fireworks, and *his own writings*. A good new play I never expect to see more; nor have seen since the 'Provoked Husband,'[2] which came out when I was at school." Goldsmith, who was extremely fond of the theatre, and felt the evils of this system, inveighed in his treatise against the wrongs experienced by

---

[1] Horace Walpole (1717-1797), a dilettante author and critic.
[2] *The Provoked Husband, or a Journey to London*, by Vanbrugh and Colley Cibber. It was brought out in 1727-28.

authors at the hands of managers. "Our poet's performance," said he, "must undergo a process truly chemical before it is presented to the public. It must be tried in the manager's fire; strained through a licenser, suffer from repeated corrections, till it may be a mere *caput mortuum*[1] when it arrives before the public." Again,—"Getting a play on even in three or four years is a privilege reserved only for the happy few who have the arts of courting the manager as well as the Muse; who have adulation to please his vanity, powerful patrons to support their merit, or money to indemnify disappointment. Our Saxon ancestors had but one name for a wit and a witch. I will not dispute the propriety of uniting those characters then; but the man who under present discouragements ventures to write for the stage, whatever claim he may have to the appellation of a wit, at least has no right to be called a conjurer." But a passage which perhaps touched more sensibly than all the rest on the sensibilities of Garrick, was the following:—

"I have no particular spleen against the fellow who sweeps the stage with the besom, or the hero who brushes it with his train. It were a matter of indifference to me, whether our heroines are in keeping, or our candle-snuffers burn their fingers, did not such make a great part of public care and polite conversation. Our actors assume all that state off the stage which they do on it; and, to use an expression borrowed from the green-room, every one is *up* in his part. I am sorry to say it, they seem to forget their real characters."

These strictures were considered by Garrick as intended for himself, and they were rankling in his mind when Goldsmith waited upon him and solicited his vote for the vacant secretaryship of the Society of Arts[2], of which the manager was

---

[1] The lifeless remains.

[2] The first exhibition of the Society of Arts was held in 1760; out of this Society grew the Royal Academy (1768), which still holds annual exhibitions of pictures in London. The purpose of the exhibition is the advancement of the interests of art.

a member. Garrick, puffed up by his dramatic renown and
his intimacy with the great, and knowing Goldsmith only by
his budding reputation, may not have considered him of
sufficient importance to be conciliated. In reply to his solicitations, he observed that he could hardly expect his friendly
exertions after the unprovoked attack he had made upon his
management. Goldsmith replied that he had indulged in no
personalities, and had only spoken what he believed to be the
truth. He made no further apology nor application; failed to
get the appointment, and considered Garrick his enemy. In
the second edition of his treatise he expunged or modified the
passages which had given the manager offence; but though
the author and actor became intimate in after years, this false
step at the outset of their intercourse was never forgotten.

About this time Goldsmith engaged with Dr. Smollett, who
was about to launch the "British Magazine." Smollett was
a complete schemer and speculator in literature, and intent
upon enterprises that had money rather than reputation in
view. Goldsmith has a good-humored hit at this propensity
in one of his papers in the "Bee," in which he represents
Johnson, Hume, and others taking seats in the stage-coach
bound for Fame, while Smollett prefers that destined for
Riches.

Another prominent employer of Goldsmith was Mr. John
Newbery, who engaged him to contribute occasional essays to
a newspaper entitled the "Public Ledger," which made its
first appearance on the 12th of January, 1760. His most valuable and characteristic contributions to this paper were his
"Chinese Letters," subsequently modified into the "Citizen of
the World." These lucubrations attracted general attention;
they were reprinted in the various periodical publications of
the day, and met with great applause. The name of the
author, however, was as yet but little known.

Being now easier in circumstances, and in receipt of frequent sums from the booksellers, Goldsmith, about the middle of 1760, emerged from his dismal abode in Green Arbor Court, and took respectable apartments in Wine-Office Court, Fleet Street.

Still he continued to look back with considerate benevolence to the poor hostess, whose necessities he had relieved by pawning his gala coat, for we are told that "he often supplied her with food from his own table, and visited her frequently with the sole purpose to be kind to her."

He now became a member of a debating club, called the Robin Hood, which used to meet near Temple Bar, and in which Burke, while yet a Temple student, had first tried his powers. Goldsmith spoke here occasionally, and is recorded in the Robin Hood archives as "a candid disputant with a clear head and an honest heart, though coming but seldom to the society." His relish was for clubs of a more social, jovial nature, and he was never fond of argument. An amusing anecdote is told of his first introduction to the club, by Samuel Derrick, an Irish acquaintance of some humor. On entering, Goldsmith was struck with the self-important appearance of the chairman ensconced in a large gilt chair. "This," said he, "must be the Lord Chancellor at least." "No, no," replied Derrick, "he's only master of the *rolls*."—The chairman was a *baker*.

CHAPTER XII

In his new lodgings in Wine-Office Court, Goldsmith began
to receive visits of ceremony, and to entertain his literary
friends. Among the latter he now numbered several names
of note, such as Guthrie, Murphy, Christopher Smart, and
Bickerstaff. He had also a numerous class of hangers-on, the
small fry of literature; how, knowing his almost utter incapacity to refuse a pecuniary request, were apt, now that he was
considered flush, to levy continual taxes upon his purse.

Among others, one Pilkington, an old college acquaintance
but now a shifting adventurer, duped him in the most ludicrous
manner. He called on him with a face full of perplexity.
A lady of the first rank having an extraordinary fancy for
curious animals, for which she was willing to give enormous
sums, he had procured a couple of white mice to be forwarded
to her from India. They were actually on board of a ship in
the river. Her grace had been apprised of their arrival, and
was all impatience to see them. Unfortunately, he had no
cage to put them in, nor clothes to appear in before a lady of
her rank. Two guineas would be sufficient for his purpose,
but where were two guineas to be procured!

The simple heart of Goldsmith was touched; but, alas! he
had but half a guinea in his pocket. It was unfortunate, but,
after a pause, his friend suggested, with some hesitation, "that
money might be raised upon his watch: it would but be the
loan of a few hours." So said, so done; the watch was deliv-

ered to the worthy Mr. Pilkington to be pledged at a neighboring pawnbroker's, but nothing farther was ever seen of him, the watch, or the white mice. The next that Goldsmith heard of the poor shifting scapegrace, he was on his death-bed, starving with want, upon which, forgetting or forgiving the trick he had played upon him, he sent him a guinea. Indeed he used often to relate with great humor the foregoing anecdote of his credulity, and was ultimately in some degree indemnified by its suggesting to him the amusing little story of Prince Bonbennin and the White Mouse in the "Citizen of the World."

In this year Goldsmith became personally acquainted with Dr. Johnson, toward whom he was drawn by strong sympathies, though their natures were widely different. Both had struggled from early life with poverty, but had struggled in different ways. Goldsmith, buoyant, heedless, sanguine, tolerant of evils, and easily pleased, had shifted along by any temporary expedient; cast down at every turn, but rising again with indomitable good-humor, and still carried forward by his talent at hoping. Johnson, melancholy, and hypochondriacal, and prone to apprehend the worst, yet sternly resolute to battle with and conquer it, had made his way doggedly and gloomily, but with a noble principle of self-reliance and a disregard of foreign aid. Both had been irregular at college: Goldsmith, as we have shown, from the levity of his nature and his social and convivial habits; Johnson, from his acerbity and gloom. When, in after life, the latter heard himself spoken of as gay and frolicsome at college, because he had joined in some riotous excesses there, "Ah, sir!" replied he, "I was mad and violent. It was bitterness which they mistook for frolic. *I was miserably poor, and I thought to fight my way by my literature and my wit.* So I disregarded all power and all authority."

Goldsmith's poverty was never accompanied by bitterness,

but neither was it accompanied by the guardian pride which kept Johnson from falling into the degrading shifts of poverty. Goldsmith had an unfortunate facility at borrowing, and helping himself along by the contributions of his friends; no doubt trusting, in his hopeful way, of one day making retribution. Johnson never hoped, and therefore never borrowed. In his sternest trials he proudly bore the ills he could not master. In his youth, when some unknown friend, seeing his shoes completely worn out, left a new pair at his chamber-door, he disdained to accept the boon, and threw them away.

Though like Goldsmith an immethodical student, he had imbibed deeper draughts of knowledge, and made himself a riper scholar. While Goldsmith's happy constitution and genial humors carried him abroad into sunshine and enjoyment, Johnson's physical infirmities and mental gloom drove him upon himself; to the resources of reading and meditation; threw a deeper though darker enthusiasm into his mind, and stored a retentive memory with all kinds of knowledge.

After several years of youth passed in the country as usher, teacher, and an occasional writer for the press, Johnson, when twenty-eight years of age, came up to London with a half-written tragedy in his pocket; and David Garrick, late his pupil, and several years his junior, as a companion, both poor and penniless,—both, like Goldsmith, seeking their fortune in the metropolis. "We rode and tied," [1] said Garrick sport-

---

[1] "They were both setting out, having agreed to ride and tie, a method of travelling much used by persons who have but one horse between them, and is thus performed. The two travellers set out together, one on horse-back, the other on foot: now as it generally happens that he on horseback outgoes him on foot, the custom is, that, when he arrives at the distance agreed on, he is to dismount, tie the horse to some gate, tree, post, or other thing, and then proceed on foot; when the other comes up to the horse he unties him, mounts, and gallops on, till, having passed by his fellow-traveller, he likewise arrives at his place of tying."—FIELDING, *Joseph Andrews*, Book II, Chap. II.

ively in after years of prosperity, when he spoke of their humble wayfaring. "I came to London," said Johnson, with "twopence halfpenny in my pocket.—"Eh, what's that you say?" cried Garrick, "with twopence halfpenny in your pocket?" "Why, yes: I came with twopence halfpenny in *my* pocket, and thou, Davy, with but three halfpence in thine." Nor was there much exaggeration in the picture; for so poor were they in purse and credit, that after their arrival they had, with difficulty, raised five pounds, by giving their joint note to a bookseller in the Strand.

Many, many years had Johnson gone on obscurely in London, "fighting his way by his literature and his wit;" enduring all the hardships and miseries of a Grub-Street writer: so destitute at one time, that he and Savage[1] the poet had walked all night about St. James's Square, both too poor to pay for a night's lodging, yet both full of poetry and patriotism, and determined to stand by their country; so shabby in dress at another time, that, when he dined at Cave's, his bookseller, when there was prosperous company, he could not make his appearance at table, but had his dinner handed to him behind a screen.

Yet through all the long and dreary struggle, often diseased in mind as well as in body, he had been resolutely self-dependent, and proudly self-respectful; he had fulfilled his college vow, he had "fought his way by his literature and wit." His "Rambler" and "Idler" had made him the great moralist of the age, and his "Dictionary and History of the English Language," that stupendous monument of individual labor, had excited the admiration of the learned world. He was now at the head of intellectual society; and had become as distinguished by his conversational as his literary powers. He had

---

[1] Richard Savage (1698-1743); there is a life of Savage by Johnson in the *Lives of the Poets.*

become as much an autocrat in his sphere as his fellow-way-farer and adventurer Garrick had become of the stage, and had been humorously dubbed by Smollett, "The Great Cham of Literature."

Such was Dr. Johnson, when on the 31st of May, 1761, he was to make his appearance as a guest at a literary supper given by Goldsmith to a numerous party at his new lodgings in Wine-Office Court. It was the opening of their acquaintance. Johnson had felt and acknowledged the merit of Goldsmith as an author, and been pleased by the honorable mention made of himself in the "Bee" and the Chinese Letters. Dr. Percy called upon Johnson to take him to Goldsmith's lodgings; he found Johnson arrayed with unusual care in a new suit of clothes, a new hat, and a well-powdered wig; and could not but notice his uncommon spruceness. "Why, sir," replied Johnson, "I hear that Goldsmith, who is a very great sloven, justifies his disregard of cleanliness and decency by quoting my practice, and I am desirous this night to show him a better example."

The acquaintance thus commenced ripened into intimacy in the course of frequent meetings in the shop of Davies, the bookseller, in Russell Street, Covent Garden. As this was one of the great literary gossiping-places of the day, especially to the circle over which Johnson presided, it is worthy of some specification. Mr. Thomas Davies, noted in after-times as the biographer of Garrick, had originally been on the stage, and though a small man, had enacted tyrannical tragedy[1] with a pomp and magniloquence beyond his size, if we may

---

[1] Irving's phrase aptly names the high-sounding, bombastic tragedy of the period, the so-called "heroic tragedy." The popularity of this sort of tragedy was largely due to Dryden who produced several very extravagant examples of it. The plays were generally improbable in action, the characters, usually kings and queens, unreal, and the language very lofty and stilted.

trust the description given of him by Churchill in the "Rosciad"[1]:—

> "Statesman all over—in plots famous grown,
> *He mouths a sentence as curs mouth a bone.*"

This unlucky sentence is said to have crippled him in the midst of his tragic career, and ultimately to have driven him from the stage. He carried into the bookselling craft somewhat of the grandiose manner of the stage, and was prone to be mouthy and magniloquent.

Churchill had intimated, that while on the stage he was more noted for his pretty wife than his good acting:

> "With him came mighty Davies; on my life,
> That fellow has a very pretty wife."

"Pretty Mrs. Davies" continued to be the load-star of his fortunes. Her tea-table became almost as much a literary lounge as her husband's shop. She found favor in the eyes of the Ursa Major of literature by her winning ways, as she poured out for him cups without stint of his favorite beverage. Indeed it is suggested that she was one leading cause of his habitual resort to this literary haunt. Others were drawn thither for the sake of Johnson's conversation, and thus it became a resort of many of the notorieties of the day. Here might occasionally be seen Bennet Langton, George Steevens, Dr. Percy, celebrated for his ancient ballads, and sometimes Warburton in prelatic state.[2] Garrick resorted to it for a time, but soon grew shy and suspicious, declaring that most of the authors who frequented Mr. Davies's shop went merely to abuse him.

---

[1] Charles Churchill (1731-1764), published his *Rosciad*, a satirical poem on actors, in 1761.

[2] For Langton, see below, p. 186-87. Steevens (1736-1800) is remembered chiefly for his Shakspere commentaries. William Warburton (1698-1779), bishop of Gloucester, was the author of a number of philosophical religious works.

Foote, the Aristophanes of the day, was a frequent visitor; his broad face beaming with fun and waggery, and his satirical eye ever on the lookout for characters and incidents for his farces. He was struck with the odd habits and appearance of Johnson and Goldsmith, now so often brought together in Davies's shop. He was about to put on the stage a farce called "The Orators," intended as a hit at the Robin Hood debating-club, and resolved to show up the two doctors in it for the entertainment of the town.

"What is the common price of an oak stick, sir?" said Johnson to Davies. "Sixpence," was the reply. "Why then, sir, give me leave to send your servant to purchase a shilling one. I'll have a double quantity, for I am told Foote means to take me off as he calls it, and I am determined the fellow shall not do it with impunity."

Foote had no disposition to undergo the criticism of the cudgel wielded by such potent hands, so the farce of "The Orators" appeared without the caricatures of the lexicographer and the essayist.

CHAPTER XIII

Notwithstanding his growing success, Goldsmith continued
to consider literature a mere makeshift, and his vagrant imagination teemed with schemes and plans of a grand but indefinite
nature. One was for visiting the East and exploring the
interior of Asia. He had, as has been before observed, a
vague notion that valuable discoveries were to be made there,
and many useful inventions in the arts brought back to the
stock of European knowledge. "Thus, in Siberian Tartary,"
observed he, in one of his writings, "the natives extract a
strong spirit from milk, which is a secret probably unknown
to the chemists of Europe. In the most savage parts of India
they are possessed of the secret of dyeing vegetable substances
scarlet, and that of refining lead into a metal which, for hard-
ness and color, is little inferior to silver."

Goldsmith adds a description of the kind of person suited
to such an enterprise, in which he evidently had himself in view.

"He should be a man of philosophical turn, one apt to
deduce consequences of general utility from particular occur-
rences; neither swoln with pride, nor hardened by prejudice;
neither wedded to one particular system, nor instructed only
in one particular science; neither wholly a botanist, nor quite
an antiquarian; his mind should be tinctured with miscellaneous knowledge, and his manners humanized by an intercourse
with men. He should be in some measure an enthusiast to

the design; fond of travelling, from a rapid imagination and an innate love of change; furnished with a body capable of sustaining every fatigue, and a heart not easily terrified at danger." [1]

In 1761, when Lord Bute became prime minister on the accession of George the Third, Goldsmith drew up a memorial on the subject, suggesting the advantages to be derived from a mission to those countries solely for useful and scientific purposes; and, the better to insure success, he preceded his application to the government by an ingenious essay to the same effect in the "Public Ledger."

His memorial and his essay were fruitless, his project most probably being deemed the dream of a visionary. Still it continued to haunt his mind, and he would often talk of making an expedition to Aleppo some time or other, when his means were greater, to inquire into the arts peculiar to the East, and to bring home such as might be valuable. Johnson, who knew how little poor Goldsmith was fitted by scientific lore for this favorite scheme of his fancy, scoffed at the project when it was mentioned to him. "Of all men," said he, "Goldsmith is the most unfit to go out upon such an inquiry, for he is utterly ignorant of such arts as we already possess, and, consequently, could not know what would be accessions to our present stock of mechanical knowledge. Sir, he would bring home a grinding-barrow, which you see in every street in London, and think that he had furnished a wonderful improvement."

His connection with Newbery the bookseller now led him into a variety of temporary jobs, such as a pamphlet on the Cock-Lane Ghost,[2] a Life of Beau Nash, the famous Master of Ceremonies at Bath, &c.: one of the best things for his

---

[1] *Citizen of the World*, Letter CVIII.

[2] See below, p. 314.

fame, however, was the remodelling and republication of his
Chinese Letters under the title of "The Citizen of the World,"
a work which has long since taken its merited stand among
the classics of the English language. "Few works," it has
been observed by one of his biographers, "exhibit a nicer perception, or more delicate delineation of life and manners. Wit,
humor, and sentiment pervade every page; the vices and
follies of the day are touched with the most playful and diverting satire; and English characteristics, in endless variety, are
hit off with the pencil of a master."

In seeking materials for his varied views of life, he often
mingled in strange scenes and got involved in whimsical situations. In the summer of 1762 he was one of the thousands
who went to see the Cherokee chiefs, whom he mentions in
one of his writings. The Indians made their appearance in
grand costume, hideously painted and besmeared. In the
course of the visit Goldsmith made one of the chiefs a present,
who, in the ecstasy of his gratitude, gave him an embrace that
left his face well bedaubed with oil and red ochre.

Towards the close of 1762 he removed to "merry Islington,"
then a country village, though now swallowed up in omnivor-
ous London. He went there for the benefit of country air,
his health being injured by literary application and confine-
ment, and to be near his chief employer, Mr. Newbery, who
resided in the Canonbury House.[1]   In this neighborhood he
used to take his solitary rambles, sometimes extending his
walks to the gardens of the "White Conduit House," so famous
among the essayists of the last century. While strolling one
day in these gardens, he met three females of the family of a
respectable tradesman to whom he was under some obligation.

---

[1] See Irving, *Tales of a Traveller*, "The Poor Devil Author," for a description of Islington and Canonbury Castle and this general region. Cf. also
below, pp. 235 ff.

With his prompt disposition to oblige, he conducted them about the garden, treated them to tea, and ran up a bill in the most open-handed manner imaginable; it was only when he came to pay that he found himself in one of his old dilemmas— he had not the wherewithal in his pocket. A scene of perplexity now took place between him and the waiter, in the midst of which came up some of his acquaintances, in whose eyes he wished to stand particularly well. This completed his mortification. There was no concealing the awkwardness of his position. The sneers of the waiter revealed it. His acquaintances amused themselves for some time at his expense, professing their inability to relieve him. When, however, they had enjoyed their banter, the waiter was paid, and poor Goldsmith enabled to convoy off the ladies with flying colors.

Among the various productions thrown off by him for the booksellers during this growing period of his reputation, was a small work in two volumes, entitled "The History of England, in a Series of Letters from a Nobleman to His Son." It was digested from Hume, Rapin, Carte, and Kennet. These authors he would read in the morning; make a few notes; ramble with a friend into the country about the skirts of "merry Islington"; return to a temperate dinner and cheerful evening; and, before going to bed, write off what had arranged itself in his head from the studies of the morning. In this way he took a more general view of the subject, and wrote in a more free and fluent style than if he had been mousing at the time among authorities. The work, like many others written by him in the earlier part of his literary career, was anonymous. Some attributed it to Lord Chesterfield, others to Lord Orrery, and others to Lord Lyttelton. The latter seemed pleased to be the putative father, and never disowned the bantling thus laid at his door; and well might he have been proud to be considered capable of producing what has been well-pronounced "the most finished and elegant summary of English history in the same compass that has been or is likely to be written."

The reputation of Goldsmith, it will be perceived, grew slowly; he was known and estimated by a few; but he had not those brilliant though fallacious qualities which flash upon the public, and excite loud but transient applause. His works were more read than cited; and the charm of style, for which he was specially noted, was more apt to be felt than talked about. He used often to repine, in a half humorous, half querulous manner, at his tardiness in gaining the laurels which he felt to be his due. "The public," he would exclaim, "will never do me justice; whenever I write anything, they make a point to know nothing about it."

About the beginning of 1763 he became acquainted with Boswell, whose literary gossipings were destined to have a deleterious effect upon his reputation. Boswell was at that time a young man, light, buoyant, pushing, and presumptuous. He had a morbid passion for mingling in the society of men noted for wit and learning, and had just arrived from Scotland, bent upon making his way into the literary circles of the metropolis. An intimacy with Dr. Johnson, the great literary luminary of the day, was the crowning object of his aspiring and somewhat ludicrous ambition. He expected to meet him at a dinner to which he was invited at Davies the bookseller's, but was disappointed. Goldsmith was present, but he was not as yet sufficiently renowned to excite the reverence of Boswell. "At this time," says he in his Notes, "I think he had published nothing with his name, though it was pretty generally understood that one Dr. Goldsmith was the author of 'An Inquiry into the Present State of Polite Learning in Europe,' and of 'The Citizen of the World,' a series of letters supposed to be written from London by a Chinese."

A conversation took place at table between Goldsmith and Mr. Robert Dodsley, compiler of the well-known collection of modern poetry, as to the merits of the current poetry of the day. Goldsmith declared there was none of superior merit. Dodsley cited his own collection in proof of the contrary. "It is true," said he, "we can boast of no palaces nowadays, like Dryden's 'Ode to St. Cecilia's Day,' but we have villages composed of very pretty houses." Goldsmith, however, maintained that there was nothing above mediocrity, an opinion in which Johnson, to whom it was repeated, concurred, and with reason, for the era was one of the dead levels of British poetry.

Boswell has made no note of this conversation; he was an unitarian in his literary devotion, and disposed to worship none but Johnson. Little Davies endeavored to console him for his disappointment, and to stay the stomach of his curiosity, by giving him imitations of the great lexicographer; mouthing his words, rolling his head, and assuming as ponderous a manner as his petty person would permit. Boswell was shortly afterwards made happy by an introduction to Johnson, of whom he became the obsequious satellite. From him he likewise imbibed a more favorable opinion of Goldsmith's merits, though he was fain to consider them derived in a great measure from his Magnus Apollo. "He had sagacity enough," says he, "to cultivate assiduously the acquaintance of Johnson, and his faculties were gradually enlarged by the contemplation of such a model. To me and many others it appeared that he studiously copied the manner of Johnson, though, indeed, upon a smaller scale." So on another occasion he calls him "one of the brightest ornaments of the Johnsonian school." "His respectful attachment to

Johnson," adds he, "was then at its height; for his own literary reputation had not yet distinguished him so much as to
excite a vain desire of competition with his great master."

What beautiful instances does the garrulous Boswell give
of the goodness of heart of Johnson, and the passing homage
to it by Goldsmith. They were speaking of a Mr. Levett,
long an intimate of Johnson's house and a dependent on his
bounty; but who, Boswell thought, must be an irksome charge
upon him. "He is poor and honest," said Goldsmith, "which
is recommendation enough to Johnson."

Boswell mentioned another person of a very bad character,
and wondered at Johnson's kindness to him. "He is now
become miserable," said Goldsmith, "and that insures the
protection of Johnson." Encomiums like these speak almost
as much for the heart of him who praises as of him who is
praised.

Subsequently, when Boswell had become more intense in
his literary idolatry, he affected to undervalue Goldsmith,
and a lurking hostility to him is discernible throughout his
writings, which some have attributed to a silly spirit of jealousy of the superior esteem evinced for the poet by Dr.
Johnson. We have a gleam of this in his account of the first
evening he spent in company with those two eminent authors
at their famous resort, the Mitre Tavern, in Fleet Street.
This took place on the 1st of July, 1763. The trio supped
together, and passed some time in literary conversation. On
quitting the tavern, Johnson, who had now been sociably
acquainted with Goldsmith for two years, and knew his merits,
took him with him to drink tea with his blind pensioner, Miss
Williams,—a high privilege among his intimates and admirers.
To Boswell, a recent acquaintance, whose intrusive syco-
phancy had not yet made its way into his confidential intimacy, he gave no invitation. Boswell felt it with all the

jealousy of a little mind. "Dr. Goldsmith," says he, in his Memoirs, "being a privileged man, went with him, strutting away, and calling to me with an air of superiority, like that of an esoteric over an exoteric disciple of a sage of antiquity, 'I go to Miss Williams.' I confess I then envied him this mighty privilege, of which he seemed to be so proud; but it was not long before I obtained the same mark of distinction."

Obtained! but how? not like Goldsmith, by the force of unpretending but congenial merit, but by a course of the most pushing, contriving, and spaniel-like subserviency. Really, the ambition of the man to illustrate his mental insignificance, by continually placing himself in juxtaposition with the great lexicographer, has something in it perfectly ludicrous. Never, since the days of Don Quixote and Sancho Panza, has there been presented to the world a more whimsically contrasted pair of associates than Johnson and Boswell.

"Who is this Scotch cur at Johnson's heels?" asked some one when Boswell had worked his way into incessant companionship. "He is not a cur," replied Goldsmith, "you are too severe; he is only a bur. Tom Davies flung him at Johnson in sport, and he has the faculty of sticking."

CHAPTER XIV

Among the intimates who used to visit the poet occasionally in his retreat at Islington, was Hogarth, the painter.
Goldsmith had spoken well of him in his essays in the "Public
Ledger," and this formed the first link in their friendship. He
was at this time upwards of sixty years of age, and is described
as a stout, active, bustling little man, in a sky-blue coat,
satirical and dogmatic, yet full of real benevolence and the
love of human nature. He was the moralist and philosopher
of the pencil; like Goldsmith he had sounded the depths of
vice and misery, without being polluted by them; and though
his picturings had not the pervading amenity of those of the
essayist, and dwelt more on the crimes and vices than the
follies and humors of mankind, yet they were all calculated,
in like manner, to fill the mind with instruction and precept,
and to make the heart better.

Hogarth does not appear to have had much of the rural
feeling with which Goldsmith was so amply endowed, and may
not have accompanied him in his strolls about hedges and
green lanes; but he was a fit companion with whom to ex-
plore the mazes of London, in which he was continually on the
lookout for character and incident. One of Hogarth's admirers speaks of having come upon him in Castle Street, engaged
in one of his street-studies, watching two boys who were

quarrelling; patting one on the back who flinched, and endeavoring to spirit him up to a fresh encounter. "At him again! D—— him, if I would take it of him! At him again!"

A frail memorial of this intimacy between the painter and the poet exists in a portrait in oil, called "Goldsmith's Hostess." It is supposed to have been painted by Hogarth in the course of his visits to Islington, and given by him to the poet as a means of paying his landlady. There are no friendships among men of talents more likely to be sincere than those between painters and poets. Possessed of the same qualities of mind, governed by the same principles of taste and natural laws of grace and beauty, but applying them to different yet mutually illustrative arts, they are constantly in sympathy, and never in collision with each other.

A still more congenial intimacy of the kind was that contracted by Goldsmith with Mr. (afterwards Sir Joshua) Reynolds. The latter was now about forty years of age, a few years older than the poet, whom he charmed by the blandness and benignity of his manners, and the nobleness and generosity of his disposition, as much as he did by the graces of his pencil and the magic of his coloring. They were men of kindred genius, excelling in corresponding qualities of their several arts, for style in writing is what color is in painting; both are innate endowments, and equally magical in their effects. Certain graces and harmonies of both may be acquired by diligent study and imitation, but only in a limited degree; whereas by their natural possessors they are exercised spontaneously, almost unconsciously, and with ever-varying fascination. Reynolds soon understood and appreciated the merits of Goldsmith, and a sincere and lasting friendship ensued between them.

At Reynolds's house Goldsmith mingled in a higher range

of company than he had been accustomed to. The fame of this celebrated artist, and his amenity of manners, were gathering round him men of talents of all kinds, and the increasing affluence of his circumstances enabled him to give full indulgence to his hospitable disposition. Poor Goldsmith had not yet, like Dr. Johnson, acquired reputation enough to atone for his external defects and his want of the air of good society. Miss Reynolds used to inveigh against his personal appearance, which gave her the idea, she said, of a low mechanic, a journeyman tailor. One evening, at a large supper-party, being called upon to give as a toast the ugliest man she knew, she gave Dr. Goldsmith, upon which a lady who sat opposite, and whom she had never met before, shook hands with her across the table, and "hoped to become better acquainted."

We have a graphic and amusing picture of Reynolds's hospitable but motley establishment, in an account given by a Mr. Courtenay to Sir James Mackintosh; though it speaks of a time after Reynolds had received the honor of knighthood. "There was something singular," said he, "in the style and economy of Sir Joshua's table that contributed to pleasantry and good-humor,—a coarse, inelegant plenty, without any regard to order and arrangement. At five o'clock precisely, dinner was served, whether all the invited guests had arrived or not. Sir Joshua was never so fashionably ill-bred as to wait an hour perhaps for two or three persons of rank or title, and put the rest of the company out of humor by this invidious distinction. His invitations, however, did not regulate the number of his guests. Many dropped in uninvited. A table prepared for seven or eight was often compelled to contain fifteen or sixteen. There was a consequent deficiency of knives, forks, plates, and glasses. The attendance was in the same style, and those who were knowing in the ways of the house took care on sitting down to call

instantly for beer, bread, or wine, that they might secure a
supply before the first course was over. He was once prevailed on to furnish the table with decanters and glasses at
dinner, to save time and prevent confusion. These gradually
were demolished in the course of service, and were never
replaced. These trifling embarrassments, however, only serve
to enhance the hilarity and singular pleasure of the entertainment. The wine, cookery, and dishes were but little
attended to; nor was the fish or venison ever talked of or
recommended. Amidst this convivial animated bustle among
his guests, our host sat perfectly composed; always attentive
to what was said, never minding what was ate or drank, but
left every one at perfect liberty to scramble for himself."

Out of the casual but frequent meeting of men of talent
at this hospitable board rose that association of wits, authors,
scholars, and statesmen, renowned as the Literary Club.
Reynolds was the first to propose a regular association of the
kind, and was eagerly seconded by Johnson, who proposed
as a model a club which he had formed many years previously
in Ivy-Lane, but which was now extinct. Like that club the
number of members was limited to nine. They were to meet
and sup together once a week, on Monday night, at the Turk's
Head on Gerard Street, Soho, and two members were to
constitute a meeting. It took a regular form in the year 1764,
but did not receive its literary appellation until several years
afterwards.

The original members were Reynolds, Johnson, Burke,
Dr. Nugent, Bennet Langton, Topham Beauclerc, Chamier,
Hawkins, and Goldsmith; and here a few words concerning
some of the members may be acceptable. Burke was at that
time about thirty-three years of age; he had mingled a little
in politics and been Under-Secretary to Hamilton at Dublin,
but was again a writer for the booksellers, and as yet but in

the dawning of his fame. Dr. Nugent was his father-in-law,
a Roman Catholic, and a physician of talent and instruction.
Mr. (afterwards Sir John) Hawkins was admitted into this
association from having been a member of Johnson's Ivy-
Lane club. Originally an attorney, he had retired from the
practice of the law, in consequence of a large fortune which
fell to him in right of his wife, and was now a Middlesex
magistrate. He was, moreover, a dabbler in literature and
music, and was actually engaged on a history of music, which
he subsequently published in five ponderous volumes. To
him we are also indebted for a biography of Johnson, which
appeared after the death of that eminent man. Hawkins was
as mean and parsimonious as he was pompous and conceited.
He forbore to partake of the suppers at the club, and begged
therefore to be excused from paying his share of the reckoning. "And was he excused?" asked Dr. Burney of Johnson.
"Oh, yes, for no man is angry with another for being inferior
to himself. We all scorned him and admitted his plea. Yet
I really believe him to be an honest man at bottom, though
to be sure he is penurious, and he is mean, and it must be
owned he has a tendency to savageness." He did not remain
above two or three years in the club; being in a manner
elbowed out in consequence of his rudeness to Burke.

Mr. Anthony Chamier was Secretary in the war-office, and
a friend to Beauclerc, by whom he was proposed. We have
left our mention of Bennet Langton and Topham Beauclerc
until the last, because we have most to say about them. They
were doubtless induced to join the club through their devotion
to Johnson, and the intimacy of these two very young and
aristocratic men with the stern and somewhat melancholy
moralist is among the curiosities of literature.

Bennet Langton was of an ancient family, who held their
ancestral estate of Langton in Lincolnshire,—a great title to

respect with Johnson. "Langton, sir," he would say, "has a grant of free-warren from Henry the Second; and Cardinal Stephen Langton, in King John's reign, was of this family."

Langton was of a mild, contemplative, enthusiastic nature. When but eighteen years of age, he was so delighted with reading Johnson's "Rambler," that he came to London chiefly with a view to obtain an introduction to the author. Boswell gives us an account of his first interview, which took place in the morning. It is not often that the personal appearance of an author agrees with the preconceived ideas of his admirer. Langton, from perusing the writings of Johnson, expected to find him a decent, well-dressed, in short a remarkably decorous philosopher. Instead of which, down from his bedchamber about noon, came, as newly risen, a large uncouth figure, with a little dark wig which scarcely covered his head, and his clothes hanging loose about him. But his conversation was so rich, so animated, and so forcible, and his religious and political notions so congenial with those in which Langton had been educated, that he conceived for him that veneration and attachment which he ever preserved.

Langton went to pursue his studies at Trinity College, Oxford, where Johnson saw much of him during a visit which he paid to the University. He found him in close intimacy with Topham Beauclerc, a youth two years older than himself, very gay and dissipated, and wondered what sympathies could draw two young men together of such opposite characters. On becoming acquainted with Beauclerc he found that, rake though he was, he possessed an ardent love of literature, an acute understanding, polished wit, innate gentility, and high aristocratic breeding. He was, moreover, the only son of Lord Sidney Beauclerc, and grandson of the Duke of St. Albans, and was thought in some particulars to have a resemblance to Charles the Second. These were high recommenda-

tions with Johnson; and when the youth testified a profound
respect for him and an ardent admiration of his talents, the
conquest was complete, so that in a "short time," says Boswell, "the moral pious Johnson and the gay dissipated Beauclerc were companions."

The intimacy begun in college chambers was continued
when the youths came to town during the vacations. The
uncouth, unwieldy moralist was flattered at finding himself an
object of idolatry to two high-born, high-bred, aristocratic
young men, and throwing gravity aside, was ready to join in
their vagaries and play the part of a "young man upon the
town." Such at least is the picture given of him by Boswell
on one occasion when Beauclerc and Langton, having supped
together at a tavern, determined to give Johnson a rouse at
three o'clock in the morning. They accordingly rapped
violently at the door of his chambers in the Temple. The
indignant sage sallied forth in his shirt, poker in hand, and a
little black wig on the top of his head, instead of helmet; prepared to wreak vengeance on the assailants of his castle; but
when his two young friends *Lanky* and *Beau*, as he used to
call them, presented themselves, summoning him forth to a
morning ramble, his whole manner changed. "What, is
it you, ye dogs?" cried he. "Faith, I'll have a frisk with you!"

So said so done. They sallied forth together into Covent
Garden; figured among the green-grocers and fruit-women,
just come in from the country with their hampers; repaired
to a neighboring tavern, where Johnson brewed a bowl of
bishop, a favorite beverage with him, grew merry over his
cups, and anathematized sleep in two lines, from Lord Lansdowne's[1] drinking song:—

> "Short, very short, be then thy reign,
> For I'm in haste to laugh and drink again."

[1] George Greville, Lord Lansdowne, (1667-1735).

They then took boat again, rowed to Billingsgate, and Johnson and Beauclerc determined, like "mad wags," to "keep
it up" for the rest of the day.   Langton, however, the most
sober-minded of the three, pleaded an engagement to breakfast with some young ladies; whereupon the great moralist
reproached him with "leaving his social friends to go and sit
with a set of wretched *un-idea'd* girls."

This madcap freak of the great lexicographer made a
sensation, as may well be supposed, among his intimates.
"I heard of your frolic t'other night," said Garrick to him;
"you'll be in the 'Chronicle.'" [1]   He uttered worse forebod-
ings to others.   "I shall have my old friend to bail out of the
round-house," said he.   Johnson, however, valued himself
upon having thus enacted a chapter in the "Rake's Progress," [2]
and crowed over Garrick on the occasion.   "*He* durst not
do such a thing!" chuckled he "his *wife* would not *let* him!"

When these two young men entered the club, Langton was
about twenty-two, and Beauclerc about twenty-four years of
age, and both were launched on London life.   Langton, however, was still the mild, enthusiastic scholar, steeped to the
lips in Greek, with fine conversational powers, and an inval-
uable talent for listening.   He was upwards of six feet high,
and very spare.   "Oh! that we could sketch him," exclaims
Miss Hawkins, in her "Memoirs," "with his mild countenance,
his elegant features, and his sweet smile, sitting with one leg
twisted round the other, as if fearing to occupy more space
than was equitable; his person inclining forward, as if wanting strength to support his weight, and his arms crossed over
his bosom, or his hands locked together on his knee."   Beauclerc, on such occasions, sportively compared him to a stork

---

[1] Probably the *St. James Chronicle*, an evening newspaper published three
times a week; see below p. 211.

[2] A series of paintings by Hogarth, telling the story indicated by the title.

in Raphael's Cartoons,[1] standing on one leg. Beauclerc was more a "man upon town," a lounger in St. James's Street, an associate with George Selwyn, with Walpole, and other aristocratic wits; a man of fashion at court; a casual frequenter of the gaming-table; yet, with all this, he alternated in the easiest and happiest manner the scholar and the man of letters; lounged into the club with the most perfect self-possession, bringing with him the careless grace and polished wit of high-bred society, but making himself cordially at home among his learned fellow-members.

The gay yet lettered rake maintained his sway over Johnson, who was fascinated by that air of the world, that ineffable tone of good society in which he felt himself deficient, especially as the possessor of it always paid homage to his superior talent. "Beauclerc," he would say, using a quotation from Pope, "has a love of folly, but a scorn of fools; everything he does shows the one, and everything he says, the other." Beauclerc delighted in rallying the stern moralist of whom others stood in awe, and no one, according to Boswell, could take equal liberty with him with impunity. Johnson, it is well known, was often shabby and negligent in his dress, and not over-cleanly in his person. On receiving a pension from the crown, his friends vied with each other in respectful congratulations. Beauclerc simply scanned his person with a whimsical glance, and hoped that, like Falstaff, "he'd in future purge and live cleanly like a gentleman." Johnson took the hint with unexpected good-humor, and profited by it.

Still Beauclerc's satirical vein, which darted shafts on every side, was not always tolerated by Johnson. "Sir," said he on one occasion, "you never open your mouth but with

---

[1] Paintings representing scenes from the lives of the Apostles; now preserved in the South Kensington Museum, London.

intention to give pain; and you have often given me pain, not from the power of what you have said, but from seeing your intention."

When it was at first proposed to enroll Goldsmith among the members of this association, there seems to have been some demur; at least so says the pompous Hawkins. "As he wrote for the booksellers we of the club looked on him as a mere literary drudge, equal to the task of compiling and translating, but little capable of original and still less of poetical composition."

Even for some time after his admission he continued to be regarded in a dubious light by some of the members. Johnson and Reynolds, of course, were well aware of his merits, nor was Burke a stranger to them; but to the others he was as yet a sealed book, and the outside was not prepossessing. His ungainly person and awkward manners were against him with men accustomed to the graces of society, and he was not sufficiently at home to give play to his humor and to that bonhomie which won the hearts of all who knew him. He felt strange and out of place in this new sphere; he felt at times the cool satirical eye of the courtly Beauclerc scanning him, and the more he attempted to appear at his ease, the more awkward he became.

CHAPTER XV

Johnson had now become one of Goldsmith's best friends
and advisers. He knew all the weak points of his character,
but he knew also his merits; and while he would rebuke him
like a child, and rail at his errors and follies, he would suffer
no one else to undervalue him. Goldsmith knew the sound-
ness of his judgment and his practical benevolence, and often
sought his counsel and aid amid the difficulties into which his
heedlessness was continually plunging him.

"I received one morning," says Johnson, "a message from
poor Goldsmith that he was in great distress, and, as it was
not in his power to come to me, begging that I would come
to him as soon as possible. I sent him a guinea, and promised to come to him directly. I accordingly went as soon as
I was dressed, and found that his landlady had arrested him
for his rent, at which he was in a violent passion: I perceived
that he had already changed my guinea, and had a bottle of
Madeira and a glass before him. I put the cork into the
bottle, desired he would be calm, and began to talk to him of
the means by which he might be extricated. He then told
me he had a novel ready for the press, which he produced
to me. I looked into it and saw its merit; told the landlady
I should soon return; and, having gone to a bookseller, sold
it for sixty pounds. I brought Goldsmith the money, and he

discharged his rent, not without rating his landlady in a high tone for having used him so ill."

The novel in question was the "Vicar of Wakefield"; the bookseller to whom Johnson sold it was Francis Newbery, nephew to John. Strange as it may seem, this captivating work, which has obtained and preserved an almost unrivalled popularity in various languages, was so little appreciated by the bookseller, that he kept it by him for nearly two years unpublished![1]

Goldsmith had, as yet, produced nothing of moment in poetry. Among his literary jobs, it is true, was an Oratorio entitled "The Captivity," founded on the bondage of the Israelites in Babylon. It was one of those unhappy offsprings of the Muse ushered into existence amid the distortions of music. Most of the Oratorio has passed into oblivion; but the following song from it will never die.

> "The wretch condemned from life to part,
>   Still, still on hope relies,
> And every pang that rends the heart
>   Bids expectation rise.
>
> "Hope, like the glimmering taper's light,
>   Illumes and cheers our way;
> And still, as darker grows the night,
>   Emits a brighter ray."

Goldsmith distrusted his qualifications to succeed in poetry, and doubted the disposition of the public mind in regard to it. "I fear," said he, "I have come too late into the world; Pope and other poets have taken up the places in the temple of Fame; and as few at any period can possess poetical reputation, a man of genius can now hardly acquire it." Again, on another occasion, he observes: "Of all kinds of ambition, as things are now circumstanced, perhaps that which pur-

---

[1] See p. 207 and note.

sues poetical fame is the wildest. What from the increased
refinement of the times, from the diversity of judgment produced by opposing systems of criticism, and from the more
prevalent divisions of opinion influenced by party, the strongest
and happiest efforts can expect to please but in a very narrow
circle." [1]

At this very time he had by him his poem of "The Traveller." The plan of it, as has already been observed, was
conceived many years before, during his travels in Switzerland, and a sketch of it sent from that country to his brother
Henry in Ireland. The original outline is said to have embraced a wider scope; but it was probably contracted through
diffidence, in the process of finishing the parts. It had laid
by him for several years in a crude state, and it was with
extreme hesitation and after much revision that he at length
submitted it to Dr. Johnson. The frank and warm approbation of the latter encouraged him to finish it for the press;
and Dr. Johnson himself contributed a few lines towards the
conclusion.

We hear much about "poetic inspiration," and the "poet's
eye in a fine phrensy rolling;" but Sir Joshua Reynolds gives
an anecdote of Goldsmith while engaged upon his poem,
calculated to cure our notions about the ardor of composition.
Calling upon the poet one day, he opened the door without
ceremony, and found him in the double occupation of turning
a couplet and teaching a pet dog to sit upon his haunches.
At one time he would glance his eye at his desk, and at another
shake his finger at the dog to make him retain his position.
The last lines on the page were still wet; they form a part of
the description of Italy:

"By sports like these are all their cares beguiled,
The sports of children satisfy the child."

---

[1] From the dedication to the *Traveller*.

Goldsmith, with his usual good-humor, joined in the laugh caused by his whimsical employment, and acknowledged that his boyish sport with the dog suggested the stanza.

The poem was published on the 19th of December, 1764, in a quarto form, by Newbery, and was the first of his works to which Goldsmith prefixed his name. As a testimony of cherished and well-merited affection, he dedicated it to his brother Henry. There is an amusing affectation of indifference as to its fate expressed in the dedication. "What reception a poem may find," says he, "which has neither abuse, party, nor blank verse to support it, I cannot tell, nor am I solicitous to know." The truth is, no one was more emulous and anxious for poetic fame; and never was he more anxious than in the present instance, for it was his grand stake. Mr. Johnson aided the launching of the poem by a favorable notice in the "Critical Review"; other periodical works came out in its favor. Some of the author's friends complained that it did not command instant and wide popularity; that it was a poem to win, not to strike: it went on rapidly increasing in favor; in three months a second edition was issued; shortly afterwards, a third; then a fourth; and, before the year was out, the author was pronounced the best poet of his time.

The appearance of "The Traveller" at once altered Goldsmith's intellectual standing in the estimation of society; but its effect upon the club, if we may judge from the account given by Hawkins, was almost ludicrous. They were lost in astonishment that a "newspaper essayist" and "bookseller's drudge" should have written such a poem. On the evening of its announcement to them Goldsmith had gone away early, after "rattling away as usual," and they knew not how to reconcile his heedless garrulity with the serene beauty, the easy grace, the sound good sense, and the occasional elevation of his poetry. They could scarcely believe that such magic

numbers had flowed from a man to whom in general, says
Johnson, "it was with difficulty they could give a hearing."
"Well," exclaimed Chamier, "I do believe he wrote this poem
himself, and let me tell you, that is believing a great deal."

At the next meeting of the club, Chamier sounded the
author a little about his poem. "Mr. Goldsmith," said he,
"what do you mean by the last word in the first line of your
'Traveller,' 'Remote, unfriended, melancholy, *slow*'?—do you
mean tardiness of locomotion?"—"Yes," replied Goldsmith,
inconsiderately, being probably flurried at the moment. "No,
sir," interposed his protecting friend Johnson, "you did not
mean tardiness of locomotion; you meant that sluggishness
of mind which comes upon a man in solitude."—"Ah," exclaimed Goldsmith, "*that* was what I meant." Chamier immediately believed that Johnson himself had written the line, and
a rumor became prevalent that he was the author of many
of the finest passages. This was ultimately set at rest by
Johnson himself, who marked with a pencil all the verses he
had contributed, nine in number, inserted towards the conclusion, and by no means the best in the poem. He moreover
with generous warmth, pronounced it the finest poem that
had appeared since the days of Pope.

But one of the highest testimonials to the charm of the
poem was given by Miss Reynolds, who had toasted poor
Goldsmith as the ugliest man of her acquaintance. Shortly
after the appearance of "The Traveller," Dr. Johnson read
it aloud from beginning to end in her presence. "Well,"
exclaimed she, when he had finished, "I never more shall
think Dr. Goldsmith ugly!"

On another occasion, when the merits of "The Traveller"
were discussed at Reynolds's board, Langton declared "there
was not a bad line in the poem, not one of Dryden's careless
verses." "I was glad," observed Reynolds, "to hear Charles

Fox say it was one of the finest poems in the English language."
"Why was[1] you glad?" rejoined Langton, "you surely had no
doubt of this before." "No," interposed Johnson, decisively;
"the merit of 'The Traveller' is so well established, that Mr.
Fox's praise cannot augment it, nor his censure diminish it."

Boswell, who was absent from England at the time of
the publication of the "Traveller," was astonished on his
return, to find Goldsmith, whom he had so much undervalued,
suddenly elevated almost to a par with his idol. He accounted
for it by concluding that much both of the sentiments and
expression of the poem had been derived from conversations
with Johnson. "He imitates you, sir," said this incarnation
of toadyism. "Why no, sir," replied Johnson, "Jack Hawks-
worth is one of my imitators, but not Goldsmith. Goldy,
sir, has great merit." "But, sir, he is much indebted to you
for his getting so high in the public estimation." "Why, sir,
he has, perhaps, got *sooner* to it by his intimacy with me."

The poem went through several editions in the course of
the first year, and received some few additions and corrections from the author's pen. It produced a golden harvest
to Mr. Newbery; but all the remuneration on record, doled
out by his niggard hand to the author, was twenty guineas!

---

[1] The construction *was* with the second person of the pronoun was used
by the best writers of the eighteenth century.

CHAPTER XVI

Goldsmith, now that he was rising in the world, and becoming a notoriety, felt himself called upon to improve his style
of living. He accordingly emerged from Wine-Office Court,
and took chambers in the Temple. It is true they were but
of humble pretensions, situated on what was then the library
staircase, and it would appear that he was a kind of inmate
with Jeffs, the butler of the society. Still he was in the Temple, that classic region rendered famous by the Spectator and
other essayists as the abode of gay wits and thoughtful men
of letters; and which, with its retired courts and embowered
gardens, in the very heart of a noisy metropolis, is, to the quiet-
seeking student and author, an oasis freshening with verdure
in the midst of a desert. Johnson, who had become a kind
of growling supervisor of the poet's affairs, paid him a visit
soon after he had installed himself in his new quarters, and
went prying about the apartment, in his near-sighted manner,
examining everything minutely. Goldsmith was fidgeted by
this curious scrutiny, and apprehending a disposition to find
fault, exclaimed, with the air of a man who had money in both
pockets, "I shall soon be in better chambers than these." The
harmless bravado drew a reply from Johnson, which touched
the chord of proper pride. "Nay, sir," said he, "never mind

that. Nil te quæsiveris extra," [1]—implying that his reputation rendered him independent of outward show. Happy
would it have been for poor Goldsmith, could he have kept
this consolatory compliment perpetually in mind, and squared
his expenses accordingly.

Among the persons of rank who were struck with the merits
of the "Traveller" was the Earl (afterwards Duke) of
Northumberland. He procured several other of Goldsmith's
writings, the perusal of which tended to elevate the author in
his good opinion, and to gain for him his good will. The
Earl held the office of Lord-Lieutenant of Ireland, and understanding Goldsmith was an Irishman, was disposed to extend
to him the patronage which his high post afforded. He intimated the same to his relative, Dr. Percy, who, he found,
was well acquainted with the poet, and expressed a wish that
the latter should wait upon him. Here, then, was another
opportunity for Goldsmith to better his fortune, had he been
knowing and worldly enough to profit by it. Unluckily the
path to fortune lay through the aristocratical mazes of Northumberland House, and the poet blundered at the outset.
The following is the account he used to give of his visit:
"I dressed myself in the best manner I could, and, after
studying some compliments I thought necessary on such an
occasion, proceeded to Northumberland House, and acquainted
the servants that I had particular business with the Duke.
They showed me into an antechamber, where, after waiting
some time, a gentleman, very elegantly dressed, made his
appearance: taking him for the Duke, I delivered all the fine
things I had composed in order to compliment him on the
honor he had done me; when, to my great astonishment, he

---

[1] Slightly altered from Persius, *Satire* I, l. 7, which reads: "Nec te quaesi-
veris extra." Johnson's version might be translated, " Seek nothing that lies
without yourself," the implication being that Goldsmith's natural gifts were
a sufficient reason for content.

told me I had mistaken him for his master, who would see me immediately. At that instant the Duke came into the apartment, and I was so confounded on the occasion that I wanted words barely sufficient to express the sense I entertained of the Duke's politeness, and went away exceedingly chagrined at the blunder I had committed."

Sir John Hawkins, in his Life of Dr. Johnson, gives some farther particulars of this visit, of which he was, in part, a witness. "Having one day," says he, "a call to make on the late Duke (then Earl) of Northumberland, I found Goldsmith waiting for an audience in an outer room: I asked him what brought him there; he told me, an invitation from his lordship. I made my business as short as I could, and, as a reason, mentioned that Dr. Goldsmith was waiting without. The Earl asked me if I was acquainted with him. I told him that I was, adding what I thought was most likely to recommend him. I retired, and stayed in the outer room to take him home. Upon his coming out, I asked him the result of his conversation. 'His lordship,' said he, 'told me he had read my poem, meaning the "Traveller," and was much delighted with it; that he was going to be lord-lieutenant of Ireland, and that, hearing I was a native of that country, he should be glad to do me any kindness.' 'And what did you answer,' said I, 'to this gracious offer?' 'Why,' said he, 'I could say nothing but that I had a brother there, a clergyman, that stood in need of help: as for myself, I have no great dependence on the promises of great men; I look to the booksellers for support; they are my best friends, and I am not inclined to forsake them for others.'" "Thus," continues Sir John, "did this idiot in the affairs of the world trifle with his fortunes, and put back the hand that was held out to assist him,"[1]

We cannot join with Sir John in his worldly sneer at the

[1] See Introduction, p. 39.

conduct of Goldsmith on this occasion. While we admire that honest independence of spirit which prevented him from asking favors for himself, we love that warmth of affection which instantly sought to advance the fortunes of a brother; but the peculiar merits of poor Goldsmith seem to have been little understood by the Hawkinses, the Boswells, and the other biographers of the day.

After all, the introduction to Northumberland House did not prove so complete a failure as the humorous account given by Goldsmith, and the cynical account given by Sir John Hawkins, might lead one to suppose. Dr. Percy, the heir male of the ancient Percies, brought the poet into the acquaintance of his kinswoman, the countess; who, before her marriage with the earl, was in her own right heiress of the House of Northumberland. "She was a lady," says Boswell, "not only of high dignity of spirit, such as became her noble blood, but of excellent understanding and lively talents." Under her auspices a poem of Goldsmith's had an aristocratical introduction to the world. This was the beautiful ballad of "The Hermit," originally published under the name of "Edwin and Angelina." It was suggested by an old English ballad beginning "Gentle Herdsman," shown him by Dr. Percy, who was at that time making his famous collection, entitled "Reliques of Ancient English Poetry," which he submitted to the inspection of Goldsmith prior to publication. A few copies only of "The Hermit" were printed at first, with the following title-page: "Edwin and Angelina: a Ballad. By Mr. Goldsmith. Printed for the Amusement of the Countess of Northumberland."[1]

All this, though it may not have been attended with any immediate pecuniary advantage, contributed to give Gold-

---

[1] The *Hermit* was afterwards inserted into the *Vicar of Wakefield;* see below, p. 211.

smith's name and poetry the high stamp of fashion, so potent in England: the circle at Northumberland House, however, was of too stately and aristocratical a nature to be much to his taste, and we do not find that he became familiar with it.

He was much more at home at Gosfield, the seat of his countryman, Robert Nugent, afterwards Baron Nugent and Viscount Clare, who appreciated his merits even more heartily than the Earl of Northumberland, and occasionally made him his guest both in town and country. Nugent is described as a jovial voluptuary, who left the Roman-Catholic for the Protestant religion, with a view to bettering his fortunes; he had an Irishman's inclination for rich widows, and an Irishman's luck with the sex; having been thrice married, and gained a fortune with each wife. He was now nearly sixty, with a remarkably loud voice, broad Irish brogue, and ready, but somewhat coarse wit. With all his occasional coarseness he was capable of high thought, and had produced poems which showed a truly poetic vein. He was long a a member of the House of Commons, where his ready wit, his fearless decision, and good-humored audacity of expression always gained him a hearing, though his tall person and awkward manner gained him the nickname of Squire Gawky among the political scribblers of the day. With a patron of this jovial temperament, Goldsmith probably felt more at ease than with those of higher refinement.

The celebrity which Goldsmith had acquired by his poem of "The Traveller" occasioned a resuscitation of many of his miscellaneous and anonymous tales and essays from the various newspapers and other transient publications in which they lay dormant. These he published in 1765, in a collected form, under the title of "Essays by Mr. Goldsmith." "The following Essays," observes he in his preface, "have already appeared at different times, and in different publications. The

pamphlets in which they were inserted being generally unsuccessful, these shared the common fate, without assisting the
booksellers' aims, or extending the author's reputation. The
public were too strenuously employed with their own follies
to be assiduous in estimating mine; so that many of my best
attempts in this way have fallen victims to the transient topic
of the times—the Ghost in Cock Lane, or the Siege of Ticon-
deroga.

"But, though they have passed pretty silently into the
world, I can by no means complain of their circulation. The
magazines and papers of the day have indeed been liberal
enough in this respect. Most of these essays have been
regularly reprinted twice or thrice a year, and conveyed to
the public through the kennel of some engaging compilation.
If there be a pride in multiplied editions, I have seen some of
my labors sixteen times reprinted, and claimed by different
parents as their own. I have seen them flourished at the
beginning with praise, and signed at the end with the names
of Philautos, Philalethes, Phileleutheros, and Philanthropos.
It is time, however, at last to vindicate my claims; and as
these entertainers of the public, as they call themselves, have
partly lived upon me for some years, let me now try if I cannot
live a little upon myself."

It was but little, in fact; for all the pecuniary emolument
he received from the volume was twenty guineas. It had a
good circulation, however, was translated into French, and
has maintained its stand among the British classics.

Notwithstanding that the reputation of Goldsmith had
greatly risen, his finances were often at a very low ebb, owing
to his heedlessness as to expense, his liability to be imposed
upon, and a spontaneous and irresistible propensity to give
to every one who asked. The very rise in his reputation had
increased these embarrassments. It had enlarged his circle

of needy acquaintances, authors poorer in pocket than himself, who came in search of literary counsel; which generally meant a guinea and a breakfast. And then his Irish hangers-on! "Our Doctor," said one of these sponges, "had a constant levee of his distressed countrymen, whose wants, as far as he was able, he always relieved; and he has often been known to leave himself without a guinea, in order to supply the necessities of others."

This constant drainage of the purse, therefore, obliged him to undertake all jobs proposed by the booksellers, and to keep up a kind of running account with Mr. Newbery; who was his banker on all occasions, sometimes for pounds, sometimes for shillings; but who was a rigid accountant, and took care to be amply repaid in manuscript. Many effusions, hastily penned in these moments of exigency, were published anonymously, and never claimed. Some of them have but recently been traced to his pen; while of many the true authorship will probably never be discovered. Among others, it is suggested, and with great probability, that he wrote for Mr. Newbery the famous nursery story of "Goody Two Shoes," which appeared in 1765, at a moment when Goldsmith was scribbling for Newbery, and much pressed for funds. Several quaint little tales introduced in his Essays show that he had a turn for this species of mock history; and the advertisement and title-page bear the stamp of his sly and playful humor.[1]

"We are desired to give notice that there is in the press, and speedily will be published, either by subscription or otherwise, as the public shall please to determine, the 'History of Little Goody Two Shoes, otherwise Mrs. Margery Two

---

[1] Welsh, in the preface to a facsimile reprint of *Goody Two Shoes* (published by Griffith, Farran, Okeden and Welsh, successors to the old firm of Newbery), sums up the evidence for Goldsmith's authorship, which seems on the whole fairly convincing.

Shoes;' with the means by which she acquired learning and
wisdom, and, in consequence thereof, her estate; set forth at
large for the benefit of those

"Who, from a state of rags and care,
And having shoes but half a pair,
Their fortune and their fame should fix,
And gallop in a coach and six."

The world is probably not aware of the ingenuity, humor,
good sense, and sly satire contained in many of the old English nursery-tales. They have evidently been the sportive
productions of able writers, who would not trust their names
to productions that might be considered beneath their dignity.
The ponderous works on which they relied for immortality
have perhaps sunk into oblivion, and carried their names
down with them; while their unacknowledged offspring, "Jack
the Giant Killer," "Giles Gingerbread," and "Tom Thumb,"
flourish in wide-spreading and never-ceasing popularity.

As Goldsmith had now acquired popularity and an extensive acquaintance, he attempted, with the advice of his friends,
to procure a more regular and ample support by resuming
the medical profession. He accordingly launched himself
upon the town in style; hired a man-servant; replenished his
wardrobe at considerable expense, and appeared in a professional wig and cane, purple silk small-clothes, and a scarlet
roquelaure buttoned to the chin: a fantastic garb, as we
should think at the present day, but not unsuited to the
fashion of the times.

With his sturdy little person thus arrayed in the unusual
magnificence of purple and fine linen, and his scarlet roquelaure flaunting from his shoulders, he used to strut into the
apartments of his patients swaying his three-cornered hat in
one hand and his medical sceptre, the cane, in the other, and
assuming an air of gravity and importance suited to the solem-

nity of his wig; at least, such is the picture given of him by the waiting gentlewoman who let him into the chamber of one of his lady-patients.

He soon, however, grew tired and impatient of the duties and restraints of his profession; his practice was chiefly among his friends, and the fees were not sufficient for his maintenance; he was disgusted with attendance on sick-chambers and capricious patients, and looked back with longing to his tavern-haunts and broad convivial meetings, from which the dignity and duties of his medical calling restrained him. At length, on prescribing to a lady of his acquaintance, who, to use a hackneyed phrase, "rejoiced" in the aristocratical name of Sidebotham, a warm dispute arose between him and the apothecary as to the quantity of medicine to be administered. The Doctor stood up for the rights and dignities of his profession, and resented the interference of the compounder of drugs. His rights and dignities, however, were disregarded; his wig and cane and scarlet roquelaure were of no avail; Mrs. Sidebotham sided with the hero of the pestle and mortar; and Goldsmith flung out of the house in a passion. "I am determined henceforth," said he to Topham Beauclerc, "to leave off prescribing for friends." "Do so, my dear Doctor," was the reply; "whenever you undertake to kill, let it be only your enemies."

This was the end of Goldsmith's medical career.

CHAPTER XVII

The success of the poem of "The Traveller," and the
popularity which it had conferred on its author, now roused
the attention of the bookseller in whose hands the novel of
"The Vicar of Wakefield" had been slumbering for nearly
two long years. The idea has generally prevailed that it was
Mr. John Newbery to whom the manuscript had been sold,
and much surprise has been expressed that he should be
insensible to its merit and suffer it to remain unpublished,
while putting forth various inferior writings by the same
author. This, however, is a mistake; it was his nephew,
Francis Newbery, who had become the fortunate purchaser.
Still the delay is equally unaccountable.[1] Some have imagined that the uncle and nephew had business arrangements
together, in which this work was included, and that the elder
Newbery, dubious of its success, retarded the publication until

---

[1] The story of the sale of the *Vicar* is still a matter of doubt. Dobson,
Life, p. 110, shows that it was probably sold in shares to three different publishers; Collins, by whom it was first printed at Salisbury, Francis Newbery, successor to John Newbery, and a third named Strahan. "That it was
sold in this way is further confirmed by the fact that some years later, according to old accounts consulted by Mr. Welsh, it still belonged to Collins and
two other shareholders, those shareholders being John Newbery's successors
and Johnson's friend Strahan. This story of the sale is perfectly in accord-
ance with eighteenth-century practice; and, except that it is difficult to
understand why the book remained so long unpublished, calls for no especial
remark. And even the delay in publication can be explained by neglect on
the author's part (not at all a fanciful supposition!) to put the finishing
touches to work which had been already paid for."

the full harvest of "The Traveller" should be reaped. Booksellers are prone to make egregious mistakes as to the merit
of works in manuscript; and to undervalue, if not reject,
those of classic and enduring excellence, when destitute of
that false brilliancy commonly called "effect." In the present instance, an intellect vastly superior to that of either of the
booksellers was equally at fault. Dr. Johnson, speaking of
the work to Boswell, some time subsequent to its publication,
observed, "I myself did not think it would have had much
success. It was written and sold to a bookseller before 'The
Traveller,' but published after, so little expectation had the
bookseller from it. Had it been sold after 'The Traveller,'
he might have had twice as much money; *though sixty guineas
was no mean price.*" [1]

Sixty guineas for the "Vicar of Wakefield"! and this could
be pronounced *no mean price* by Dr. Johnson, at that time
the arbiter of British talent, and who had had an opportunity
of witnessing the effect of the work upon the public mind; for
its success was immediate. It came out on the 27th of March,
1766; before the end of May a second edition was called for;
in three months more, a third; and so it went on, widening
in a popularity that has never flagged. Rogers, the Nestor
of British literature, whose refined purity of taste and exquisite
mental organization rendered him eminently calculated to
appreciate a work of the kind, declared that of all the books
which through the fitful changes of three generations he had
seen rise and fall, the charm of the "Vicar of Wakefield" had
alone continued as at first; and could he revisit the world
after an interval of many more generations, he should as
surely look to find it undiminished. Nor has its celebrity
been confined to Great Britain. Though so exclusively a
picture of British scenes and manners, it has been translated

---

[1] Boswell, *Life of Johnson*, ed. Hill, Vol. III, p. 321.

into almost every language, and everywhere its charm has been the same. Goethe, the great genius of Germany, declared in his eighty-first year, that it was his delight at the age of twenty, that it had in a manner formed a part of his education, influencing his taste and feelings throughout life, and that he had recently read it again from beginning to end—with renewed delight, and with a grateful sense of the early benefit derived from it.

It is needless to expatiate upon the qualities of a work which has thus passed from country to country, and language to language, until it is now known throughout the whole reading-world and is become a household book in every hand. The secret of its universal and enduring popularity is undoubtedly its truth to nature, but to nature of the most amiable kind, to nature such as Goldsmith saw it. The author, as we have occasionally shown in the course of this memoir, took his scenes and characters in this, as in his other writings, from originals in his own motley experience; but he has given them as seen through the medium of his own indulgent eye, and has set them forth with the colorings of his own good head and heart. Yet how contradictory it seems that this, one of the most delightful pictures of home and home-felt happiness should be drawn by a homeless man; that the most amiable picture of domestic virtue and all the endearments of the married state should be drawn by a bachelor, who had been severed from domestic life almost from boyhood; that one of the most tender, touching, and affecting appeals on behalf of female loveliness should have been made by a man whose deficiency in all the graces of person and manner seemed to mark him out for a cynical disparager of the sex.

We cannot refrain from transcribing from the work a short passage illustrative of what we have said, and which within a wonderfully small compass comprises a world of beauty of imagery, tenderness of feeling, delicacy and refinement of thought, and matchless purity of style. The two stanzas which conclude it, in which are told a whole history of woman's wrongs and sufferings, is, for pathos, simplicity, and euphony, a gem in the language. The scene depicted is where the poor Vicar is gathering around him the wrecks of his shattered family, and endeavoring to rally them back to happiness.

"The next morning the sun arose with peculiar warmth for the season, so that we agreed to breakfast together on the honeysuckle bank; where, while we sat, my youngest daughter at my request joined her voice to the concert on the trees about us. It was in this place my poor Olivia first met her seducer, and every object served to recall her sadness. But that melancholy which is excited by objects of pleasure, or inspired by sounds of harmony, soothes the heart instead of corroding it. Her mother, too, upon this occasion, felt a pleasing distress, and wept and loved her daughter as before. 'Do, my pretty Olivia,' cried she, 'let us have that melancholy air your father was so fond of; your sister Sophy has already obliged us. Do, child, it will please your old father.' She complied in a manner so exquisitely pathetic as moved me.

> " 'When lovely woman stoops to folly,
>   And finds too late that men betray,
>   What charm can soothe her melancholy,
>   What art can wash her guilt away?
>
> " 'The only art her guilt to cover,
>   To hide her shame from every eye,
>   To give repentance to her lover,
>   And wring his bosom—is to die.' "

Scarce had the "Vicar of Wakefield" made its appearance and been received with acclamation, than its author was subjected to one of the usual penalties that attend success. He was attacked in the newspapers. In one of the chapters he had introduced his ballad of "The Hermit," of which, as we have mentioned, a few copies had been printed some considerable time previously for the use of the Countess of Northumberland. This brought forth the following article in a fashionable journal of the day:—

" *To the Printer of the 'St. James's Chronicle.'*

"SIR,—In the 'Reliques of Ancient Poetry,' published about two years ago, is a very beautiful little ballad, called 'A Friar of Orders Gray.' The ingenious editor, Mr. Percy, supposes that the stanzas sung by Ophelia in the play of 'Hamlet' were parts of some ballad well known in Shakspeare's time, and from these stanzas, with the addition of one or two of his own to connect them, he has formed the above-mentioned ballad; the subject of which is, a lady comes to a convent to inquire for her love who had been driven there by her disdain. She is answered by a friar that he is dead:—

> " 'No, no, he is dead, gone to his death's bed.
> He never will come again.'

The lady weeps and laments her cruelty; the friar endeavors to comfort her with morality and religion, but all in vain; she expresses the deepest grief and the most tender sentiments of love, till at last the friar discovers himself:—

> " 'And lo! beneath this gown of gray
> Thy own true love appears.'

"This catastrophe is very fine, and the whole, joined with the greatest tenderness, has the greatest simplicity; yet, though this ballad was so recently published in the 'Ancient Reliques,' Dr Goldsmith has been hardy enough to publish a poem called 'The Hermit,' where the circumstances and catastrophe are exactly the same, only with this difference, that the natural simplicity and tenderness of the original are almost entirely lost in the languid smoothness and tedious paraphrase of the copy, which is as short of the merits of Mr. Percy's ballad as the insipidity of negus is to the genuine flavor of champagne.

"I am, sir, yours, &c.,
"DETECTOR."

This attack, supposed to be by Goldsmith's constant persecutor, the malignant Kenrick, drew from him the following note to the editor:—

"SIR,—As there is nothing I dislike so much as newspaper controversy, particularly upon trifles, permit me to be as concise as possible in informing a correspondent of yours that I recommended 'Blainville's Travels' because I thought the book was a good one; and I think so still. I said I was told by the bookseller that it was then first published; but in that it seems I was misinformed, and my reading was not extensive enough to set me right.

"Another correspondent of yours accuses me of having taken a ballad I published some time ago, from one by the ingenious Mr. Percy. I do not think there is any great resemblance between the two pieces in question. If there be any, his ballad was taken from mine. I read it to Mr. Percy some years ago; and he, as we both considered these things as trifles at best, told me, with his usual good-humor, the next time I saw him, that he had taken my plan to form the fragments of Shakspeare into a ballad of his own. He then read me his little Cento,[1] if I may so call it, and I highly approved it. Such petty anecdotes as these are scarcely

---

[1] A patch-work of quotations.

worth printing; and, were it not for the busy disposition of
some of your correspondents, the public should never have
known that he owes me the hint of his ballad, or that I am
obliged to his friendship and learning for communications
of a much more important nature.

"I am, sir, yours, &c.,

"OLIVER GOLDSMITH." [1]

The unexpected circulation of the "Vicar of Wakefield"
enriched the publisher, but not the author.[2] Goldsmith no
doubt thought himself entitled to participate in the profits
of the repeated editions; and a memorandum, still extant,
shows that he drew upon Mr. Francis Newbery, in the month
of June, for fifteen guineas, but that the bill was returned
dishonored. He continued, therefore, his usual job-work for
the booksellers, writing introductions, prefaces, and head and
tail-pieces for new works; revising, touching up, and modifying travels and voyages; making compilations of prose and
poetry, and "building books," as he sportively termed it.
These tasks required little labor or talent, but that taste and
touch which are the magic of gifted minds. His terms began
to be proportioned to his celebrity. If his price was at any

---

[1] "The reply is perfect in tone, and shows once more how unfailing is
Goldsmith's skill when he took pen in hand. Percy, it may be added, con
firmed this story, with but little variation, in a note which he appended to
the 'Friar of Orders Gray,' in the 1775 edition of the 'Reliques,' and also in
the 'Memoir' of Goldsmith, prefixed to the 'Miscellaneous Works' of 1801."
DOBSON, *Life*, p. 125:

[2] There were three editions of the *Vicar* in the year of its publication,
1766. The fourth edition appeared in 1770, and according to the account
books of the publishers, it started with a loss. So little commercial value
had the book that after the appearance of the fourth edition a third share
was sold for five guineas. A fifth edition appeared in 1774, and a sixth in
1779. "Assuming the fifth to have been like the fourth, limited to one thousand copies, it took nearly nine years to sell two thousand copies."—DOBSON,
Life, p. 120. The book therefore did not have as large a circulation as Irving
supposed, and Goldsmith received a very fair share of the profits. Probably
not more than five thousand copies were sold before Goldsmith's death.

time objected to, "Why, sir," he would say, "it may seem large; but then a man may be many years working in obscurity before his taste and reputation are fixed or estimated; and then he is, as in other professions, only paid for his previous labors."

He was, however, prepared to try his fortune in a different walk of literature from any he had yet attempted. We have repeatedly adverted to his fondness for the drama; he was a frequent attendant at the theatres; though, as we have shown, he considered them under gross mismanagement. He thought, too, that a vicious taste prevailed among those who wrote for the stage. "A new species of dramatic composition," says he, in one of his essays, "has been introduced under the name of *sentimental comedy*, in which the virtues of private life are exhibited rather than the vices exposed; and the distresses rather than the faults of mankind make our interest in the piece. In these plays almost all the characters are good, and exceedingly generous; they are lavish enough of their tin money on the stage; and though they want humor, have abundance of sentiment and feeling. If they happen to have faults or foibles, the spectator is taught not only to pardon, but to applaud them in consideration of the goodness of their hearts; so that folly, instead of being ridiculed, is commended, and the comedy aims at touching our passions, without the power of being truly pathetic. In this manner we are likely to lose one great source of entertainment on the stage; for while the comic poet is invading the province of the tragic muse, he leaves her lively sister quite neglected. Of this, however, he is no ways solicitous, as he measures his fame by his profits. . . .

"Humor at present seems to be departing from the stage; and it will soon happen that our comic players will have nothing left for it but a fine coat and a song. It depends upon the audience whether they will actually drive these poor merry creatures from the stage, or sit at a play as gloomy as at the tabernacle. It is not easy to recover an art when once lost; and it will be a just punishment, that when, by our being too fastidious, we have banished humor from the stage, we should ourselves be deprived of the art of laughing." [1]

Symptoms of reform in the drama had recently taken place. The comedy of the "Clandestine Marriage," the joint production of Colman and Garrick, and suggested by Hogarth's inimitable pictures of *Mariage à la mode*, had taken the town by storm, crowded the theatre with fashionable audiences, and formed one of the leading literary topics of the year. Goldsmith's emulation was roused by its success. The comedy was, in what he considered the legitimate line, totally different from the sentimental school; it presented pictures of real life, delineations of character and touches of humor, in which he felt himself calculated to excel. The consequence was, that in the course of this year (1766) he commenced a comedy of the same class, to be entitled the "Good-Natured Man," at which he diligently wrought whenever the hurried occupation of "book-building" allowed him leisure.

[1] The so-called sentimental comedy arose as a reaction from the comedy of Wycherley, Congreve, Vanbrugh and other writers of the end of the seventeenth century. This seventeenth century comedy was characterized by sparkling wit, coupled however with the most flagrant immorality in plot and dialogue. The sentimental comedy, founded by Richard Steele (*The Conscious Lovers*, 1722), attempted to reform the morals of the stage but unfortunately went to the other extreme, and resulted in what Hazlitt, in his *English Comic Writers*, calls, "*do-me-good*, lack-a-daisical, whining, make-believe comedies." True comedy, that is, a truthful portrayal of characters and manners in brilliant dialogue, revived under Sheridan and Goldsmith; in the comedies of these two writers, we have wit, a sufficient truth to nature, and a healthful morality. The passage is quoted from *Unacknowledged Essays*, No. XXVII.

CHAPTER XVIII

The social position of Goldsmith had undergone a material change since the publication of "The Traveller."
Before that event he was but partially known as the author
of some clever anonymous writings, and had been a tolerated member of the club and the Johnson circle, without
much being expected from him. Now he had suddenly
risen to literary fame, and become one of the *lions* of the
day. The highest regions of intellectual society were now
open to him; but he was not prepared to move in them
with confidence and success. Ballymahon had not been a
good school of manners at the outset of life; nor had his
experience as a "poor student" at colleges and medical
schools contributed to give him the polish of society. He
had brought from Ireland, as he said, nothing but his
"brogue and his blunders," and they had never left him.
He had travelled, it is true; but the Continental tour which
in those days gave the finishing grace to the education of a
patrician youth, had, with poor Goldsmith, been little better
than a course of literary vagabondizing. It had enriched
his mind, deepened and widened the benevolence of his
heart, and filled his memory with enchanting pictures, but
it had contributed little to disciplining him for the polite
intercourse of the world. His life in London had hitherto
been a struggle with sordid cares and sad humiliations.
"You scarcely can conceive," wrote he some time previously
to his brother, "how much eight years of disappointment,

anguish, and study have worn me down." Several more.
years had since been added to the term during which he had
trod the lowly walks of life. He had been a tutor, an
apothecary's drudge, a petty physician of the suburbs, a
bookseller's hack, drudging for daily bread. Each separate
walk had been beset by its peculiar thorns and humiliations. It is wonderful how his heart retained its gentleness
and kindness through all these trials; how his mind rose
above the "meannesses of poverty," to which, as he says,
he was compelled to submit; but it would be still more
wonderful, had his manners acquired a tone corresponding
to the innate grace and refinement of his intellect. He was
near forty years of age when he published "The Traveller,"
and was lifted by it into celebrity. As is beautifully said
of him by one of his biographers, "he has fought his way to
consideration and esteem; but he bears upon him the scars
of his twelve years' conflict; of the mean sorrows through
which he has passed; and of the cheap indulgences he has
sought relief and help from. There is nothing plastic in
his nature now. His manners and habits are completely
formed; and in them any further success can make little
favorable change, whatever it may effect for his mind or
genius."*

We are not to be surprised, therefore, at finding him
make an awkward figure in the elegant drawing-rooms which
were now open to him, and disappointing those who had
formed an idea of him from the fascinating ease and
gracefulness of his poetry.

Even the literary club, and the circle of which it formed
a part, after their surprise at the intellectual flights of which
he showed himself capable, fell into a conventional mode of
judging and talking of him, and of placing him in absurd

---

* Forster's Goldsmith.

.and whimsical points of view. His very celebrity operated here to his disadvantage. It brought him into continual comparison with Johnson, who was the oracle of that circle and had given it a tone. Conversation was the great staple there, and of this Johnson was a master. He had been a reader and thinker from childhood: his melancholy temperament, which unfitted him for the pleasures of youth, had made him so. For many years past the vast variety of works he had been obliged to consult in preparing his Dictionary, had stored an uncommonly retentive memory with facts on all kinds of subjects; making it a perfect colloquial armory. "He had all his life," says Boswell, "habituated himself to consider conversation as a trial of intellectual vigor and skill. He had disciplined himself as a talker as well as a writer, making it a rule to impart whatever he knew in the most forcible language he could put it in, so that by constant practice and never suffering any careless expression to escape him, he had attained an extraordinary accuracy and command of language."

His conversation in all companies, according to Sir Joshua Reynolds, was such as to secure him universal attention, something above the usual colloquial style being always expected from him.

"I do not care," said Orme, the historian of Hindostan, "on what subject Johnson talks; but I love better to hear him talk than anybody. He either gives you new thoughts or a new coloring."

A stronger and more graphic eulogium is given by Dr. Percy. "The conversation of Johnson," says he, "is strong and clear, and may be compared to an antique statue, where every vein and muscle is distinct and clear."

Such was the colloquial giant with which Goldsmith's celebrity and his habits of intimacy brought him into con-

tinual comparison; can we wonder that he should appear to
disadvantage? Conversation grave, discursive, and disputatious, such as Johnson excelled and delighted in, was to
him a severe task, and he never was good at a task of any
kind. He had not, like Johnson, a vast fund of acquired
facts to draw upon; nor a retentive memory to furnish them
forth when wanted. He could not, like the great lexicographer, mould his ideas and balance his periods while talking. He had a flow of ideas, but it was apt to be hurried
and confused; and, as he said of himself, he had contracted
a hesitating and disagreeable manner of speaking. He
used to say that he always argued best when he argued
alone; that is to say, he could master a subject in his study,
with his pen in his hand; but when he came into company
he grew confused, and was unable to talk about it. Johnson made a remark concerning him to somewhat of the same
purport. "No man," said he, "is more foolish than Goldsmith when he has not a pen in his hand, or more wise when
he has." Yet with all this conscious deficiency he was continually getting involved in colloquial contests with Johnson
and other prime talkers of the literary circle. He felt that
he had become a notoriety, that he had entered the lists and
was expected to make fight; so with that heedlessness
which characterized him in everything else he dashed on at
a venture, trusting to chance in this as in other things, and
hoping occasionally to make a lucky hit. Johnson perceived
his hap-hazard temerity, but gave him no credit for the real
diffidence which lay at bottom. "The misfortune of Goldsmith in conversation," said he, "is this, he goes on without
knowing how he is to get off. His genius is great, but his
knowledge is small. As they say of a generous man it is a
pity he is not rich, we may say of Goldsmith it is a pity he
is not knowing. He would not keep his knowledge to him-

self." And, on another occasion, he observes: "Goldsmith, rather than not talk, will talk of what he knows himself to be ignorant, which can only end in exposing him. If in company with two founders, he would fall a-talking on the method of making cannon, though both of them would soon see that he did not know what metal a cannon is made of." And again: "Goldsmith should not be forever attempting to shine in conversation; he has not temper for it, he is so much mortified when he fails. Sir, a game of jokes is composed partly of skill, partly of chance; a man may be beat at times by one who has not the tenth part of his wit. Now Goldsmith, putting himself against another, is like a man laying a hundred to one, who cannot spare the hundred. It is not worth a man's while. A man should not lay a hundred to one unless he can easily spare it, though he has a hundred chances for him; he can get but a guinea, and he may lose a hundred. Goldsmith is in this state. When he contends, if he gets the better, it is a very little addition to a man of his literary reputation; if he does not get the better, he is miserably vexed."

Johnson was not·aware how much he was himself to blame in producing this vexation. "Goldsmith," said Miss Reynolds, "always appeared to be overawed by Johnson, particularly when in company with people of any consequence; always as if impressed with fear of disgrace; and indeed well he might. I have been witness to many mortifications he has suffered in Dr. Johnson's company."

It may not have been disgrace that he feared, but rudeness. The great lexicographer, spoiled by the homage of society, was still more prone than himself to lose temper when the argument went against him. He could not brook appearing to be worsted, but would attempt to bear down his adversary by the rolling thunder of his periods, and, when that failed, would become downright insulting. Boswell called it "having recourse to some sudden mode of robust sophistry"; but Goldsmith designated it much more happily. "There is no arguing with Johnson," said he, *"for, when his pistol misses fire, he knocks you down with the butt-end of it."**

In several of the intellectual collisions recorded by Boswell as triumphs of Dr. Johnson, it really appears to us that Goldsmith had the best both of the wit and the argument, and especially of the courtesy and good-nature.

On one occasion he certainly gave Johnson a capital reproof as to his own colloquial peculiarities. Talking of fables, Goldsmith observed that the animals introduced in them seldom talked in character. "For instance," said he, "the fable of the little fishes, who saw birds fly over their heads, and, envying them, petitioned Jupiter to be changed into birds. The skill consists in making them talk like little fishes." Just then observing that Dr. Johnson was shaking his sides and laughing, he immediately added, "Why, Dr. Johnson, this is not so easy as you seem to think; for, if you were to make little fishes talk, they would talk like whales."

But though Goldsmith suffered frequent mortifications in society from the overbearing, and sometimes harsh, conduct of Johnson, he always did justice to his benevolence. When royal pensions were granted to Dr. Johnson and Dr. Shebbeare, a punster remarked, that the king had pensioned a *she-bear* and a *he-bear;* to which Goldsmith replied, "Johnson, to be sure, has a roughness in his manner, but no

---

* The following is given by Boswell, as an instance of robust sophistry:—
"Once, when I was pressing upon him with visible advantage, he stopped me thus—'My dear Boswell, let's have no more of this; you'll make nothing of it; I'd rather hear you whistle a Scotch tune.' "

man alive has a more tender heart. *He has nothing of the bear but the skin.*"

Goldsmith, in conversation, shone most when he least thought of shining; when he gave up all effort to appear wise and learned, or to cope with the oracular sententiousness of Johnson, and gave way to his natural impulses. Even Boswell could perceive his merits on these occasions. "For my part," said he, condescendingly, "I like very well to hear *honest* Goldsmith talk away carelessly;" and many a much wiser man than Boswell delighted in those outpourings of a fertile fancy and a generous heart. In his happy moods, Goldsmith had an artless simplicity and buoyant good-humor, that led to a thousand amusing blunders and whimsical confessions, much to the entertainment of his intimates; yet in his most thoughtless garrulity there was occasionally the gleam of the gold and the flash of the diamond.

CHAPTER XIX

Though Goldsmith's pride and ambition led him to mingle occasionally with high society, and to engage in the colloquial conflicts of the learned circle, in both of which he was ill at ease and conscious of being undervalued, yet he had some social resorts in which he indemnified himself for their restraints by indulging his humor without control. One of them was a shilling whist-club, which held its meetings at the Devil Tavern, near Temple Bar, a place rendered classic, we are told, by a club held there in old times, to which "rare Ben Jonson" had furnished the rules. The company was of a familiar, unceremonious kind, delighting in that very questionable wit which consists in playing off practical jokes upon each other. Of one of these Goldsmith was made the butt. Coming to the club one night in a hackney-coach, he gave the coachman by mistake a guinea instead of a shilling, which he set down at a dead loss, for there was no likelihood, he said, that a fellow of this class would have the honesty to return the money. On the next club-evening he was told a person at the street-door wished to speak with him. He went forth, but soon returned with a radiant countenance. To his surprise and delight the coachman had actually brought back the guinea. While he launched forth in praise of this unlooked-for piece of honesty, he declared it ought not to go unrewarded. Col-

lecting a small sum from the club, and no doubt increasing
it largely from his own purse, he dismissed the Jehu with
many encomiums on his good conduct. He was still chant-
ing his praises, when one of the club requested a sight of the
guinea thus honestly returned. To Goldsmith's confusion
it proved to be a counterfeit. The universal burst of
laughter which succeeded, and the jokes by which he was
assailed on every side, showed him that the whole was a
hoax, and the pretended coachman as much a counterfeit as
the guinea. He was so disconcerted, it is said, that he soon
beat a retreat for the evening.

Another of those free and easy clubs met on Wednesday
evenings at the Globe Tavern in Fleet Street. It was somewhat in the style of the Three Jolly Pigeons: songs, jokes,
dramatic imitations, burlesque parodies, and broad sallies
of humor, formed a contrast to the sententious morality,
pedantic casuistry, and polished sarcasm of the learned
circle. Here a huge "tun of man," by the name of Gordon,
used to delight Goldsmith by singing the jovial song of
Nottingham Ale, and looking like a butt of it. Here, too,
a wealthy pig-butcher, charmed, no doubt, by the mild
philanthropy of "The Traveller," aspired to be on the
most sociable footing with the author; and here was Tom
King, the comedian, recently risen to consequence by his
performance of Lord Ogleby in the new comedy of "The
Clandestine Marriage." [1]

A member of more note was one Hugh Kelly, a second-
rate author, who, as he became a kind of competitor of
Goldsmith's, deserves particular mention. He was an Irishman, about twenty-eight years of age, originally apprenticed
to a staymaker in Dublin; then writer to a London attorney;
then a Grub-Street hack; scribbling for magazines and

---

[1] See below, p. 239.

newspapers. Of late he had set up for theatrical censor and
satirist, and in a paper called "Thespis," in emulation of
Churchill's "Rosciad," had harassed many of the poor actors without mercy, and often without wit; but had lavished
his incense on Garrick, who, in consequence, took him into
favor. He was the author of several works of superficial
merit, but which had sufficient vogue to inflate his vanity.
This, however, must have been mortified on his first introduction to Johnson; after sitting a short time he got up to
take leave, expressing a fear that a longer visit might be
troublesome. "Not in the least, sir," said the surly moralist, "I had forgotten you were in the room." Johnson used to
speak of him as a man who had written more than he had read.

A prime wag of this club was one of Goldsmith's poor
countrymen and hangers-on, by the name of Glover. He
had originally been educated for the medical profession, but
had taken in early life to the stage, though apparently without much success. While performing at Cork, he undertook,
partly in jest, to restore life to the body of a malefactor, who
had just been executed. To the astonishment of every one,
himself among the number, he succeeded. The miracle
took wind. He abandoned the stage, resumed the wig and
cane, and considered his fortune as secure. Unluckily, there
were not many dead people to be restored to life in Ireland;
his practice did not equal his expectation, so he came to
London, where he continued to dabble indifferently, and
rather unprofitably, in physic and literature.

He was a great frequenter of the Globe and Devil taverns, where he used to amuse the company by his talent at
story-telling and his powers of mimicry, giving capital imitations of Garrick, Foote, Colman, Sterne, and other public
characters of the day. He seldom happened to have money
enough to pay his reckoning, but was always sure to find

some ready purse among those who had been amused by his
humors. Goldsmith, of course, was one of the readiest. It
was through him that Glover was admitted to the Wednesday Club, of which his theatrical imitations became the
delight. Glover, however, was a little anxious for the dignity of his patron, which appeared to him to suffer from the
over-familiarity of some of the members of the club. He
was especially shocked by the free and easy tone in which
Goldsmith was addressed by the pig-butcher. "Come,
Noll," would he say, as he pledged him, "here's my service
to you, old boy!"

Glover whispered to Goldsmith, that he "should not allow
such liberties."   "Let him alone," was the reply, "you'll see
how civilly I'll let him down."   After a time, he called out,
with marked ceremony and politeness, "Mr. B., I have the
honor of drinking your good health." Alas! dignity was
not poor Goldsmith's forte: he could keep no one at a distance. "Thank'ee, thank'ee, Noll," nodded the pig-butcher,
scarce taking the pipe out of his mouth. "I don't see the
effect of your reproof," whispered Glover. "I give it up,"
replied Goldsmith, with a good-humored shrug; "I ought to
have known before now there is no putting a pig in the
right way."

Johnson used to be severe upon Goldsmith for mingling
in those motley circles, observing, that, having been originally poor, he had contracted a love for low company. Goldsmith, however, was guided not by a taste for what was low,
but for what was comic and characteristic. It was the
feeling of the artist; the feeling which furnished out some
of his best scenes in familiar life; the feeling with which
"rare Ben Jonson" sought these very haunts and circles in
days of yore, to study "Every Man in his Humor." [1]

---

[1] The title of one of Ben Jonson's earliest plays.

It was not always, however, that the humor of these associates was to his taste: as they became boisterous in their
merriment, he was apt to become depressed. "The company of fools," says he, in one of his essays, "may at first
make us smile, but at last never fails of making us melancholy." "Often he would become moody," says Glover,
"and would leave the party abruptly to go home and brood
over his misfortune."

It is possible, however, that he went home for quite a
different purpose: to commit to paper some scene or passage
suggested for his comedy of "The Good-natured Man."
The elaboration of humor is often a most serious task; and
we have never witnessed a more perfect picture of mental
misery than was once presented to us by a popular dramatic
writer—still, we hope, living—whom we found in the agonies
of producing a farce which subsequently set the theatres in a
roar.

⚊ CHAPTER XX

THE GREAT CHAM OF LITERATURE AND THE KING — SCENE AT SIR
JOSHUA REYNOLDS'S — GOLDSMITH ACCUSED OF JEALOUSY —
NEGOTIATIONS WITH GARRICK — THE AUTHOR AND THE ACTOR;
THEIR CORRESPONDENCE.

The comedy of "The Good-natured Man" was completed
by Goldsmith early in 1767, and submitted to the perusal
of Johnson, Burke, Reynolds, and others of the literary
club, by whom it was heartily approved.   Johnson, who was
seldom halfway either in censure or applause, pronounced
it the best comedy that had been written since "The Provoked Husband," [1] and promised to furnish the prologue.
This immediately became an object of great solicitude with
Goldsmith, knowing the weight an introduction from the
Great Cham of literature would have with the public; but
circumstances occurred which he feared might drive the
comedy and the prologue from Johnson's thoughts.   The
latter was in the habit of visiting the royal library at the
Queen's (Buckingham) House, a noble collection of books,
in the formation of which he had assisted the librarian, Mr.
Bernard, with his advice.   One evening, as he was seated
there by the fire reading, he was surprised by the entrance of
the King (George III.), then a young man, who sought this
occasion to have a conversation with him.   The conversation was varied and discursive, the king shifting from subject to subject according to his wont.   "During the whole
interview," says Boswell, "Johnson talked to his Majesty
with profound respect, but still in his open, manly manner,

---

[1] See above, p. 163.

with a sonorous voice, and never in that subdued tone which is commonly used at the levee and in the drawing-room. 'I found his Majesty wished I should talk,' said he, 'and I made it my business to talk. I find it does a man good to be talked to by his sovereign. In the first place, a man cannot be in a passion.' " It would have been well for Johnson's colloquial disputants, could he have often been under such decorous restraint. Profoundly monarchical in his principles, he retired from the interview highly gratified with the conversation of the King and with his gracious behavior. "Sir," said he to the librarian, "they may talk of the King as they will, but he is the finest gentleman I have ever seen."—"Sir," said he subsequently to Bennet Langton, "his manners are those of as fine a gentleman as we may suppose Louis the Fourteenth or Charles the Second."

While Johnson's face was still radiant with the reflex of royalty, he was holding forth one day to a listening group at Sir Joshua Reynolds's, who were anxious to hear every particular of this memorable conversation. Among other questions, the King had asked him whether he was writing anything. His reply was, that he thought he had already done his part as a writer. "I should have thought so, too," said the King, "if you had not written so well."—"No man," said Johnson, commenting on this speech, "could have made a handsomer compliment; and it was fit for a King to pay. It was decisive."—"But did you make no reply to this high compliment?" asked one of the company. "No, sir," replied the profoundly deferential Johnson; "when the King had said it, it was to be so. It was not for me to bandy civilities with my sovereign."

During all the time that Johnson was thus holding forth, Goldsmith, who was present, appeared to take no interest in the royal theme, but remained seated on a sofa at a distance, in a moody fit of abstraction; at length recollecting himself, he sprang up, and advancing, exclaimed, with what Boswell calls his usual "frankness and simplicity,"—"Well, you acquitted yourself in this conversation better than I should have done, for I should have bowed and stammered through the whole of it." He afterwards explained his seeming inattention by saying that his mind was completely occupied about his play, and by fears lest Johnson, in his present state of royal excitement, would fail to furnish the much-desired prologue.

How natural and truthful is this explanation. Yet Boswell presumes to pronounce Goldsmith's inattention affected, and attributes it to jealousy. "It was strongly suspected," says he, "that he was fretting with chagrin and envy at the singular honor Dr. Johnson had lately enjoyed." It needed the littleness of mind of Boswell to ascribe such pitiful motives to Goldsmith, and to entertain such exaggerated notions of the honor paid to Dr. Johnson.

"The Good-natured Man" was now ready for performance, but the question was, how to get it upon the stage. The affairs of Covent Garden, for which it had been intended, were thrown into confusion by the recent death of Rich, the manager. Drury Lane was under the management of Garrick; but a feud, it will be recollected, existed between him and the poet, from the animadversions of the latter on the mismanagement of theatrical affairs, and the refusal of the former to give the poet his vote for the secretaryship of the Society of Arts. Times, however, were changed. Goldsmith, when that feud took place, was an anonymous writer, almost unknown to fame, and of no circulation in society. Now he had become a literary lion; he was a member of the Literary Club; he was the associate

of Johnson, Burke, Topham Beauclerc, and other mag-
nates,—in a word, he had risen to consequence in the public
eye, and of course was of consequence in the eyes of David
Garrick. Sir Joshua Reynolds saw the lurking scruples of
pride existing between the author and actor, and thinking it
a pity that two men of such congenial talents, and who might
be so serviceable to each other, should be kept asunder by a
worn-out pique, exerted his friendly offices to bring them
together. The meeting took place in Reynolds's house in
Leicester Square. Garrick, however, could not entirely put
off the mock majesty of the stage; he meant to be civil, but
he was rather too gracious and condescending. Tom Davies,
in his "Life of Garrick," gives an amusing picture of the
coming together of these punctilious parties. "The manager," says he, "was fully conscious of his (Goldsmith's)
merit, and perhaps more ostentatious of his abilities to serve
a dramatic author than became a man of his prudence;
Goldsmith was, on his side, as fully persuaded of his own
importance and independent greatness. Mr. Garrick, who
had so long been treated with the complimentary language
paid to a successful patentee and admired actor, expected
that the writer would esteem the patronage of his play a
favor; Goldsmith rejected all ideas of kindness in a bargain
that was intended to be of mutual advantage to both parties,
and in this he was certainly justifiable; Mr. Garrick could
reasonably expect no thanks for the acting a new play,
which he would have rejected if he had not been convinced
it would have amply rewarded his pains and expense. I
believe the manager was willing to accept the play, but he
wished to be courted to it; and the Doctor was not disposed
to purchase his friendship by the resignation of his sincerity." They separated, however, with an understanding
on the part of Goldsmith that his play would be acted.

The conduct of Garrick subsequently proved evasive, not
through any lingerings of past hostility, but from habitual
indecision in matters of the kind, and from real scruples of
delicacy. He did not think the piece likely to succeed on
the stage, and avowed that opinion to Reynolds and Johnson,—but hesitated to say as much to Goldsmith, through
fear of wounding his feelings. A further misunderstanding
was the result of this want of decision and frankness;
repeated interviews and some correspondence took place
without bringing matters to a point, and in the meantime
the theatrical season passed away.

Goldsmith's pocket, never well supplied, suffered griev-
ously by this delay, and he considered himself entitled to
call upon the manager, who still talked of acting the play,
to advance him forty pounds upon a note of the younger
Newbery. Garrick readily complied, but subsequently suggested certain important alterations in the comedy as indis-
pensable to its success; these were indignantly rejected by
the author, but pertinaciously insisted on by the manager.
Garrick proposed to leave the matter to the arbitration of
Whitehead,[1] the laureate, who officiated as his "reader" and
elbow-critic. Goldsmith was more indignant than ever, and
a violent dispute ensued, which was only calmed by the
interference of Burke and Reynolds.

Just at this time, order came out of confusion in the
affairs of Covent Garden. A pique having risen between
Colman and Garrick, in the course of their joint authorship
of "The Clandestine Marriage," the former had become
manager and part-proprietor of Covent Garden, and was
preparing to open a powerful competition with his former
colleague. On hearing of this, Goldsmith made overtures

---

[1] William Whitehead (1715-1785), one of the "illustrious obscure", published poems in 1754.

to Colman; who, without waiting to consult his fellow pro-
prietors, who were absent, gave instantly a favorable reply.
Goldsmith felt the contrast of this warm, encouraging conduct, to the chilling delays and objections of Garrick. He
at once abandoned his piece to the discretion of Colman.
"Dear sir," says he, in a letter dated Temple Garden Court,
July 9th, "I am very much obliged to you for your kind
partiality in my favor, and your tenderness in shortening the
interval of my expectation. That the play is liable to many
objections I well know, but I am happy that it is in hands
the most capable in the world of removing them. If then,
dear sir, you will complete your favor by putting the piece
into such a state as it may be acted, or of directing me how
to do it, I shall ever retain a sense of your goodness to me.
And indeed, though most probably this be the last I shall
ever write, yet I can't help feeling a secret satisfaction that
poets for the future are likely to have a protector who
declines taking advantage of their dreadful situation—and
scorns that importance which may be acquired by trifling
with their anxieties."

The next day Goldsmith wrote to Garrick, who was at
Litchfield, informing him of his having transferred his piece
to Covent Garden, for which it had been originally written,
and by the patentee of which it was claimed, observing,
"As I found you had very great difficulties about that piece,
I complied with his desire. . . . I am extremely sorry that
you should think me warm at our last meeting: your judgment certainly ought to be free, especially in a matter which
must in some measure concern your own credit and interest.
I assure you, sir, I have no disposition to differ with you on
this or any other account, but am, with an high opinion of
your abilities, and a very real esteem, sir, your most obedient humble servant. OLIVER GOLDSMITH."

In his reply, Garrick observed, "I was, indeed, much hurt that your warmth at our last meeting mistook my sincere and friendly attention to your play for the remains of a former misunderstanding, which I had as much forgot as if it had never existed. What I said to you at my own house I now repeat, that I felt more pain in giving my sentiments than you possibly would in receiving them. It has been the business, and ever will be, of my life to live on the best terms with men of genius; and I know that Dr. Goldsmith will have no reason to change his previous friendly disposition towards me, as I shall be glad of every future opportunity to convince him how much I am his obedient servant and well-wisher. D. GARRICK."

CHAPTER XXI

MORE HACK-AUTHORSHIP—TOM DAVIES AND THE ROMAN HISTORY—
CANONBURY CASTLE — POLITICAL AUTHORSHIP — PECUNIARY
TEMPTATION—DEATH OF NEWBERY THE ELDER.

Though Goldsmith's comedy was now in train to be performed, it could not be brought out before Christmas; in
the meantime he must live. Again, therefore, he had to
resort to literary jobs for his daily support. These obtained
for him petty occasional sums, the largest of which was ten
pounds, from the elder Newbery, for an historical compilation; but this scanty rill of quasi patronage, so sterile in its
products, was likely soon to cease; Newbery being too ill
to attend to business, and having to transfer the whole
management of it to his nephew.

At this time Tom Davies, the sometime Roscius, sometime bibliopole, stepped forward to Goldsmith's relief, and
proposed that he should undertake an easy popular history
of Rome in two volumes. An arrangement was soon made.
Goldsmith undertook to complete it in two years, if possible, for two hundred and fifty guineas, and forthwith set
about his task with cheerful alacrity. As usual, he sought
a rural retreat during the summer months, where he might
alternate his literary labors with strolls about the green
fields. "Merry Islington" was again his resort, but he now
aspired to better quarters than formerly, and engaged the
chambers occupied occasionally by Mr. Newbery, in Canonbury House, or Castle, as it is popularly called. This had
been a hunting-lodge of Queen Elizabeth, in whose time it
was surrounded by parks and forests. In Goldsmith's day,

nothing remained of it but an old brick tower; it was still in the country amid rural scenery, and was a favorite nestling-place of authors, publishers, and others of the literary order.* A number of these he had for fellow-occupants of the castle; and they formed a temporary club, which held its meetings at the Crown Tavern, on the Islington lower road; and here he presided in his own genial style, and was the life and delight of the company.

The writer of these pages visited old Canonbury Castle some years since, out of regard to the memory of Goldsmith.[1] The apartment was still shown which the poet had inhabited, consisting of a sitting-room and small bedroom, with panelled wainscots and Gothic windows. The quaintness and quietude of the place were still attractive. It was one of the resorts of citizens on their Sunday walks, who would ascend to the top of the tower and amuse themselves with reconnoitering the city through a telescope. Not far from this tower were the gardens of the White Conduit House, a Cockney Elysium, where Goldsmith used to figure in the humbler days of his fortune. In the first edition of his Essays he speaks of a stroll in these gardens, where he at that time, no doubt, thought himself in perfectly genteel society. After his rise in the world, however, he became too knowing to speak of such plebeian haunts. In a new

---

*See on the distant slope, majestic shows
Old Canonbury's tower, an ancient pile,
To various fates assigned; and where by turns
Meanness and grandeur have alternate reign'd;
Thither, in later days, hath genius fled
From yonder city to respire and die.
There the sweet bard of Auburn sat, and tuned
The plaintive moanings of his village dirge.
There learned Chambers treasured lore for *men*,
And Newberry there his A-B-C's for *babes*.[2]

[1] See above, p. 176, note.
[2] Ascribed to Fox by Welsh, *Book-seller of the Last Century*, p. 47.

edition of his Essays, therefore, the White Conduit House and its gardens disappear, and he speaks of "a stroll in the Park."

While Goldsmith was literally living from hand to mouth by the forced drudgery of the pen, his independence of spirit was subjected to a sore pecuniary trial. It was the opening of Lord North's administration, a time of great political excitement. The public mind was agitated by the question of American taxation, and other questions of like irritating tendency. Junius[1] and Wilkes[2] and other powerful writers were attacking the administration with all their force; Grub Street was stirred up to its lowest depths; inflammatory talent of all kinds was in full activity, and the kingdom was deluged with pamphlets, lampoons, and libels of the grossest kinds. The ministry were looking anxiously round for literary support. It was thought that the pen of Goldsmith might be readily enlisted. His hospitable friend and countryman, Robert Nugent, politically known as Squire Gawky, had come out strenuously for colonial taxation; had been selected for a lordship of the board of trade, and raised to the rank of Baron Nugent and Viscount Clare. His example, it was thought, would be enough of itself to bring Goldsmith into the ministerial ranks; and then what writer of the day was proof against a full purse or a pension? Accordingly one Parson Scott, chaplain to Lord Sandwich, and author of "Anti Sejanus Panurge," and other political libels in support of the administration, was sent to negotiate with the poet, who at this time was returned to town. Dr. Scott, in after-years, when his political subserviency had been rewarded by two fat crown-livings, used to make what he

---

[1] See below, p. 320.

[2] John Wilkes (1727-1797), a writer on political subjects and champion of the popular cause.

considered a good story out of this embassy to the poet.
"I found him," said he, "in a miserable suit of chambers,
in the Temple. I told him my authority: I told how I was
empowered to pay most liberally for his exertions; and,
would you believe it! he was so absurd as to say, 'I can earn
as much as will supply my wants without writing for any
party; the assistance you offer is therefore unnecessary to
me;'—and so I left him in his garret!" Who does not
admire the sturdy independence of poor Goldsmith toiling
in his garret for nine guineas the job, and smile with contempt
at the indignant wonder of the political divine, albeit his subserviency *was* repaid by two fat crown-livings?

Not long after this occurrence, Goldsmith's old friend,
though frugal-handed employer, Newbery, of picture-book
renown, closed his mortal career. The poet has celebrated
him as the friend of all mankind; he certainly lost nothing
by his friendship. He coined the brains of his authors in
the times of their exigency, and made them pay dear for the
plank put out to keep them from drowning. It is not likely
his death caused much lamentation among the scribbling
tribe; we may express decent respect for the memory of the
just, but we shed tears only at the grave of the generous.

CHAPTER XXII

THEATRICAL MANŒUVRING—THE COMEDY OF "FALSE DELICACY"
— FIRST PERFORMANCE OF "THE GOOD-NATURED MAN" —
CONDUCT OF JOHNSON — CONDUCT OF THE AUTHOR — INTER-
MEDDLING OF THE PRESS.

The comedy of "The Good-natured Man" was doomed
to experience delays and difficulties to the very last. Garrick, notwithstanding his professions, had still a lurking
grudge against the author, and tasked his managerial arts
to thwart him in his theatrical enterprise. For this purpose
he undertook to build up Hugh Kelly, Goldsmith's boon
companion of the Wednesday club, as a kind of rival. Kelly
had written a comedy called "False Delicacy," in which
were embodied all the meretricious qualities of the sentimental school. Garrick, though he had decried that school,
and had brought out his comedy of "The Clandestine
Marriage" in opposition to it, now lauded "False Delicacy"
to the skies, and prepared to bring it out at Drury Lane with
all possible stage-effect. He even went so far as to write a
prologue and epilogue for it, and to touch up some parts of
the dialogue. He had become reconciled to his former colleague, Colman, and it is intimated that one condition in the
treaty of peace between these potentates of the realms of
pasteboard (equally prone to play into each other's hands
with the confederate potentates on the great theatre of life)
was, that Goldsmith's play should be kept back until Kelly's
had been brought forward.

In the meantime the poor author, little dreaming of the
deleterious influence at work behind the scenes, saw the

appointed time arrive and pass by without the performance
of his play; while "False Delicacy" was brought out at
Drury Lane (January 23, 1768) with all the trickery of
managerial management. Houses were packed to applaud
it to the echo; the newspapers vied with each other in their
venal praises, and night after night seemed to give it a fresh
triumph.

While "False Delicacy" was thus borne on the full tide
of fictitious prosperity, "The Good-natured Man" was creeping through the last rehearsals at Covent Garden. The
success of the rival piece threw a damp upon author, manager,
and actors. Goldsmith went about with a face full of anxiety; Colman's hopes in the piece declined at each rehearsal;
as to his fellow-proprietors, they declared they never entertained any. All the actors were discontented with their
parts, excepting Ned Shuter, an excellent low comedian, and
a pretty actress named Miss Walford; both of whom the
poor author ever afterward held in grateful recollection.

Johnson, Goldsmith's growling monitor and unsparing
castigator in times of heedless levity, stood by him at present
with that protecting kindness with which he ever befriended
him in time of need. He attended the rehearsals; he furnished the prologue according to promise; he pish'd and
pshaw'd at any doubts and fears on the part of the author,
but gave him sound counsel, and held him up with a steadfast and manly hand. Inspirited by his sympathy, Goldsmith plucked up new heart, and arrayed himself for the
grand trial with unusual care. Ever since his elevation into
the polite world, he had improved in his wardrobe and toilet.
Johnson could do no longer accuse him of being shabby in his
appearance; he rather went to the other extreme. On the
present occasion there is an entry in the books of his tailor,
Mr. William Filby, of a suit of "Tyrian bloom, satin grain,

and garter blue silk breeches, £8. 2s. 7d." Thus magnificently attired, he attended the theatre and watched the reception of the play, and the effect of each individual scene, with that vicissitude of feeling incident to his mercurial nature.

Johnson's prologue was solemn in itself, and being delivered by Brinsley in lugubrious tones suited to the ghost in "Hamlet," seemed to throw a portentous gloom on the audience. Some of the scenes met with great applause, and at such times Goldsmith was highly elated; others went off coldly, or there were slight tokens of disapprobation, and then his spirits would sink. The fourth act saved the piece; for Shuter, who had the main comic character of Croaker, was so varied and ludicrous in his execution of the scene in which he reads an incendiary letter, that he drew down thunders of applause. On his coming behind the scenes, Goldsmith greeted him with an overflowing heart; declaring that he exceeded his own idea of the character, and made it almost as new to him as to any of the audience.

On the whole, however, both the author and his friends were disappointed at the reception of the piece, and considered it a failure. Poor Goldsmith left the theatre with his towering hopes completely cut down. He endeavored to hide his mortification, and even to assume an air of unconcern while among his associates; but the moment he was alone with Dr. Johnson, in whose rough but magnanimous nature he reposed unlimited confidence, he threw off all restraint and gave way to an almost childlike burst of grief. Johnson, who had shown no want of sympathy at the proper time, saw nothing in the partial disappointment of overrated expectations to warrant such ungoverned emotions, and rebuked him sternly for what he termed a silly affectation, saying that "No man should be expected to sympathize with the sorrows of vanity."

When Goldsmith had recovered from the blow, he, with his usual unreserve, made his past distress a subject of amusement to his friends. Dining one day, in company with Dr. Johnson, at the chaplain's table at St. James's Palace, he entertained the company with a particular and comic account of all his feelings on the night of representation, and his despair when the piece was hissed. How he went, he said, to the Literary Club; chatted gayly, as if nothing had gone amiss; and, to give a greater idea of his unconcern, sang his favorite song about an old woman tossed in a blanket seventeen   times as high as the moon. . . . "All this while," added he, "I was suffering horrid tortures, and, had I put a bit in my mouth, I verily believe it would have strangled me on the spot, I was so excessively ill; but I made more noise than usual to cover all that; so they never perceived my not eating, nor suspected the anguish of my heart; but when all were gone except Johnson here, I burst out a-crying, and even swore that I would never write again."

Dr. Johnson sat in amaze at the odd frankness and childlike self-accusation of poor Goldsmith. When the latter had come to a pause, "All this, Doctor," said he, dryly, "I thought had been a secret between you and me, and I am sure I would not have said anything about it for the world." But Goldsmith had no secrets: his follies, his weaknesses, his errors were all thrown to the surface; his heart was really too guileless and innocent to seek mystery and concealment. It is too often the false, designing man that is guarded in his conduct and never offends proprieties.

It is singular, however, that Goldsmith, who thus in conversation could keep nothing to himself, should be the author of a maxim which would inculcate the most thorough dissimulation. "Men of the world," says he in one of the papers of the "Bee," "maintain that the true end of speech

is not so much to express our wants as to conceal them." [1]
How often is this quoted as one of the subtle remarks of the
fine-witted Talleyrand!

"The Good-natured Man" was performed for ten nights
in succession; the third, sixth, and ninth nights were for the
author's benefit; the fifth night it was commanded by their
Majesties; after this it was played occasionally, but rarely,
having always pleased more in the closet than on the stage.

As to Kelly's comedy, Johnson pronounced it entirely
devoid of character, and it has long since passed into oblivion.
Yet it is an instance how an inferior production, by dint of
puffing and trumpeting, may be kept up for a time on the
surface of popular opinion, or rather of popular talk. What
had been done for "False Delicacy" on the stage was continued by the press. The booksellers vied with the manager
in launching it upon the town. They announced that the
first impression of three thousand copies was exhausted
before two o'clock on the day of publication; four editions,
amounting to ten thousand copies, were sold in the course
of the season; a public breakfast was given to Kelly at the
Chapter Coffee House, and a piece of plate presented to him
by the publishers. The comparative merits of the two plays
were continually subjects of discussion in green-rooms,
coffee-houses, and other places where theatrical questions
were discussed.

Goldsmith's old enemy, Kenrick, that "viper of the press,"
endeavored on this, as on many other occasions, to detract
from his well-earned fame; the poet was excessively sensitive to these attacks, and had not the art and self-command
to conceal his feelings.

Some scribblers on the other side insinuated that Kelly
had seen the manuscript of Goldsmith's play, while in the

---

[1] *The Bee*, No. III.

hands of Garrick or elsewhere, and had borrowed some of the situations and sentiments. Some of the wags of the day took a mischievous pleasure in stirring up a feud between the two authors. Goldsmith became nettled, though he could scarcely be deemed jealous of one so far his inferior. He spoke disparagingly, though no doubt sincerely, of Kelly's play: the latter retorted. Still, when they met one day behind the scenes of Covent Garden, Goldsmith, with his customary urbanity, congratulated Kelly on his success. "If I thought you sincere, Mr. Goldsmith," replied the other, abruptly, "I should thank you." Goldsmith was not a man to harbor spleen or ill-will, and soon laughed at this unworthy rivalship; but the jealousy and envy awakened in Kelly's mind long continued. He is even accused of having given vent to his hostility by anonymous attacks in the newspapers, the basest resource of dastardly and malignant spirits; but of this there is no positive proof.

CHAPTER XXIII

The profits resulting from "The Good-natured Man"
were beyond any that Goldsmith had yet derived from his
works. He netted about four hundred pounds from the
theatre, and one hundred pounds from his publisher.

Five hundred pounds! and all at one miraculous draught!
It appeared to him wealth inexhaustible. It at once opened
his heart and hand, and led him into all kinds of extravagance. The first symptom was ten guineas sent to Shuter
for a box-ticket for his benefit, when "The Good-natured
Man" was to be performed. The next was an entire change
in his domicile. The shabby lodgings with Jeffs, the butler,
in which he had been worried by Johnson's scrutiny, were
now exchanged for chambers more becoming a man of his
ample fortune. The apartments consisted of three rooms
on the second floor of No. 2 Brick Court, Middle Temple,
on the right hand ascending the staircase, and overlooked the
umbrageous walks of the Temple garden. The lease he
purchased for £400, and then went on to furnish his rooms
with mahogany sofas, card-tables, and bookcases; with curtains, mirrors, and Wilton carpets. His awkward little
person was also furnished out in style befitting his apartment;
for, in addition to his suit of "Tyrian bloom, satin grain,"

we find another charged about this time, in the books of Mr. Filby, in no less gorgeous terms, being "lined with silk and furnished with gold buttons," Thus lodged and thus arrayed, he invited the visits of his most aristocratic acquaintances, and no longer quailed beneath the courtly eye of Beauclerc. He gave dinners to Johnson, Reynolds, Percy, Bickerstaff, and other friends of note; and supper-parties to young folks of both sexes. These last were preceded by round games of cards, at which there was more laughter than skill, and in which the sport was to cheat each other; or by romping games of forfeits and blind-man's-buff, at which he enacted the lord of misrule. Blackstone, whose chambers were immediately below, and who was studiously occupied on his "Commentaries," used to complain of the racket made overhead by his revelling neighbor.

Sometimes Goldsmith would make up a rural party, composed of four or five of his "jolly-pigeon" friends, to enjoy what he humorously called a "shoemaker's holiday."[1] These would assemble at his chambers in the morning, to partake of a plentiful and rather expensive breakfast; the remains of which, with his customary benevolence, he generally gave to some poor woman in attendance. The repast ended, the party would set out on foot, in high spirits, making extensive rambles by foot-paths and green lanes to Blackheath, Wandsworth, Chelsea, Hampton Court, Highgate, or some other pleasant resort, within a few miles of London. A simple but gay and heartily relished dinner, at a country inn, crowned the excursion. In the evening they strolled back to town, all the better in health and spirits for a day spent in rural and social enjoyment. Occasionally, when extravagantly

---

[1] The allusion is derived from Thomas Dekker's comedy, *The Shoemakers' Holiday* (1600), in which the guild of shoemakers is granted a holiday which they spend roaming over London.

inclined, they adjourned from dinner to drink tea at the White Conduit House; and, now and then, concluded their festive day by supping at the Grecian or Temple Exchange Coffee-Houses, or at the Globe Tavern, in Fleet Street. The whole expenses of the day never exceeded a crown, and were often from three and sixpence to four shillings; for the best part of their entertainment, sweet air and rural scenes, excellent exercise and joyous conversation, cost nothing.

One of Goldsmith's humble companions, on these excursions, was his occasional amanuensis, Peter Barlow, whose quaint peculiarities afforded much amusement to the company. Peter was poor but punctilious, squaring his expenses according to his means. He always wore the same garb; fixed his regular expenditure for dinner at a trifling sum, which, if left to himself, he never exceeded, but which he always insisted on paying. His oddities always made him a welcome companion on the "shoemaker's holidays." The dinner, on these occasions, generally exceeded considerably his tariff; he put down, however, no more than his regular sum, and Goldsmith made up the difference.

Another of these hangers-on, for whom, on such occasions, he was content to "pay the shot," was his countryman Glover, of whom mention has already been made as one of the wags and sponges of the Globe and Devil taverns, and a prime mimic at the Wednesday Club.

This vagabond genius has bequeathed us a whimsical story of one of his practical jokes upon Goldsmith, in the course of a rural excursion in the vicinity of London. They had dined at an inn on Hampstead Heights, and were descending the hill, when, in passing a cottage, they saw through the open window a party at tea. Goldsmith, who was fatigued, cast a wistful glance at the cheerful tea-table. "How I should like to be of that party," exclaimed he. "Nothing more easy," replied Glover; "allow me to introduce you." So saying, he entered the house with an air of the most perfect familiarity, though an utter stranger, and was followed by the unsuspecting Goldsmith, who supposed, of course, that he was a friend of the family. The owner of the house rose on the entrance of the strangers. The undaunted Glover shook hands with him in the most cordial manner possible, fixed his eye on one of the company who had a peculiarly good-natured physiognomy, muttered something like a recognition, and forthwith launched into an amusing story, invented at the moment, of something which he pretended had occurred upon the road. The host supposed the new-comers were friends of his guests; the guests, that they were friends of the host. Glover did not give them time to find out the truth. He followed one droll story with another; brought his powers of mimicry into play, and kept the company in a roar. Tea was offered and accepted; an hour went off in the most sociable manner imaginable, at the end of which Glover bowed himself and his companion out of the house with many facetious last words, leaving the host and his company to compare notes, and to find out what an impudent intrusion they had experienced.

Nothing could exceed the dismay and vexation of Goldsmith when triumphantly told by Glover that it was all a hoax, and that he did not know a single soul in the house. His first impulse was to return instantly and vindicate himself from all participation in the jest; but a few words from his free-and-easy companion dissuaded him. "Doctor," said he, coolly, "we are unknown; you quite as much as I; if you return and tell the story, it will be in the newspapers to-morrow; nay, upon recollection, I remember in one of their offices the face of that squinting fellow who sat in the corner as if he was treasuring up my stories for future use, and we shall be sure of being exposed; let us therefore keep our own counsel."

This story was frequently afterward told by Glover, with rich dramatic effect, repeating and exaggerating the conversation, and mimicking, in ludicrous style, the embarrassment surprise, and subsequent indignation of Goldsmith.

It is a trite saying that a wheel cannot run in two ruts; nor a man keep two opposite sets of intimates. Goldsmith sometimes found his old friends of the "jolly-pigeon" order turning up rather awkwardly when he was in company with his new aristocratic acquaintances. He gave a whimsical account of the sudden apparition of one of them at his gay apartments in the Temple, who may have been a welcome visitor at his squalid quarters in Green Arbor Court. "How do you think he served me?" said he to a friend. "Why, sir, after staying away two years, he came one evening into my chambers, half drunk, as I was taking a glass of wine with Topham Beauclerc and General Oglethorpe[1]; and sitting himself down, with most intolerable assurance inquired after my health and literary pursuits, as if we were upon the most friendly footing. I was at first so much ashamed of ever having known such a fellow, that I stifled my resentment, and drew him into a conversation on such topics as I knew he could talk upon; in which, to do him justice, he acquitted himself very reputably; when all of a sudden, as if recollecting something, he pulled two papers out of his pocket, which he presented to me with great ceremony, saying, 'here, my dear friend, is a quarter of a pound of tea, and a half pound of sugar, I have brought you; for though it is not in my power at present to pay you the two guineas you so generously lent me, you, nor any man else, shall ever have it to

---

[1]See below, p. 310.

say that I want gratitude.' This," added Goldsmith, "was too much. I could no longer keep in my feelings, but desired him to turn out of my chambers directly; which he very coolly did, taking up his tea and sugar; and I never saw him afterwards."

CHAPTER XXIV

The heedless expenses of Goldsmith, as may easily be
supposed, soon brought him to the end of his "prize-money,"
but when his purse gave out he drew upon futurity, obtaining
advances from his booksellers and loans from his friends in
the confident hope of soon turning up another trump. The
debts which he thus thoughtlessly incurred in consequence
of a transient gleam of prosperity embarrassed him for the
rest of his life; so that the success of the "Good-natured
Man" may be said to have been ruinous to him.

He was soon obliged to resume his old craft of book-
building, and set about his "History of Rome," undertaken
for Davies.

It was his custom, as we have shown, during the summer-
time, when pressed by a multiplicity of literary jobs, or
urged to the accomplishment of some particular task, to take
country lodgings a few miles from town, generally on the
Harrow or Edgeware roads, and bury himself there for weeks
and months together. Sometimes he would remain closely
occupied in his room, at other times he would stroll out along
the lanes and hedgerows, and taking out paper and pencil,
note down thoughts to be expanded and connected at home.
His summer retreat for the present year, 1768, was a little
cottage with a garden, pleasantly situated about eight miles
from town on the Edgeware road. He took it in conjunction
with a Mr. Edmond Botts, a barrister and man of letters, his

neighbor in the Temple, having rooms immediately opposite
him on the same floor. They had become cordial intimates,
and Botts was one of those with whom Goldsmith now and
then took the friendly but pernicious liberty of borrowing.

The cottage which they had hired belonged to a rich shoemaker of Piccadilly, who had embellished his little domain
of half an acre with statues, and jets, and all the decorations
of landscape gardening; in consequence of which Goldsmith
gave it the name of The Shoemaker's Paradise. As his
fellow-occupant, Mr. Botts, drove a gig, he sometimes, in an
interval of literary labor, accompanied him to town, partook
of a social dinner there, and returned with him in the evening.
On one occasion, when they had probably lingered too long
at the table, they came near breaking their necks on their
way homeward by driving against a post on the side-walk,
while Botts was proving by the force of legal eloquence that
they were in the very middle of the broad Edgeware road.

In the course of this summer, Goldsmith's career of gayety
was suddenly brought to a pause by intelligence of the death
of his brother Henry, then but forty-five years of age. He
had led a quiet and blameless life amid the scenes of his
youth, fulfilling the duties of village pastor with unaffected
piety; conducting the school at Lissoy with a degree of
industry and ability that gave it celebrity, and acquitting himself in all the duties of life with undeviating rectitude and the
mildest benevolence. How truly Goldsmith loved and vener-
ated him is evident in all his letters and throughout his
works; in which his brother continually forms his model for
an exemplification of all the most endearing of the Christian virtues; yet his affection at his death was embittered by
the fear that he died with some doubt upon his mind of the
warmth of his affection. Goldsmith had been urged by his
friends in Ireland, since his elevation in the world, to use his

influence with the great, which they supposed to be all-powerful, in favor of Henry, to obtain for him church-pre-ferment. He did exert himself as far as his diffident nature would permit, but without success; we have seen that, in the case of the Earl of Northumberland, when, as Lord-Lieutenant of Ireland, that nobleman proffered him his patronage, he asked nothing for himself, but only spoke on behalf of his brother. Still some of his friends, ignorant of what he had done and of how little he was able to do, accused him of negligence. It is not likely, however, that his amiable and estimable brother joined in the accusation.

To the tender and melancholy recollections of his early days awakened by the death of this loved companion of his childhood, we may attribute some of the most heartfelt passages in his "Deserted Village." Much of that poem we are told was composed this summer, in the course of solitary strolls about the green lanes and beautiful rural scenes of the neighborhood; and thus much of the softness and sweetness of English landscape became blended with the ruder features of Lissoy. It was in these lonely and subdued moments, when tender regret was half-mingled with self-upbraiding, that he poured forth that homage of the heart rendered as it were at the grave of his brother. The picture of the village pastor in this poem, which we have already hinted was taken in part from the character of his father, embodied likewise the recollections of his brother Henry; for the natures of the father and son seem to have been identical. In the following lines, however, Goldsmith evidently contrasted the quiet settled life of his brother, passed at home in the benevolent exercise of the Christian duties, with his own restless vagrant career:—

"Remote from towns he ran his godly race,
Nor e'er had changed, nor wished to change his place."

To us the whole character seems traced as it were in an expiatory spirit; as if, conscious of his own wandering restlessness, he sought to humble himself at the shrine of excellence which he had not been able to practise:—

"At church with meek and unaffected grace,
His looks adorn'd the venerable place;
Truth from his lips prevail'd with double sway,
And fools, who came to scoff, remain'd to pray.
The service past, around the pious man,
With steady zeal, each honest rustic ran;
Even children follow'd, with endearing wile,
And pluck'd his gown, to share the good man's smile:
His ready smile a parent's warmth express'd,
Their welfare pleas'd him, and their cares distress'd
To them his heart, his love, his griefs were given,
But all his serious thoughts had rest in heaven.

.   .   .   .

And, as a bird each fond endearment tries
To tempt its new-fledged offspring to the skies,
He tried each art, reproved each dull delay,
Allured to brighter worlds, *and led the way.*"

CHAPTER XXV

In October Goldsmith returned to town and resumed
his usual haunts. We hear of him at a dinner given by his
countryman Isaac Bickerstaff, author of "Love in a Village,"
"Lionel and Clarissa," and other successful dramatic pieces.
The dinner was to be followed by the reading by Bickerstaff
of a new play. Among the guests was one Paul Hiffernan,
likewise an Irishman; somewhat idle and intemperate; who
lived nobody knew how nor where, sponging wherever he had
a chance, and often of course upon Goldsmith, who was
ever the vagabond's friend, or rather victim. Hiffernan was
something of a physician, and elevated the emptiness of his
purse into the dignity of a disease, which he termed *impe-
cuniosity*, and against which he claimed a right to call for
relief from the healthier purses of his friends. He was a
scribbler for the newspapers, and latterly a dramatic critic,
which had probably gained him an invitation to the dinner
and reading. The wine and wassail, however, befogged his
senses. Scarce had the author got into the second act of
his play, when Hiffernan began to nod, and at length snored
outright. Bickerstaff was embarrassed, but continued to
read in a more elevated tone. The louder he read, the
louder Hiffernan snored; until the author came to a pause.
"Never mind the brute, Bick, but go on," cried Goldsmith.

"He would have served Homer just so if he were here and reading his own works."

Kenrick, Goldsmith's old enemy, travestied this anecdote in the following lines, pretending that the poet had compared his countryman Bickerstaff to Homer.

> "What are your Bretons, Romans, Grecians,
> Compared with thorough-bred Milesians!
> Step into Griffin's shop, he'll tell ye
> Of Goldsmith, Bickerstaff, and Kelly .
> And, take one Irish evidence for t'other,
> Ev'n Homer's self is but their foster-brother."

Johnson was a rough consoler to a man when wincing under an attack of this kind. "Never mind, sir," said he to Goldsmith, when he saw that he felt the sting. "A man whose business it is to be talked of is much helped by being attacked. Fame, sir, is a shuttlecock; if it be struck only at one end of the room, it will soon fall to the ground; to keep it up, it must be struck at both ends."

Bickerstaff, at the time of which we are speaking, was in high vogue, the associate of the first wits of the day; a few years afterwards he was obliged to fly the country to escape the punishment of an infamous crime. Johnson expressed great astonishment at hearing the offence for which he had fled. "Why, sir?" said Thrale; "he had long been a suspected man." Perhaps there was a knowing look on the part of the eminent brewer, which provoked a somewhat contemptuous reply. "By those who look close to the ground," said Johnson, "dirt will sometimes be seen; I hope I see things from a greater distance."

We have already noticed the improvement, or rather the increased expense, of Goldsmith's wardrobe since his elevation into polite society. "He was fond," says one of his contemporaries, "of exhibiting his muscular little person in

the gayest apparel of the day, to which was added a bag-
wig and sword." Thus arrayed, he used to figure about in
the sunshine in the Temple Gardens, much to his own satisfaction, but to the amusement of his acquaintances.

Boswell, in his memoirs, has rendered one of his suits
forever famous. That worthy, on the 16th of October in
this same year, gave a dinner to Johnson, Goldsmith, Reynolds, Garrick, Murphy, Bickerstaff, and Davies. Goldsmith
was generally apt to bustle in at the last moment, when the
guests were taking their seats at table; but on this occasion
he was unusually early. While waiting for some lingerers
to arrive, "he strutted about," says Boswell, "bragging of
his dress, and I believe was seriously vain of it, for his mind
was undoubtedly prone to such impressions. 'Come, come,'
said Garrick, 'talk no more of that. You are perhaps the
worst—eh, eh?' Goldsmith was eagerly attempting to interrupt him, when Garrick went on, laughing ironically. 'Nay,
you will always *look* like a gentleman; but I am talking of
your being well or *ill dressed.*' 'Well, let me tell you,' said
Goldsmith, 'when the tailor brought home my bloom-
colored coat, he said, "Sir, I have a favor to beg of you;
when anybody asks you who made your clothes, be pleased
to mention John Filby, at the Harrow, in Water Lane." '
'Why, sir,' cried Johnson, 'that was because he knew the
strange color would attract crowds to gaze at it, and thus
they might hear of him, and see how well he could make a
coat of so absurd a color.' "

But though Goldsmith might permit this raillery on the
part of his friends, he was quick to resent any personalities
of the kind from strangers. As he was one day walking the
Strand in grand array with bag-wig and sword, he excited
the merriment of two coxcombs, one of whom called to the
other to "look at that fly with a long pin stuck through it."

Stung to the quick, Goldsmith's first retort was to caution
the passers-by to be on their guard against "that brace of
disguised pickpockets,"—his next was to step into the middle
of the street, where there was room for action, half-draw
his sword, and beckon the joker, who was armed in like
manner, to follow him. This was literally a war of wit
which the other had not anticipated. He had no inclination
to push the joke to such an extreme, but abandoning the
ground, sneaked off with his brother-wag amid the hootings
of the spectators.

This proneness to finery in dress, however, which Boswell and others of Goldsmith's contemporaries, who did not
understand the secret plies of his character, attributed to
vanity, arose, we are convinced, from a widely different
motive. It was from a painful idea of his own personal
defects, which had been cruelly stamped upon his mind in
his boyhood, by the sneers and the jeers of his playmates, and
had been grounded deeper into it by rude speeches made
to him in every step of his struggling career, until it had
become a constant cause of awkwardness and embarrassment.
This he had experienced the more sensibly since his reputation had elevated him into polite society; and he was constantly endeavoring by the aid of dress to acquire that personal
acceptability, if we may use the phrase, which nature had denied
him. If ever he betrayed a little self-complacency on first
turning out in a new suit, it may, perhaps, have been because
he felt as if he had achieved a triumph over his ugliness.

There were circumstances too, about the time of which
we are treating, which may have rendered Goldsmith more
than usually attentive to his personal appearance. He had
recently made the acquaintance of a most agreeable family
from Devonshire, which he met at the house of his friend,
Sir Joshua Reynolds. It consisted of Mrs. Horneck, widow

of Captain Kane Horneck; two daughters, seventeen and nineteen years of age; and an only son, Charles, *the Captain in Lace*, as his sisters playfully and somewhat proudly called him, he having lately entered the Guards. The daughters are described as uncommonly beautiful, intelligent, sprightly, and agreeable. Catharine, the eldest, went among her friends by the name of *Little Comedy*, indicative, very probably, of her disposition. She was engaged to William Henry Bunbury, second son of a Suffolk baronet. The hand and heart of her sister Mary were yet unengaged, although she bore the by-name among her friends of the *Jessamy Bride*. This family was prepared, by their intimacy with Reynolds and his sister, to appreciate the merits of Goldsmith. The poet had always been a chosen friend of the eminent painter; and Miss Reynolds, as we have shown, ever since she had heard his poem of "The Traveller" read aloud, had ceased to consider him ugly. The Hornecks were equally capable of forgetting his person in admiring his works. On becoming acquainted with him, too, they were delighted with his guileless simplicity, his buoyant good-nature, and his innate benevolence; and an enduring intimacy soon sprang up between them. For once poor Goldsmith had met with polite society, with which he was perfectly at home, and by which he was fully appreciated; for once he had met with lovely women, to whom his ugly features were not repulsive. A proof of the easy and playful terms in which he was with them, remains in a whimsical epistle in verse, of which the following was the occasion. A dinner was to be given to their family by a Dr. Baker, a friend of their mother's, at which Reynolds and Angelica Kauffman[1] were to be present.

---

[1] Angelica Kauffman (1740-1807), achieved some distinction as an artist, chiefly as a portrait painter; she was of German birth but lived in London from 1766 to 1781.

The young ladies were eager to have Goldsmith of the party, and their intimacy with Dr. Baker allowing them to take the liberty, they wrote a joint invitation to the poet at the last moment. It came too late, and drew from him the following reply; on the top of which was scrawled, "This *is* a poem! This *is* a copy of verses!"

> "Your mandate I got,
>   You may all go to pot;
> Had your senses been right,
> You'd have sent before night:
> So tell Horneck and Nesbitt,
> And Baker and his bit,
> And Kauffman beside,
> And the *Jessamy Bride*,
> With the rest of the crew,
> The Reynoldses too,
>
> *Little Comedy's* face,
> And the *Captain in Lace,*—
> Tell each other to rue
> Your Devonshire crew,
> For sending so late
> To one of my state.
> But 'tis Reynolds's way
> From wisdom to stay,
> And Angelica's whim
> To befrolic like him;
>
> But alas! your good worships, how could they be wiser,
> When both have been spoil'd in to-day's 'Advertiser'?"*

It has been intimated that the intimacy of poor Goldsmith with the Miss Hornecks, which began in so sprightly a vein, gradually assumed something of a more tender nature, and that he was not insensible to the fascinations of the younger sister. This may account for some of the phenomena which about this time appeared in his wardrobe and toilet. During the first year of his acquaintance with these lovely girls, the tell-tale book of his tailor, Mr. William Filby, displays

---

*The following lines had appeared in that day's "Advertiser," on the portrait of Sir Joshua by Angelica Kauffman:—

> "While fair Angelica, with matchless grace,
>   Paints Conway's burly form and Stanhope's face:
> Our hearts to beauty willing homage pay,
> We praise, admire, and gaze our souls away.
> But when the likeness she hath done for thee,
> O Reynolds! with astonishment we see,
> Forced to submit, with all our pride we own,
> Such strength, such harmony, excelled by none,
> And thou art rivalled by thyself alone."

entries of four or five full suits, besides separate articles of dress. Among the items we find a green half-trimmed frock and breeches, lined with silk; a queen's-blue dress suit; a half-dress suit of ratteen, lined with satin; a pair of silk stocking-breeches, and another pair of a bloom-color. Alas! poor Goldsmith! how much of this silken finery was dictated, not by vanity, but humble consciousness of thy defects; how much of it was to atone for the uncouthness of thy person, and to win favor in the eyes of the Jessamy Bride!

CHAPTER XXVI

In the winter of 1768–69 Goldsmith occupied himself at
his quarters in the Temple, slowly "building up" his Roman
History. We have pleasant views of him in this learned and
half-cloistered retreat of wits and lawyers and legal students,
in the reminiscences of Judge Day of the Irish Bench, who,
in his advanced age, delighted to recall the days of his youth,
when he was a Templar, and to speak of the kindness with
which he and his fellow-student, Grattan, were treated by
the poet. "I was just arrived from college," said he, "full
freighted with academic gleanings, and our author did not
disdain to receive from me some opinions and hints towards
his Greek and Roman histories. Being then a young man,
I felt much flattered by the notice of so celebrated a person.
He took great delight in the conversation of Grattan, whose
brilliancy in the morning of life furnished full earnest of the
unrivalled splendor which awaited his meridian; and finding
us dwelling together in Essex Court, near himself, where he
frequently visited my immortal friend, his warm heart became
naturally prepossessed towards the associate of one whom
he so much admired."

The Judge goes on, in his reminiscences, to give a picture
of Goldsmith's social habits, similar in style to those already
furnished. He frequented much the Grecian Coffee-House,

then the favorite resort of the Irish and Lancashire Templars. He delighted in collecting his friends around him at evening parties at his chambers, where he entertained them with a cordial and unostentatious hospitality. "Occasionally," adds the Judge, "he amused them with his flute, or with whist, neither of which he played well, particularly the latter, but, on losing his money, he never lost his temper. In a run of bad luck and worse play, he would fling his cards upon the floor and exclaim, '*Byefore* George, I ought forever to renounce thee, fickle, faithless fortune.' "

The Judge was aware, at the time, that all the learned labor of poor Goldsmith upon his Roman History was mere hack-work to recruit his exhausted finances. "His purse replenished," adds he, "by labors of this kind, the season of relaxation and pleasure took its turn, in attending the theatres, Ranelagh, Vauxhall, and other scenes of gayety and amusement. Whenever his funds were dissipated,—and they fled more rapidly from being the dupe of many artful persons, male and female, who practised upon his benevolence,—he returned to his literary labors, and shut himself up from society to provide fresh matter for his bookseller, and fresh supplies for himself."

How completely had the young student discerned the characteristics of poor, genial, generous, drudging, holiday-loving Goldsmith; toiling, that he might play; earning his bread by the sweat of his brains, and then throwing it out of the window.

The Roman History was published in the middle of May, in two volumes of five hundred pages each. It was brought out without parade or pretension, and was announced as for the use of schools and colleges; but, though a work written for bread, not fame, such is its ease, perspicuity, good sense, and the delightful simplicity of its style, that it was well received

by the critics, commanded a prompt and extensive sale, and
has ever since remained in the hands of young and old.

Johnson, who, as we have before remarked, rarely praised
or dispraised things by halves, broke forth in a warm eulogy
of the author and the work, in a conversation with Boswell,
to the great astonishment of the latter. "Whether we take
Goldsmith," said he, "as a poet, as a comic writer, or as an
historian, he stands in the first class." Boswell.—"An historian! My dear sir, you surely will not rank his compilation
of the Roman History with the works of other historians of
this age." Johnson.—"Why, who are before him?" Boswell.—"Hume—Robertson—Lord Lyttelton." Johnson (his
antipathy against the Scotch beginning to rise).—"I have not
read Hume; but doubtless Goldsmith's History is better than
the verbiage of Robertson, or the foppery of Dalrymple."
Boswell.—"Will you not admit the superiority of Robertson,
in whose history we find such penetration, such painting?"
Johnson.—"Sir, you must consider how that penetration and
that painting are employed. It is not history, it is imagination. He who describes what he never saw, draws from
fancy. Robertson paints minds as Sir Joshua paints faces,
in a history-piece; he imagines an heroic countenance. You
must look upon Robertson's work as romance, and try it
by that standard. History it is not. Besides, sir, it is the
great excellence of a writer to put into his book as much as
his book will hold. Goldsmith has done this in his History.
Now Robertson might have put twice as much in his book.
Robertson is like a man who has packed gold in wool; the
wool takes up more room than the gold. No, sir, I always
thought Robertson would be crushed with his own weight—
would be buried under his own ornaments. Goldsmith tells
you shortly all you want to know; Robertson detains you a
great deal too long. No man will read Roberston's cum-

brous detail a second time; but Goldsmith's plain narrative
will please again and again. I would say to Robertson what
an old tutor of a college said to one of his pupils, 'Read over
your compositions, and whenever you meet with a passage
which you think is particularly fine, strike it out!' Goldsmith's abridgment is better than that of Lucius Florus or
Eutropius; and I will venture to say, that, if you compare
him with Vertot in the same places of the Roman History,
you will find that he excels Vertot. Sir, he has the art of
compiling, and of saying everything he has to say in a pleasing
manner. He is now writing a Natural History, and will make
it as entertaining as a Persian tale."

The Natural History to which Johnson alluded was the
"History of Animated Nature," which Goldsmith commenced
in 1769, under an engagement with Griffin, the bookseller,
to complete it as soon as possible in eight volumes, each containing upwards of four hundred pages, in pica; a hundred
guineas to be paid to the author on the delivery of each volume
in manuscript.

He was induced to engage in this work by the urgent
solicitations of the booksellers, who had been struck by the
sterling merits and captivating style of an introduction which
he wrote to Brookes's "Natural History." It was Goldsmith's
intention originally to make a translation of Pliny, with a
popular commentary; but the appearance of Buffon's work
induced him to change his plan, and make use of that author
for a guide and model.

Cumberland, speaking of this work, observes: "Distress
drove Goldsmith upon undertakings neither congenial with
his studies nor worthy of his talents. I remember him when
in his chambers in the Temple, he showed me the beginning
of his 'Animated Nature'; it was with a sigh, such as genius
draws when hard necessity diverts it from its bent to drudge

for bread, and talk of birds, and beasts, and creeping things, which Pidock's showman would have done as well. Poor fellow, he hardly knows an ass from a mule, nor a turkey from a goose, but when he sees it on the table."

Others of Goldsmith's friends entertained similar ideas with respect to his fitness for the task, and they were apt now and then to banter him on the subject, and to amuse themselves with his easy credulity. The custom among the natives of Otaheite of eating dogs being once mentioned in company, Goldsmith observed that a similar custom prevailed in China; that a dog-butcher is as common there as any other butcher; and that, when he walks abroad, all the dogs fall on him. Johnson.—"That is not owing to his killing dogs; sir, I remember a butcher at Litchfield, whom a dog that was in the house where I lived always attacked. It is the smell of carnage which provokes this, let the animals he has killed be what they may." Goldsmith.—"Yes, there is a general abhorrence in animals at the signs of massacre. If you put a tub full of blood into a stable, the horses are likely to go mad." Johnson.—"I doubt that." Goldsmith.—"Nay, sir, it is a fact well authenticated." Thrale.—"You had better prove it before you put it into your book on Natural History. You may do it in my stable if you will." Johnson.—"Nay, sir, I would not have him prove it. If he is content to take his information from others, he may get through his book with little trouble, and without much endangering his reputation. But if he makes experiments for so comprehensive a book as his, there would be no end to them; his erroneous assertions would fall then upon himself; and he might be blamed for not having made experiments as to every particular."

Johnson's original prediction, however, with respect to this work, that Goldsmith would make it as entertaining as a Persian tale, was verified, and though much of it was borrowed from Buffon, and but little of it written from his own observation,—though it was by no means profound, and was chargeable with many errors, yet the charms of his style and the play of his happy disposition throughout have continued to render it far more popular and readable than many works on the subject of much greater scope and science. Cumberland was mistaken, however, in his notion of Goldsmith's ignorance and lack of observation as to the characteristics of animals. On the contrary, he was a minute and shrewd observer of them; but he observed them with the eye of a poet and moralist as well as a naturalist. We quote two passages from his works illustrative of this fact, and we do so the more readily because they are in a manner a part of his history, and give us another peep into his private life in the Temple,—of his mode of occupying himself in his lonely and apparently idle moments, and of another class of acquaintances which he made there.

Speaking in his "Animated Nature" of the habitudes of Rooks, "I have often amused myself," says he, "with observing their plans of policy from my window in the Temple, that looks upon a grove, where they have made a colony in the midst of a city. At the commencement of spring the rookery, which during the continuance of winter seemed to have been deserted, or only guarded by about five or six, like old soldiers in a garrison, now begins to be once more frequented, and in a short time all the bustle and hurry of business will be fairly commenced."

The other passage, which we take the liberty to quote at some length, is from an admirable paper in the "Bee," and relates to the House Spider.

"Of all the solitary insects I have ever remarked, the spider is the most sagacious, and its motions to me, who have attentively considered them, seem almost to exceed belief. . . .

I perceived, about four years ago, a large spider in one corner of my room making its web; and, though the maid frequently levelled her broom against the labors of the little animal, I had the good fortune then to prevent its destruction, and I may say it more than paid me by the entertainment it afforded.

"In three days the web was, with incredible diligence, completed; nor could I avoid thinking that the insect seemed to exult in its new abode. It frequently traversed it round, examined the strength of every part of it, retired into its hole, and came out very frequently. The first enemy, however, it had to encounter was another and a much larger spider, which, having no web of its own, and having probably exhausted all its stock in former labors of this kind, came to invade the property of its neighbor. Soon, then, a terrible encounter ensued, in which the invader seemed to have the victory, and the laborious spider was obliged to take refuge in its hole. Upon this I perceived the victor using every art to draw the enemy from its stronghold. He seemed to go off, but quickly returned; and when he found all arts in vain, began to demolish the new web without mercy. This brought on another battle, and, contrary to my expectations, the laborious spider became conqueror, and fairly killed his antagonist.

"Now, then, in peaceable possession of what was justly its own, it waited three days with the utmost impatience, repairing the breaches of its web, and taking no sustenance that I could perceive. At last, however, a large blue fly fell into the snare, and struggled hard to get loose. The spider gave it leave to entangle itself as much as possible, but it seemed to be too strong for the cobweb. I must own I was greatly surprised when I saw the spider immediately sally out, and in less than a minute weave a new net round its captive, by which the motion of its wings was stopped; and, when it was fairly hampered in this manner, it was seized and dragged into the hole.

"In this manner it lived, in a precarious state; and Nature seemed to have fitted it for such a life, for upon a single fly it subsisted for more than a week. I once put a wasp into the net; but when the spider came out in order to seize it as usual, upon perceiving what kind of an enemy it had to deal with, it instantly broke all the bands that held it fast, and contributed all that lay in its power to disengage so formidable an antagonist. When the wasp was set at liberty, I expected the spider would have set about repairing the breaches that were made in its net; but those, it seems, were irreparable; wherefore the cobweb was now entirely forsaken, and a new one begun, which was completed in the usual time.

"I had now a mind to try how many cobwebs a single spider could furnish; wherefore I destroyed this, and the insect set about another. When I destroyed the other also, its whole stock seemed entirely exhausted, and it could spin no more. The arts it made use of to support itself, now deprived of its great means of subsistence, were indeed surprising. I have seen it roll up its legs like a ball, and lie motionless for hours together, but cautiously watching all the time; when a fly happened to approach sufficiently near, it would dart out all at once, and often seize its prey.

"Of this life, however, it soon began to grow weary, and resolved to invade the possession of some other spider, since it could not make a web of its own. It formed an attack upon a neighboring fortification with great vigor, and at first was as vigorously repulsed. Not daunted, however, with one defeat, in this manner it continued to lay siege to another's web for three days, and at length, having killed the defendant, actually took possession. When smaller flies happen to fall into the snare, the spider does not sally out at once, but very patiently waits till it is sure of them; for, upon his immediately approaching, the terror of his appearance might give the captive strength sufficient to get loose; the manner, then, is to wait patiently, till, by ineffectual and impotent struggles, the captive has wasted all its strength, and then he becomes a certain and easy conquest.

"The insect I am now describing lived three years; every year it changed its skin and got a new set of legs. I have sometimes plucked off a leg, which grew again in two or three days. At first it dreaded my approach to its web, but at last it became so familiar as to take a fly out of my hand; and, upon my touching any part of the web, would immediately leave its hole, prepared either for a defence or an attack." [1]

---

[1] *The Bee*, No. VI.

CHAPTER XXVII

HONORS AT THE ROYAL ACADEMY — LETTER TO HIS BROTHER
MAURICE — FAMILY FORTUNES — JANE CONTARINE AND THE
MINIATURE—PORTRAITS AND ENGRAVINGS—SCHOOL ASSOCIA-
TIONS—JOHNSON AND GOLDSMITH IN WESTMINSTER ABBEY.

The latter part of the year 1768 had been made memorable
in the world of taste by the institution of the Royal Academy
of Arts, under the patronage of the King and the direction
of forty of the most distinguished artists. Reynolds, who
had been mainly instrumental in founding it, had been
unanimously elected president, and had thereupon received
the honor of knighthood.* Johnson was so delighted with
his friend's elevation that he broke through a rule of total
abstinence with respect to wine, which he had maintained
for several years, and drank bumpers on the occasion. Sir
Joshua eagerly sought to associate his old and valued friends
with him in his new honors, and it is supposed to be through
his suggestions that, on the first establishment of professor-
ships, which took place in December, 1769, Johnson was
nominated to that of Ancient Literature, and Goldsmith
to that of History. They were mere honorary titles, without
emolument, but gave distinction, from the noble institution
to which they appertained. They also gave the possessors
honorable places at the annual banquet, at which were
assembled many of the most distinguished persons of rank

---

* We must apologize for the anachronism we have permitted ourselves
in the course of this memoir, in speaking of Reynolds as *Sir Joshua*, when
treating of circumstances which occurred prior to his being dubbed ; but it
is so customary to speak of him by that title, that we found it difficᵗ ᵗ to
dispense with it.

and talent, all proud to be classed among the patrons of the arts.

The following letter of Goldsmith to his brother alludes to the foregoing appointment, and to a small legacy bequeathed to him by his uncle Contarine.

"*To Mr. Maurice Goldsmith, at James Lawder's, Esq., at Kilmore, near Carrick-on-Shannon.*

"January, 1770.

"DEAR BROTHER,—I should have answered your letter sooner, but, in truth, I am not fond of thinking of the necessities of those I love, when it is so very little in my power to help them.   I am sorry to find you are every way unprovided for; and what adds to my uneasiness is, that I have received a letter from my sister Johnson, by which I learn that she is pretty much in the same circumstances. As to myself, I believe I think I could get both you and my poor brother-in-law something like that which you desire, but I am determined never to ask for little things, nor exhaust any little interest I may have, until I can serve you, him, and myself more effectually.   As yet, no opportunity has offered; but I believe you are pretty well convinced that I will not be remiss when it arrives.

"'The King has lately been pleased to make me professor of Ancient History in the royal academy of painting which he has just established, but there is no salary annexed; and I took it rather as a compliment to the Institution than any benefit to myself.   Honors to one in my situation are something like ruffles to one that wants a shirt.

"You tell me that there are fourteen or fifteen pounds left me in the hands of my cousin Lawder, and you ask me what I would have done with them. My dear brother, I would by no means give any directions to my dear worthy relations at Kilmore how to dispose of money which is, properly speaking, more theirs than mine. All that I can say is, that I entirely, and this letter will serve to witness, give up any right and title to it; and I am sure they will dispose of it to the best advantage. To them I entirely leave it; whether they or you may think the whole necessary to fit you out, or whether our poor sister Johnson may not want the half, I leave entirely to their and your discretion. The kindness of that good couple to our shattered family demands our sincerest gratitude; and, though they have almost forgotten me, yet, if good things at last arrive, I hope one day to return and increase their good-humor by adding to my own.

"I have sent my cousin Jenny a miniature picture of myself, as I believe it is the most acceptable present I can offer. I have ordered it to be left for her at George Faulkner's, folded in a letter. The face, you well know, is ugly enough, but it is finely painted. I will shortly also send my friends over the Shannon some mezzotinto prints of myself, and some more of my friends here, such as Burke, Johnson, Reynolds, and Colman. I believe I have written a hundred letters to different friends in your country, and never received an answer to any of them. I do not know how to account for this, or why they are unwilling to keep up for me those regards which I must ever retain for them.

"If, then, you have a mind to oblige me, you will write often, whether I answer you or not. Let me particularly have the news of our family and old acquaintances. For instance, you may begin by telling me about the family where you reside, how they spend their time, and whether they ever make mention of me. Tell me about my mother, my brother Hodson and his son, my brother Harry's son and daughter, my sister Johnson, the family of Ballyoughter, what is become of them, where they live, and how they do. You

talked of being my only brother: I don't understand you.
Where is Charles?   A sheet of paper occasionally filled with
the news of this kind would make me very happy, and would
keep you nearer my mind.   As it is, my dear brother, believe
me to be

"Yours, most affectionately,

"OLIVER GOLDSMITH."

By this letter we find the Goldsmiths the same shifting,
shiftless race as formerly; a "shattered family," scrambling
on each other's back as soon as any rise above the surface.
Maurice is "every way unprovided for"; living upon cousin
Jane and her husband; and, perhaps, amusing himself by
hunting otter in the river Inny.   Sister Johnson and her
husband are as poorly off as Maurice, with, perhaps, no one
at hand to quarter themselves upon; as to the rest, "what is
become of them? where do they live? and how do they do?
what has become of Charles?"   What forlorn, hap-hazard
life is implied by these questions!   Can we wonder that,
with all the love for his native place which is shown throughout Goldsmith's writings, he had not the heart to return
there?   Yet his affections are still there.   He wishes to know
whether the Lawders (which means his cousin Jane, his early
Valentine) ever made mention of him; he sends Jane his
miniature; he believes "it is the most acceptable present he can
offer"; he evidently, therefore, does not believe she has almost
forgotten him, although he intimates that he does: in his
memory she is still Jane Contarine, as he last saw her,
when he accompanied her harpsichord with his flute.
Absence, like death, sets a seal on the image of those we
have loved; we cannot realize the intervening changes which
time may have effected.

As to the rest of Goldsmith's relatives, he abandons his

legacy of fifteen pounds, to be shared among them. It is
all he has to give. His heedless improvidence is eating up
the pay of the booksellers in advance. With all his literary
success, he has neither money nor influence; but he has
empty fame, and he is ready to participate with them; he
is honorary professor, without pay; his portrait is to be
engraved in mezzotint, in company with those of his friends,
Burke, Reynolds, Johnson, Colman, and others, and he will
send prints of them to his friends over the Channel, though
they may not have a house to hang them up in. What a
motley letter! How indicative of the motley character of
the writer! By the by, the publication of a splendid mezzotinto engraving of his likeness by Reynolds was a great matter
of glorification to Goldsmith, especially as it appeared in such
illustrious company. As he was one day walking the streets
in a state of high elation, from having just seen it figuring in
the print-shop windows, he met a young gentleman with a
newly married wife hanging on his arm, whom he immediately
recognized for Master Bishop, one of the boys he had petted
and treated with sweetmeats when a humble usher at Milner's
school. The kindly feelings of old times revived, and he
accosted him with cordial familiarity, though the youth may
have found some difficulty in recognizing in the personage,
arrayed, perhaps, in garments of Tyrian dye, the dingy
pedagogue of the Milners. "Come, my boy," cried Goldsmith, as if still speaking to a school-boy,—"come, Sam, I
am delighted to see you. I must treat you to something—
what shall it be? Will you have some apples?" glancing
at an old woman's stall; then, recollecting the print-shop
window: "Sam," said he, "have you seen my picture by
Sir Joshua Reynolds? Have you seen it, Sam? Have you
got an engraving?" Bishop was caught; he equivocated;
he had not yet bought it; but he was furnishing his house,

and had fixed upon the place where it was to be hung. "Ah, Sam!" rejoined Goldsmith reproachfully, "if your picture had been published, I should not have waited an hour without having it."

After all, it was honest pride, not vanity, in Goldsmith, that was gratified at seeing his portrait deemed worthy of being perpetuated by the classic pencil of Reynolds, and "hung up in history" beside that of his revered friend Johnson. Even the great moralist himself was not insensible to a feeling of this kind. Walking one day with Goldsmith, in Westminster Abbey, among the tombs of monarchs, warriors, and statesmen, they came to the sculptured mementos of literary worthies in poets' corner. Casting his eye round upon these memorials of genius, Johnson muttered in a low tone to his companion,—

"Forsitan et nostrum nomen miscebitur istis." [1]

Goldsmith treasured up the intimated hope, and shortly afterwards, as they were passing by Temple Bar, where the heads of Jacobite rebels, executed for treason, were mouldering aloft on spikes, pointed up to the grizzly mementos, and echoed the intimation,

"Forsitan et nostrum nomen miscebitur *istis.*"

---

[1] Perhaps also our name shall be mingled with these.

CHAPTER XXVIII

Several years had now elapsed since the publication of
"The Traveller," and much wonder was expressed that the
great success of that poem had not excited the author to
further poetic attempts. On being questioned at the annual
dinner of the Royal Academy by the Earl of Lisburn, why
he neglected the Muses to compile histories and write novels,
"My Lord," replied he, "by courting the Muses I shall
starve, but by my other labors I eat, drink, have good clothes,
and can enjoy the luxuries of life." So, also, on being asked
by a poor writer what was the most profitable mode of exercising the pen,—"My dear fellow," replied he, good-humor-
edly, "pay no regard to the draggle-tailed Muses; for my
part I have found productions in prose much more sought
after and better paid for."

Still, however, as we have heretofore shown, he found
sweet moments of dalliance to steal away from his prosaic
toils, and court the Muse among the green lanes and hedgerows in the rural environs of London, and on the 26th of May,
1770, he was enabled to bring his "Deserted Village" before
the public.

The popularity of "The Traveller" had prepared the
way for this poem, and its sale was instantaneous and immense. The first edition was immediately exhausted; in a
few days a second was issued; in a few days more a third,
and by the 16th of August the fifth edition was hurried
through the press. As is the case with popular writers,

he had become his own rival, and critics were inclined
to give the preference to his first poem; but with the
public at large we believe the "Deserted Village" has
ever been the greatest favorite. Previous to its publication the bookseller gave him in advance a note for the price
agreed upon, one hundred guineas. As the latter was returning home he met a friend to whom he mentioned the circumstance, and who, apparently judging of poetry by quantity
rather than quality, observed that it was a great sum for so
small a poem. "In truth," said Goldsmith, "I think so too;
it is much more than the honest man can afford or the piece
is worth. I have not been easy since I received it."   In fact,
he actually returned the note to the bookseller, and left it
to him to graduate the payment according to the success of
of the work.[1] The bookseller, as may well be supposed,
soon repaid him in full with many acknowledgments of his
disinterestedness. This anecdote has been called in question,
we know not on what grounds; we see nothing in it incom-
patible with the character of Goldsmith, who was very im-
pulsive, and prone to acts of inconsiderate generosity.

As we do not pretend in this summary memoir to go into
a criticism or analysis of any of Goldsmith's writings, we shall
not dwell upon the peculiar merits of this poem; we cannot
help noticing, however, how truly it is a mirror of the author's
heart, and of all the fond pictures of early friends and early
life forever present there. It seems to us as if the very last
accounts received from home, of his "shattered family,"
and the desolation that seemed to have settled upon the
haunts of his childhood, had cut the roots of one feebly

---

[1] "What Goldsmith was paid for *The Deserted Village* is uncertain.
Glover says it was a hundred guineas, and adds that Goldsmith gave the
money back to his publisher, because some one thought it was too much.
Whether such a story is wholly credible, may be left to the judicious reader
to decide."—DOBSON, *Life*, p. 153.

cherished hope, and produced the following exquisitely tender and mournful lines:—

> "In all my wand'rings round this world of care,
> In all my griefs—and God has giv'n my share—
> I still had hopes my latest hours to crown,
> Amid these humble bowers to lay me down;
> To husband out life's taper at the close,
> And keep the flame from wasting by repose;
> I still had hopes, for pride attends us still,
> Amid the swains to show my book-learn'd skill,
> Around my fire an ev'ning group to draw,
> And tell of all I felt and all I saw;
> And as a hare, whom hounds and horns pursue,
> Pants to the place from whence at first she flew;
> I still had hopes, my long vexations past,
> Here to return—*and die at home at last.*"

How touchingly expressive are the succeeding lines, wrung from a heart which all the trials and temptations and buffetings of the world could not render worldly; which, amid a thousand follies and errors of the head, still retained its childlike innocence; and which, doomed to struggle on to the last amidst the din and turmoil of the metropolis, had ever been cheating itself with a dream of rural quiet and seclusion:—

> "Oh bless'd retirement! friend to life's decline,
> Retreats from care, *that never must be mine,*
> How blest is he who crowns, in shades like these,
> A youth of labor with an age of ease;
> Who quits a world where strong temptations try,
> And, since 'tis hard to combat, learns to fly!
> For him no wretches, born to work and weep,
> Explore the mine, or tempt the dangerous deep;
> Nor surly porter stands, in guilty state,
> To spurn imploring famine from the gate;
> But on he moves to meet his latter end,
> Angels around befriending virtue's friend;

Sinks to the grave with unperceived decay,
While resignation gently slopes the way;
And all his prospects brightening to the last,
His heaven commences ere the world be past."

NOTE

The following article, which appeared in a London periodical, shows the effect of Goldsmith's poem in renovating the fortunes of Lissoy.

"About three miles from Ballymahon, a very central town in the sister-kingdom, is the mansion and village of Auburn, so called by their present possessor, Captain Hogan. Through the taste and improvement of this gentleman, it is now a beautiful spot, although fifteen years since it presented a very bare and unpoetical aspect. This, however, was owing to a cause which serves strongly to corroborate the assertion, that Goldsmith had this scene in view when he wrote his poem of 'The Deserted Village.' The then possessor, General Napier, turned all his tenants out of their farms that he might enclose them in his own private domain. Littleton, the mansion of the General, stands not far off, a complete emblem of the desolating spirit lamented by the poet, dilapidated and converted into a barrack.

"The chief object of attraction is Lissoy, once the parsonage-house of Henry Goldsmith, that brother to whom the poet dedicated his 'Traveller,' and who is represented as a village pastor,

" 'Passing rich with forty pounds a year.'

"When I was in the country, the lower chambers were inhabited by pigs and sheep, and the drawing-rooms by oats. Captain Hogan, however, has, I believe, got it since into his possession, and has, of course, improved its condition.

"Though at first strongly inclined to dispute the identity

of Auburn, Lissoy House overcame my scruples. As I
clambered over the rotten gate, and crossed the grass-grown
lawn or court, the tide of association became too strong for
casuistry: here the poet dwelt and wrote, and here his
thoughts fondly recurred when composing his 'Traveller' in
a foreign land. Yonder was the decent church, that literally
'topped the neighboring hill.' Before me lay the little hill
of Knockrue, on which he declares, in one of his letters, he
had rather sit with a book in hand than mingle in the proudest assemblies. And, above all, startlingly true, beneath my
feet was

> " 'Yonder copse, where once the garden smiled,
> And still where many a garden-flower grows wild.'

"A painting from the life could not be more exact. 'The
stubborn currant-bush' lifts its head above the rank grass,
and the proud hollyhock flaunts where its sisters of the
flower-knot are no more.

"In the middle of the village stands the old 'hawthorn-
tree,' built up with masonry to distinguish and preserve it;
it is old and stunted, and suffers much from the depreda-
tions of post-chaise travellers, who generally stop to procure
a twig. Opposite to it is the village ale-house; over the door
of which swings 'The Three Jolly Pigeons.' Within, everything is arranged according to the letter:—

> " 'The whitewash'd wall, the nicely-sanded floor,
> The varnish'd clock that click'd behind the door;
> The chest, contrived a double debt to pay,
> A bed by night, a chest of drawers by day;
> The pictures placed for ornament and use,
> The twelve good rules, the royal game of goose.'

"Captain Hogan, I have heard, found great difficulty in
obtaining 'the twelve good rules,' but at length purchased

them at some London book-stall to adorn the white-washed
parlor of 'The Three Jolly Pigeons.'   However laudable this
may be, nothing shook my faith in the reality of Auburn
so much as this exactness, which had the disagreeable air of
being got up for the occasion.   The last object of pilgrimage
is the quondam habitation of the schoolmaster,

> " 'There, in his noisy mansion, skill'd to rule.'

It is surrounded with fragrant proofs of identity in

> " 'The blossom'd furze, unprofitably gay.'

There is to be seen the chair of the poet, which fell into
the hands of its present possessors at the wreck of the parsonage-house; they have frequently refused large offers of
purchase; but more, I dare say, for the sake of drawing
contributions from the curious than from any reverence for
the bard.   The chair is of oak, with back and seat of cane,
which precluded all hopes of a secret drawer, like that lately
discovered in Gay's.   There is no fear of its being worn out
by the devout earnestness of sitters—as the cocks and hens
have usurped undisputed possession of it, and protest most
clamorously against all attempts to get it cleansed or to seat
one's self.   ·

"The controversy concerning the identity of this Auburn
was formerly a standing theme of discussion among the
learned of the neighborhood; but, since the *pros* and *cons*
have been all ascertained, the argument has died away.   Its
abettors plead the singular agreement between the local
history of the place and the Auburn of the poem, and the
exactness with which the scenery of the one answers to the
description of the other.   To this is opposed the mention of
the nightingale,

> " 'And fill'd each pause the nightingale had made;'

there being no such bird in the island. The objection is slighted, on the other hand, by considering the passage as a mere poetical license. 'Besides,' say they, 'the robin is the Irish nightingale.' And if it be hinted how unlikely it was that Goldsmith should have laid the scene in a place from which he was and had been so long absent, the rejoinder is always, 'Pray, sir, was Milton in hell when he built Pandemonium?'

"The line is naturally drawn between; there can be no doubt that the poet intended England by

> " 'The land to hast'ning ills a prey,
> Where wealth accumulates and men decay.'

But it is very natural to suppose that, at the same time, his imagination had in view the scenes of his youth, which give such strong features of resemblance to the picture." [1]

Best, an Irish clergyman, told Davis, the traveller in America, that the hawthorn-bush mentioned in the poem was still remarkably large. "I was riding once," said he, "with Brady, titular Bishop of Ardagh, when he observed to me, 'Ma foy, Best, this huge overgrown bush is mightily in the way. I will order it to be cut down.'—'What, sir!' replied I, 'cut down the bush that supplies so beautiful an image in "The Deserted Village"?'—'Ma foy!' exclaimed

---

[1] The attempt to identify Auburn and the places described in the poem is vain. Macaulay probably states the truth of the matter: "The village in its happy days is a true English village. The village in its decay is an Irish village. The felicity and the misery which Goldsmith has brought close together belong to two different countries; and to two different stages in the progress of society. He had assuredly never seen in his native island such a rural paradise, such a seat of plenty, content, and tranquillity, as his "Auburn." He had assuredly never seen in England all the inhabitants of such a paradise turned out of their homes in one day and forced to emigrate in a body to America. The hamlet he had probably seen in Kent; the ejectment he had probably seen in Munster; but, by joining the two, he has produced something which never was and never will be seen in any part of the world."

the bishop, 'is that the hawthorn bush?   Then let it be sacred
from the edge of the axe, and evil be to him that should cut
off a branch.' "—The hawthorn-bush, however, has long
since been cut up, root and branch, in furnishing relics to
literary pilgrims.

CHAPTER XXIX

THE POET AMONG THE LADIES; DESCRIPTION OF HIS PERSON AND
MANNERS—EXPEDITION TO PARIS WITH THE HORNECK FAMILY
— THE TRAVELLER OF TWENTY AND THE TRAVELLER OF
FORTY — HICKEY, THE SPECIAL ATTORNEY — AN UNLUCKY
EXPLOIT.

The "Deserted Village" had shed an additional poetic
grace round the homely person of the author; he was becoming more and more acceptable in ladies' eyes, and finding
himself more and more at ease in their society; at least in
the society of those whom he met in the Reynolds circle,
among whom he particularly affected the beautiful family
of the Hornecks.

But let us see what were really the looks and manners of
Goldsmith about this time, and what right he had to aspire
to ladies' smiles; and in so doing let us not take the sketches
of Boswell and his compeers, who had a propensity to represent him in caricature; but let us take the apparently truthful and discriminating picture of him as he appeared to
Judge Day, when the latter was a student in the Temple.

"In person," says the Judge, "he was short; about five
feet five or six inches; strong, but not heavy in make; rather
fair in complexion, with brown hair; such, at least, as could
be distinguished from his wig. His features were plain, but
not repulsive,—certainly not so when lighted up by conversation. His manners were simple, natural, and perhaps on
the whole, we may say, not polished; at least without the
refinement and good breeding which the exquisite polish
of his compositions would lead us to expect. He was always

cheerful and animated, often, indeed, boisterous in his mirth; entered with spirit into convivial society; contributed largely to its enjoyments by solidity of information, and the naïveté and originality of his character; talked often without premeditation, and laughed loudly without restraint."

This, it will be recollected, represents him as he appeared to a young Templar, who probably saw him only in Temple coffee-houses, at students' quarters, or at the jovial supper-parties given at the poet's own chambers. Here, of course, his mind was in its rough dress; his laugh may have been loud and his mirth boisterous; but we trust all these matters became softened and modified when he found himself in polite drawing-rooms and in female society.

But what say the ladies themselves of him? and here fortunately, we have another sketch of him, as he appeared at the time to one of the Horneck circle; in fact, we believe, to the Jessamy Bride herself. After admitting, apparently, with some reluctance, that "he was a very plain man," she goes on to say, "but had he been much more so, it was impossible not to love and respect his goodness of heart, which broke out on every occasion. His benevolence was unquestionable, and *his countenance bore every trace of it:* no one that knew him intimately could avoid admiring and loving his good qualities." When to all this we add the idea of intellectual delicacy and refinement associated with him by his poetry and the newly-plucked bays that were flourishing round his brow, we cannot be surprised that fine and fashionable ladies should be proud of his attentions, and that even a young beauty should not be altogether displeased with the thoughts of having a man of his genius in her chains.

We are led to indulge some notions of the kind from finding him in the month of July, but a few weeks after the publication of the "Deserted Village," setting off on a six

weeks' excursion to Paris, in company with Mrs. Horneck
and her two beautiful daughters. A day or two before his
departure, we find another new gala suit charged to him on
the books of Mr. William Filby. Were the bright eyes of
the Jessamy Bride responsible for this additional extravagance of wardrobe? Goldsmith had recently been editing
the works of Parnell;[1] had he taken courage from the example of Edwin in the Fairy tale?—

> "Yet spite of all that nature did
> To make his uncouth form forbid,
>   This creature dared to love.
> He felt the force of Edith's eyes,
> Nor wanted hope to gain the prize
>   *Could ladies look within*"——

All this we throw out as mere hints and surmises, leaving
it to our readers to draw their own conclusions. It will be
found, however, that the poet was subjected to shrewd bantering among his contemporaries about the beautiful Mary
Horneck, and that he was extremely sensitive on the subject.

It was in the month of June that he set out for Paris with
his fair companions, and the following letter was written by
him to Sir Joshua Reynolds, soon after the party landed
at Calais:—

"MY DEAR FRIEND,—

"We had a very quick passage from Dover to Calais,
which we performed in three hours and twenty minutes, all
of us extremely sea-sick, which must necessarily have happened, as my machine to prevent sea-sickness was not completed. We were glad to leave Dover, because we hated
to be imposed upon; so were in high spirits at coming to
Calais, where we were told that a little money would go a
great way.

---

[1] Thomas Parnell (1679-1718); see below, p. 295.

"Upon landing, with two little trunks, which was all we carried with us, we were surprised to see fourteen or fifteen fellows all running down to the ship to lay their hands upon them; four got under each trunk, the rest surrounded and held the hasps; and in this manner our little baggage was conducted, with a kind of funeral solemnity, till it was safely lodged at the custom-house. We were well enough pleased with the people's civility till they came to be paid; every creature that had the happiness of touching our trunks with their finger expected sixpence, and they had so pretty and civil a manner of demanding it, that there was no refusing them.

"When we had done with the porters, we had next to speak with the custom-house officers, who had their pretty civil way too. We were directed to the Hôtel d'Angleterre, where a valet-de-place came to offer his service, and spoke to me ten minutes before I once found out that he was speaking English. We had no occasion for his services, so we gave him a little money because he spoke English, and because he wanted it. I cannot help mentioning another circumstance: I bought a new riband for my wig at Canterbury, and the barber at Calais broke it in order to gain sixpence by buying me a new one."

An incident which occurred in the course of this tour has been tortured by that literary magpie, Boswell, into a proof of Goldsmith's absurd jealousy of any admiration shown to others in his presence. While stopping at a hotel in Lisle, they were drawn to the windows by a military parade in front. The extreme beauty of the Miss Hornecks immediately attracted the attention of the officers, who broke forth with enthusiastic speeches and compliments intended for their ears. Goldsmith was amused for a while, but at length affected impatience at this exclusive admiration of his beautiful companions, and exclaimed, with mock severity of aspect, "Elsewhere I also would have my admirers."

It is difficult to conceive the obtuseness of intellect necessary to misconstrue so obvious a piece of mock petulance and dry humor into an instance of mortified vanity and jealous self-conceit.

Goldsmith jealous of the admiration of a group of gay officers for the charms of two beautiful young women! This even out-Boswells Boswell: yet this is but one of several similar absurdities, evidently misconceptions of Goldsmith's peculiar vein of humor, by which the charge of envious jealousy has been attempted to be fixed upon him. In the present instance it was contradicted by one of the ladies herself, who was annoyed that it had been advanced against him. "I am sure," said she, "from the peculiar manner of his humor, and assumed frown of countenance, what was often uttered in jest was mistaken, by those who did not know him, for earnest." No one was more prone to err on this point than Boswell. He had a tolerable perception of wit, but none of humor.

The following letter to Sir Joshua Reynolds was subsequently written:

"*To Sir Joshua Reynolds.*
"Paris, July 29, [1770.]

"MY DEAR FRIEND,—I began a long letter to you from Lisle, giving a description of all that we had done and seen, but, finding it very dull, and knowing that you would show it again, I threw it aside and it was lost. You see by the top of this letter that we are at Paris, and (as I have often heard you say) we have brought our own amusement with us, for the ladies do not seem to be very fond of what we have yet seen.

"With regard to myself, I find that travelling at twenty and forty are very different things. I set out with all my

confirmed habits about me, and can find nothing on the
Continent so good as when I formerly left it. One of our
chief amusements here is scolding at everything we meet
with, and praising everything and every person we left at
home. You may judge, therefore, whether your name is
not frequently bandied at table among us. To tell you the
truth, I never thought I could regret your absence so much
as our various mortifications on the road have often taught
me to do. I could tell you of disasters and adventures without number; of our lying in barns, and of my being half
poisoned with a dish of green peas; of our quarrelling with
postilions, and being cheated by our landladies; but I reserve all this for a happy hour which I expect to share with
you upon my return.

"I have little to tell you more, but that we are at present
all well, and expect returning when we have stayed out one
month, which I did not care if it were over this very day.
I long to hear from you all, how you yourself do, how Johnson,
Burke, Dyer, Chamier, Colman, and every one of the club
do. I wish I could send you some amusement in this letter,
but I protest I am so stupefied by the air of this country (for
I am sure it cannot be natural) that I have not a word to
say. I have been thinking of the plot of a comedy, which
shall be entitled 'A Journey to Paris,' in which a family shall
be introduced with a full intention of going to France to save
money. You know there is not a place in the world more
promising for that purpose. As for the meat of this country,
I can scarce eat it; and though we pay two good shillings a
head for our dinner, I find it all so tough that I have spent less
time with my knife than my picktooth. I said this as a good
thing at the table, but it was not understood. I believe it
to be a good thing.

"As for our intended journey to Devonshire, I find it out

of my power to perform it; for, as soon at I arrive at Dover, I intend to let the ladies go on, and I will take a country-lodging somewhere near that place in order to do some business.   I have so outrun the constable that I must mortify a little to bring it up again.   For God's sake, the night you receive this take your pen in your hand and tell me some-thing about yourself and myself, if you know anything that has happened.   About Miss Reynolds, about Mr. Bickerstaff, my nephew, or anybody that you regard.   I beg you will send to Griffin the bookseller to know if there be any letters left for me, and be so good as to send them to me at Paris.   They may perhaps be left for me at the Porter's Lodge, opposite the pump in Temple Lane.   The same messenger will do. I expect one from Lord Clare, from Ireland.   As for the others, I am not much uneasy about.

"Is there anything I can do for you at Paris?   I wish you would tell me.   The whole of my own purchases here is one silk coat, which I have put on, and which makes me look like a fool.   But no more of that.   I find that Colman has gained his lawsuit.   I am glad of it.   I suppose you often meet. I will soon be among you, better pleased with my situation at home than I ever was before.   And yet I must say, that, if anything could make France pleasant, the very good women with whom I am at present would certainly do it.   I could say more about that, but I intend showing them the letter before I send it away.   What signifies teasing you longer with moral observations, when the business of my writing is over?   I have one thing only more to say, and of that I think every hour in the day, namely, that I am your most sincere and most affectionate friend,

"OLIVER GOLDSMITH."

"Direct to me at the Hotel de Danemarc, }
  Rue Jacob, Fauxbourg St. Germains." }

A word of comment on this letter:—

Travelling is, indeed, a very different thing with Goldsmith the poor student at twenty, and Goldsmith the poet
and Professor at forty. At twenty, though obliged to trudge
on foot from town to town, and country to country, paying
for a supper and a bed by a tune on the flute, everything
pleased, everything was good; a truckle-bed in a garret was
a couch of down, and the homely fare of the peasant a feast
fit for an epicure. Now, at forty, when he posts through the
country in a carriage, with fair ladies by his side, everything
goes wrong: he has to quarrel with postilions, he is cheated
by landladies, the hotels are barns, the meat is too tough to
be eaten, and he is half poisoned by green peas! A line in
his letter explains the secret: "the ladies do not seem to be
very fond of what we have seen." "One of our chief amusements is scolding at everything we meet with, and praising
everything and every person we have left at home!"—
the true English travelling amusement. Poor Goldsmith!
he has "all his *confirmed habits* about him"; that is
to say, he has recently risen into high life, and acquired high-bred notions; he must be fastidious like his
fellow-travellers; he dare not be pleased with what pleased
the vulgar tastes of his youth. He is unconsciously illus-
trating the trait so humorously satirized by him in Ned Tibbs,
the shabby beau, who can find "no such dressing as he had
at Lord Crump's or Lady Crimp's"; whose very senses have
grown genteel, and who no longer "smacks at wretched
wine or praises detestable custard." [1] A lurking thorn, too,
is worrying him throughout this tour; he has "outrun the
constable"; that is to say, his expenses have outrun his
means, and he will have to make up for this butterfly flight
by toiling like a grub on his return.

---

[1] *Citizen of the World*, Letter LXXI.

Another circumstance contributes to mar the pleasure he
had promised himself in this excursion. At Paris the party
is unexpectedly joined by a Mr. Hickey, a bustling attorney,
who is well acquainted with that metropolis and its environs,
and insists on playing the cicerone on all occasions. He
and Goldsmith did not relish each other, and they have
several petty altercations. The lawyer is too much a man
of business and method for the careless poet, and is disposed
to manage everything. He has perceived Goldsmith's whimsical peculiarities without properly appreciating his merits,
and is prone to indulge in broad bantering and raillery
at his expense, particularly irksome if indulged in the
presence of the ladies. He makes himself merry on his
return to England, by giving the following anecdote as
illustrative of Goldsmith's vanity:—

"Being with a party at Versailles, viewing the water-
works, a question arose among the gentlemen present,
whether the distance from whence they stood to one of the
little islands was within the compass of a leap. Goldsmith
maintained the affirmative; but, being bantered on the subject, and remembering his former prowess as a youth, attempted the leap, but, falling short, descended into the water,
to the great amusement of the company."

Was the Jessamy Bride a witness of this unlucky exploit?

This same Hickey is the one of whom Goldsmith, some
time subsequently, gave a good-humored sketch, in his poem
of "The Retaliation."

> "Here Hickey reclines, a most blunt, pleasant creature,
> And slander itself must allow him good-nature;
> He cherish'd his friend, and he relish'd a bumper,
> Yet one fault he had, and that one was a thumper.
> Perhaps you may ask if the man was a miser;
> I answer, No, no, for he always was wiser;

Too courteous, perhaps, or obligingly flat?
His very worst foe can't accuse him of that;
Perhaps he confided in men as they go,
And so was too foolishly honest? Ah, no!
Then what was his failing? Come, tell it, and burn ye—
He was, could he help it? a special attorney."

One of the few remarks extant made by Goldsmith during his tour is the following, of whimsical import, in his "Animated Nature."

"In going through the towns of France, some time since, I could not help observing how much plainer their parrots spoke than ours, and how very distinctly I understood their parrots speak French, when I could not understand our own, though they spoke my native language. I at first ascribed it to the different qualities of the two languages, and was for entering into an elaborate discussion on the vowels and consonants; but a friend that was with me solved the difficulty at once, by assuring me that the French women scarce did anything else the whole day than sit and instruct their feathered pupils; and that the birds were thus distinct in their lessons in consequence of continual schooling."

His tour does not seem to have left in his memory the most fragrant recollections; for, being asked, after his return, whether travelling on the Continent repaid "an Englishman for the privations and annoyances attendant on it," he replied, "I recommend it by all means to the sick, if they are without the sense of *smelling*, and to the poor if they are without the sense of *feeling*, and to both if they can discharge from their minds all idea of what in England we term comfort."

It is needless to say that the universal improvement in the art of living on the Continent has at the present day taken away the force of Goldsmith's reply, though even at the time it was more humorous than correct.

CHAPTER XXX

DEATH OF GOLDSMITH'S MOTHER — BIOGRAPHY OF PARNELL —
AGREEMENT WITH DAVIES FOR THE HISTORY OF ROME — LIFE
OF BOLINGBROKE — THE HAUNCH OF VENISON.

On his return to England, Goldsmith received the melancholy tidings of the death of his mother. Notwithstanding the fame as an author to which he had attained, she seems to have been disappointed in her early expectations from him. Like others of his family, she had been more vexed by his early follies than pleased by his proofs of genius; and in subsequent years, when he had risen to fame and to intercourse with the great, had been annoyed at the ignorance of the world and want of management, which prevented him from pushing his fortune. He had always, however, been an affectionate son, and in the latter years of her life, when she had become blind, contributed from his precarious resources to prevent her from feeling want.

He now resumed the labors of his pen, which his recent excursion to Paris rendered doubly necessary. We should have mentioned a "Life of Parnell," published by him shortly after the "Deserted Village." It was, as usual, a piece of job-work, hastily got up for pocket-money. Johnson spoke slightingly of it, and the author himself thought proper to apologize for its meagreness,—yet, in so doing, used a simile, which for beauty of imagery and felicity of language is enough of itself to stamp a value upon the essay.

"Such," says he, "is the very unpoetical detail of the life of a poet. Some dates and some few facts, scarcely more interesting than those that make the ornaments of a country

tombstone, are all that remain of one whose labors now begin
to excite universal curiosity. A poet, while living is seldom
an object sufficiently great to attract much attention; his
real merits are known but to a few, and these are generally
sparing in their praises. When his fame is increased by
time, it is then too late to investigate the peculiarities of his
disposition; *the dews of morning are past, and we vainly try
to continue the chase by the meridian splendor.*"

He now entered into an agreement with Davies to prepare
an abridgement, in one volume duodecimo, of his "History
of Rome"; but first to write a work for which there was a
more immediate demand. Davies was about to republish
Lord Bolingbroke's "Dissertation on Parties," which he
conceived would be exceedingly applicable to the affairs of
the day, and make a probable *hit* during the existing state of
violent political excitement; to give it still greater effect and
currency, he engaged Goldsmith to introduce it with a prefa-
tory life of Lord Bolingbroke.

About this time Goldsmith's friend and countryman,
Lord Clare, was in great affliction, caused by the death of
his only son, Colonel Nugent, and stood in need. of the
sympathies of a kind-hearted friend. At his request, therefore, Goldsmith paid him a visit at his seat of Gosfield,
taking his tasks with him. Davies was in a worry lest
Gosfield Park should prove a Capua[1] to the poet, and the
time be lost. "Dr. Goldsmith," writes he to a friend, "has
gone with Lord Clare into the country, and I am plagued to
get the proofs from him of the 'Life of Lord Bolingbroke.'"
The proofs, however, were furnished in time for the publication of the work in December. The "Biography," though

---

[1] After a great victory at Cannae (216 B.C.), Hannibal, instead of following up his advantage, took quarters in the rich city of Capua, where his
army gave itself up to riotous living.

written during a time of political turmoil, and introducing a work intended to be thrown into the arena of politics, maintained that freedom from party prejudice observable in all the writings of Goldsmith. It was a selection of facts, drawn from many unreadable sources, and arranged into a clear, flowing narrative, illustrative of the career and character of one who, as he intimates, "seemed formed by Nature to take delight in struggling with opposition; whose most agreeable hours were passed in storms of his own creating; whose life was spent in a continual conflict of politics, and, as if that was too short for the combat, has left his memory as a subject of lasting contention." The sum received by the author for this memoir is supposed, from circumstances, to have been forty pounds.

Goldsmith did not find the residence among the great unattended with mortifications. He had now become accustomed to be regarded in London as a literary lion, and was annoyed at what he considered a slight, on the part of Lord Camden. He complained of it on his return to town at a party of his friends. "I met him," said he, "at Lord Clare's house in the country; and he took no more notice of me than if I had been an ordinary man." "The company," says Boswell, "laughed heartily at this piece of 'diverting simplicity.'" And foremost among the laughers was doubtless the rattle-pated Boswell. Johnson, however, stepped forward, as usual, to defend the poet, whom he would allow no one to assail but himself; perhaps in the present instance he thought the dignity of literature itself involved in the question. "Nay, gentlemen," roared he, "Dr. Goldsmith is in the right. A nobleman ought to have made up to such a man as Goldsmith, and I think it is much against Lord Camden that he neglected him."

After Goldsmith's return to town he received from Lord

Clare a present of game, which he has celebrated and perpetuated in his amusing verses entitled the "Haunch of
Venison." Some of the lines pleasantly set forth the embarrassment caused by the appearance of such an aristocratic
delicacy in the humble kitchen of a poet, accustomed to look
up to mutton as a treat:—

"Thanks, my lord, for your venison; for finer or fatter
Never rang'd in a forest, or smok'd in a platter:
The haunch was a picture for painters to study,
The fat was so white, and the lean was so ruddy;
Though my stomach was sharp, I could scarce help regretting
To spoil such a delicate picture by eating:
I had thought in my chambers to place it in view,
To be shown to my friends as a piece of virtu;
As in some Irish houses where things are so-so,
One gammon of bacon hangs up for a show;
But, for eating a rasher, of what they take pride in,
They'd as soon think of eating the pan it was fry'd in.
.   .   .   .
But hang it—to poets, who seldom can eat,
Your very good mutton's a very good treat;
Such dainties to them, their health it might hurt;
It's like sending them ruffles, when wanting a shirt."

We have an amusing anecdote of one of Goldsmith's
blunders, which took place on a subsequent visit to Lord
Clare's, when that nobleman was residing in Bath.

Lord Clare and the Duke of Northumberland had houses
next to each other, of similar architecture. Returning home
one morning from an early walk, Goldsmith, in one of his frequent fits of absence, mistook the house, and walked up into
the Duke's dining-room, where he and the Duchess were
about to sit down to breakfast. Goldsmith, still supposing
himself in the house of Lord Clare, and that they were
visitors, made them an easy salutation, being acquainted
with them, and threw himself on a sofa in the lounging man-

ner of a man perfectly at home. The Duke and Duchess soon perceived his mistake, and, while they smiled internally, endeavored, with the considerateness of well-bred people, to prevent any awkward embarrassment. They accordingly chatted sociably with him about matters in Bath, until, breakfast being served, they invited him to partake. The truth at once flashed upon poor heedless Goldsmith; he started up from his free-and-easy position, made a confused apology for his blunder, and would have retired perfectly disconcerted, had not the Duke and Duchess treated the whole as a lucky occurrence to throw him in their way, and exacted a promise from him to dine with them.

This may be hung up as a companion-piece to his blunder on his first visit to Northumberland House.

CHAPTER XXXI

DINNER AT THE ROYAL ACADEMY—THE ROWLEY CONTROVERSY—
HORACE WALPOLE'S CONDUCT TO CHATTERTON—JOHNSON AT
REDCLIFFE CHURCH—GOLDSMITH'S HISTORY OF ENGLAND—
DAVIES'S CRITICISM—LETTER TO BENNET LANGTON.

On St. George's day of this year (1771), the first annual
banquet of the Royal Academy was held in the exhibition-
room; the walls of which were covered with works of art,
about to be submitted to public inspection. Sir Joshua
Reynolds, who first suggested this elegant festival, presided
in his official character; Drs. Johnson and Goldsmith, of
course, were present, as Professors of the Academy; and,
besides the Academicians, there was a large number of the
most distinguished men of the day as guests. Goldsmith
on this occasion drew on himself the attention of the company
by launching out with enthusiasm on the poems recently
given to the world by Chatterton, as the works of an ancient
author by the name of Rowley, discovered in the tower of
Redcliffe Church, at Bristol.[1] Goldsmith spoke of them with
rapture, as a treasure of old English poetry. This immediately raised the question of their authenticity; they having
been pronounced a forgery of Chatterton's. Goldsmith was
warm for their being genuine. When he considered, he said,
the merit of the poetry, the acquaintance with life and the
human heart displayed in them, the antique quaintness of
the language and the familiar knowledge of historical events,

---

[1] Thomas Chatterton (1752-1770) published poems, which he attributed to
Rowley, from 1764 to 1770; they were collected in 1777. It is now established
that the poems were of Chatterton's own composition, and that the language
and style of the poems are an imperfect imitation of earlier English poetry.

of their supposed day, he could not believe it possible they could be the work of a boy of sixteen, of narrow education, and confined to the duties of an attorney's office. They must be the productions of Rowley.

Johnson, who was a stout unbeliever in Rowley, as he had been in Ossian,[1] rolled in his chair and laughed at the enthusiasm of Goldsmith. Horace Walpole, who sat near by, joined in the laugh and jeer as soon as he found that the "*trouvaille*," [2] as he called it, "of *his friend* Chatterton," was in question. This matter, which had excited the simple admiration of Goldsmith, was no novelty to him, he said. "He might, had he pleased, have had the honor of ushering the great discovery to the learned world." And so he might, had he followed his first impulse in the matter, for he himself had been an original believer; had pronounced some speci-men verses sent to him by Chatterton wonderful for their harmony and spirit; and had been ready to print them and publish them to the world with his sanction. When he found, however, that his unknown correspondent was a mere boy, humble in sphere and indigent in circumstances, and when Gray and Mason pronounced the poems forgeries, he had changed his whole conduct towards the unfortunate author, and by his neglect and coldness had dashed all his sanguine hopes to the ground.

Exulting in his superior discernment, this cold-hearted man of society now went on to divert himself, as he says, with the credulity of Goldsmith, whom he was accustomed to pronounce "an inspired idiot"; but his mirth was soon dashed, for on asking the poet what had become of this Chatterton, he was answered, doubtless in the feeling

---

[1] An early Celtic poet to whom James Macpherson (1738-1796) ascribed the poems published under the title, *Fragments of Ancient Poetry Collected in the Highlands*, 1760.

[2] Discovery.

tone of one who had experienced the pangs of despondent genius, that "he had been to London, and had destroyed himself."

The reply struck a pang of self-reproach even to the cold heart of Walpole; a faint blush may have visited his cheek at his recent levity. "The persons of honor and veracity who were present," said he in after years, when he found it necessary to exculpate himself from the charge of heartless neglect of genius, "will attest with what surprise and concern I thus first heard of his death." Well might he feel concern. His cold neglect had doubtless contributed to madden the spirit of that youthful genius, and hurry him towards his untimely end; nor have all the excuses and palliations of Walpole's friends and admirers been ever able entirely to clear this stigma from his fame.

But what was there in the enthusiasm and credulity of honest Goldsmith in this matter, to subject him to the laugh of Johnson or the raillery of Walpole? Granting the poems were not ancient, were they not good? Granting they were not the productions of Rowley, were they the less admirable for being the productions of Chatterton? Johnson himself testified to their merits and the genius of their composer, when, some years afterwards, he visited the tower of Redcliffe Church, and was shown the coffer in which poor Chatterton had pretended to find them. "This," said he, "is the most extraordinary young man that has encountered my knowledge. *It is wonderful how the whelp has written such things.*"

As to Goldsmith, he persisted in his credulity, and had subsequently a dispute with Dr. Percy on the subject, which interrupted and almost destroyed their friendship. After all, his enthusiasm was of a generous, poetic kind; the poems remain beautiful monuments of genius, and it is even now

difficult to persuade one's self that they could be entirely
the productions of a youth of sixteen.

In the month of August was published anonymously the
"History of England," on which Goldsmith had been for
some time employed. It was in four volumes, compiled
chiefly, as he acknowledged in the preface, from Rapin,
Carte, Smollett, and Hume, each of whom," says he, "have
their admirers, in proportion as the reader is studious of
political antiquities, fond of minute anecdote, a warm parti-
san, or a deliberate reasoner." It possessed the same kind
of merit as his other historical compilations; a clear, succinct
narrative, a simple, easy, and graceful style, and an agreeable arrangement of facts; but was not remarkable for either
depth of observation or minute accuracy of research. Many
passages were transferred, with little if any alteration, from
his "Letters from a Nobleman to his Son" on the same
subject. The work, though written without party feeling,
met with sharp animadversions from political scribblers. The
writer was charged with being unfriendly to liberty, disposed
to elevate monarchy above its proper sphere; a tool of minis-
ters; one who would betray his country for a pension. Tom
Davies, the publisher, the pompous little bibliopole of Russell Street, alarmed lest the book should prove unsalable,
undertook to protect it by his pen, and wrote a long article
in its defence in "The Public Advertiser." He was vain of
his critical effusion, and sought by nods and winks and
innuendoes to intimate his authorship. "Have you seen," said
he, in a letter to a friend, "'An Impartial Account of Goldsmith's History of England'? If you want to know who was
the writer of it, you will find him in Russell Street; —*but mum!*"

The History, on the whole, however, was well received;
some of the critics declared that English history had never
before been so usefully, so elegantly, and agreeably epito-

mized, "and, like his other historical writings, it has kept its ground" in English literature.

Goldsmith had intended this summer, in company with Sir Joshua Reynolds, to pay a visit to Bennet Langton, at his seat in Lincolnshire, where he was settled in domestic life, having the year previously married the Countess Dowager of Rothes. The following letter, however, dated from his chambers in the Temple, on the 7th of September, apologizes for putting off the visit, while it gives an amusing account of his summer occupations and of the attacks of the critics on his "History of England":—

"MY DEAR SIR,—

"Since I had the pleasure of seeing you last, I have been almost wholly in the country, at a farmer's house, quite alone, trying to write a comedy. It is now finished; but when or how it will be acted, or whether it will be acted at all, are questions I cannot resolve. I am therefore so much employed upon that, that I am under the necessity of putting off my intended visit to Lincolnshire for this season. Reynolds is just returned from Paris, and finds himself now in the case of a truant that must make up for his idle time by diligence. We have therefore agreed to postpone our journey till next summer, when we hope to have the honor of waiting upon Lady Rothes and you, and staying double the time of our late intended visit. We often meet, and never without remembering you. I see Mr. Beauclerc very often both in town and country. He is now going directly forward to become a second Boyle: deep in chemistry and physics. Johnson has been down on a visit to a country parson, Doctor Taylor, and is returned to his old haunts at Mrs. Thrale's. Burke is a farmer, *en attendant*[1] a better

---

[1] Awaiting.

place; but visiting about too. Every soul is visiting about
and merry but myself. And that is hard too, as I have been
trying these three months to do something to make people
laugh. There have I been strolling about the hedges,
studying jests with a most tragical countenance. The
'Natural History' is about half finished, and I will shortly
finish the rest. God knows I am tired of this kind of finishing, which is but bungling work; and that not so much my
fault as the fault of my scurvy circumstances. They begin
to talk in town of the Opposition's gaining ground; the cry
of liberty is still as loud as ever. I have published, or Davies
has published for me, an 'Abridgement of the History of
England,' for which I have been a good deal abused in the
newspapers, for betraying the liberties of the people. God
knows I had no thought for or against liberty in any head;
my whole aim being to make up a book of a decent size, that,
as 'Squire Richard says, *would do no harm to nobody*. However, they set me down as an arrant Tory and consequently
an honest man. When you come to look at any part of it,
you'll say that I am a sore Whig. God bless you, and with
my most respectful compliments to her Ladyship, I remain,
dear Sir, your most affectionate humble servant,

"OLIVER GOLDSMITH."

CHAPTER XXXII

Though Goldsmith found it impossible to break from his
literary occupations to visit Bennet Langton, in Lincolnshire,
he soon yielded to attractions from another quarter, in which
somewhat of sentiment may have mingled. Miss Catharine
Horneck, one of his beautiful fellow-travellers, otherwise
called *Little Comedy*, had been married in August to Henry
William Bunbury, Esq., a gentleman of fortune, who has
become celebrated for the humorous productions of his
pencil. Goldsmith was shortly afterwards invited to pay
the newly married couple a visit at their seat, at Barton, in
Suffolk. How could he resist such an invitation—especially
as the Jessamy Bride would, of course, be among the guests?
It is true, he was hampered with work; he was still more
hampered with debt; his accounts with Newbery were perplexed; but all must give way. New advances are procured
from Newbery, on the promise of a new tale in the style of
the "Vicar of Wakefield," of which he showed him a few
roughly-sketched chapters; so, his purse replenished in the
old way, "by hook or by crook," he posted off to visit the bride
at Barton. He found there a joyous household, and one
where he was welcomed with affection. Garrick was there,
and played the part of master of the revels, for he was an
intimate friend of the master of the house. Notwithstanding
early misunderstandings, a social intercourse between the
actor and the poet had grown up of late, from meeting

together continually in the same circle. A few particulars have reached us concerning Goldsmith while on this happy visit. We believe the legend has come down from Miss Mary Horneck herself. "While at Barton," she says, "his manners were always playful and amusing, taking the lead in promoting any scheme of innocent mirth, and usually prefacing the invitation with 'Come, now, let us play the fool a little.' At cards, which was commonly a round game, and the stake small, he was always the most noisy, affected great eagerness to win, and teased his opponents of the gentler sex with continual jest and banter on their want of spirit in not risking the hazards of the game. But one of his most favorite enjoyments was to romp with the children, when he threw off all reserve, and seemed one of the most joyous of the group.

"One of the means by which he amused us was his songs, chiefly of the comic kind, which were sung with some taste and humor; several, I believe, were of his own composition, and I regret that I neither have copies, which might have been readily procured from him at the time, nor do I remember their names."

His perfect good-humor made him the object of tricks of all kinds; often in retaliation of some prank which he himself had played off. Unluckily, these tricks were sometimes made at the expense of his toilet, which, with a view peradventure to please the eye of a certain fair lady, he had again enriched to the impoverishment of his purse. "Being at all times gay in his dress," says this ladylike legend, "he made his appearance at the breakfast-table in a smart black silk coat with an expensive pair of ruffles; the coat some one contrived to soil, and it was sent to be cleansed; but, either by accident, or probably by design, the day after it came home, the sleeves became daubed with paint, which was not discovered until the ruffles also, to his great mortification, were irretrievably disfigured.

"He always wore a wig, a peculiarity which those who judge of his appearance only from the fine poetical head of Reynolds would not suspect; and on one occasion some person contrived seriously to injure this important adjunct to dress. It was the only one he had in the country, and the misfortune seemed irreparable until the services of Mr. Bunbury's valet were called in, who, however, performed his functions so indifferently, that poor Goldsmith's appearance became the signal for a general smile."

This was wicked waggery, especially when it was directed to mar all the attempts of the unfortunate poet to improve his personal appearance, about which he was at all times dubiously sensitive, and particularly when among the ladies.

We have in a former chapter recorded his unlucky tumble into a fountain at Versailles, when attempting a feat of agility in presence of the fair Hornecks. Water was destined to be equally baneful to him on the present occasion. "Some difference of opinion," says the fair narrator, "having arisen with Lord Harrington respecting the depth of a pond, the poet remarked that it was not so deep but that, if anything valuable was to be found at the bottom, he would not hesitate to pick it up. His lordship, after some banter, threw in a guinea; Goldsmith, not to be outdone in this kind of bravado, in attempting to fulfil his promise without getting wet, accidentally fell in to the amusement of all present; but persevered, brought out the money, and kept it, remarking that he had abundant objects on whom to bestow any farther proofs of his lordship's whim or bounty."

All this is recorded by the beautiful Mary Horneck, the Jessamy Bride herself; but while she gives these amusing pictures of poor Goldsmith's eccentricities, and of the mischievous pranks played off upon him, she bears unqualified testimony, which we have quoted elsewhere, to the qualities of his head and heart, which shone forth in his countenance, and gained him the love of all who knew him.

Among the circumstances of this visit, vaguely called to mind by this fair lady in after years, was that Goldsmith read to her and her sister the first part of a novel which he had in hand. It was doubtless the manuscript mentioned at the beginning of this chapter, on which he had obtained an advance of money from Newbery to stave off some pressing debts, and to provide funds for this very visit. It never was finished. The bookseller, when he came afterwards to examine the manuscript, objected to it as a mere narrative version of the "Good-natured Man." Goldsmith, too easily put out of conceit of his writings, threw it aside, forgetting that this was the very Newbery who kept his "Vicar of Wakefield" by him nearly two years, through doubts of its success. The loss of the manuscript is deeply to be regretted; it doubtless would have been properly wrought up before given to the press, and might have given us new scenes of life and traits of character, while it could not fail to bear traces of his delightful style. What a pity he had not been guided by the opinions of his fair listeners at Barton, instead of that of the astute Mr. Newbery!

CHAPTER XXXIII

DINNER AT GENERAL OGLETHORPE'S—ANECDOTES OF THE GEN-
ERAL—DISPUTE ABOUT DUELLING—GHOST STORIES.

We have mentioned old General Oglethorpe as one of
Goldsmith's aristocratical acquaintances. This veteran, born
in 1698, had commenced life early, by serving, when a mere
stripling, under Prince Eugene, against the Turks. He had
continued in military life, and been promoted to the rank of
major-general in 1745, and received a command during the
Scottish rebellion. Being of strong Jacobite tendencies, he
was suspected and accused of favoring the rebels; and
though acquitted by a court of inquiry, was never afterwards
employed; or, in technical language, was shelved. He had
since been repeatedly a member of Parliament, and had always
distinguished himself by learning, taste, active benevolence,
and high Tory principles. His name, however, has become
historical, chiefly from his transactions in America, and the
share he took in the settlement of the colony of Georgia. It
lies embalmed in honorable immortality in a single line of
Pope's:—

> "One, driven *by strong benevolence of soul,*
>   Shall fly, like Oglethorpe, from pole to pole."

The veteran was now seventy-four years of age, but
healthy and vigorous, and as much the preux chevalier as in
his younger days, when he served with Prince Eugene. His
table was often the gathering-place of men of talent. Johnson was frequently there, and delighted in drawing from the
General details of his various "experiences." He was anxious that he should give the world his life. "I know no man,"

said he, "whose life would be more interesting." Still the
vivacity of the General's mind and the variety of his knowledge made him skip from subject to subject too fast for the
Lexicographer. "Oglethorpe," growled he, "never com-
pletes what he has to say."

Boswell gives us an interesting and characteristic account
of a dinner-party at the General's (April 10th, 1772,) at
which Goldsmith and Johnson were present. After dinner,
when the cloth was removed, Oglethorpe, at Johnson's request,
gave an account of the siege of Belgrade, in the true veteran
style. Pouring a little wine upon the table, he drew his lines
and parallels with a wet finger, describing the positions of
the opposing forces. "Here were we—here were the Turks,"
to all which Johnson listened with the most earnest attention,
poring over the plans and diagrams with his usual purblind
closeness.

In the course of conversation the General gave an anecdote
of himself in early life, when serving under Prince Eugene.
Sitting at table once in company with a prince of Wurtem-
berg, the latter gave a fillip to a glass of wine, so as to make
some of it fly in Oglethorpe's face. The manner in which
it was done was somewhat equivocal. How was it to be
taken by the stripling officer? If seriously, he must challenge the Prince; but in so doing he might fix on himself the
character of a drawcansir.[1] If passed over without notice,
he might be charged with cowardice. His mind was made
up in an instant. "Prince," said he, smiling, "that is an
excellent joke; but we do it much better in England." So
saying, he threw a whole glass of wine in the Prince's face.
"Il a bien fait, mon Prince," cried an old General present,

---

[1] The word is derived from a character in Buckingham's burlesque called
The Rehearsal. The character Drawcansir, a bully and braggart, is a
parody on the character Almanzor in Dryden's *Conquest of Granada*.

"vous l'avez commencé." (He has done right, my Prince; you commenced it.) The Prince had the good sense to acquiesce in the decision of the veteran, and Oglethorpe's retort in kind was taken in good part.

It was probably at the close of this story that the officious Boswell, ever anxious to promote conversation for the benefit of his note-book, started the question whether duelling were consistent with moral duty. The old General fired up in an instant. "Undoubtedly," said he, with a lofty air; "undoubtedly a man has a right to defend his honor." Goldsmith immediately carried the war into Boswell's own quarters, and pinned him with the question, "what he would do if affronted?" The pliant Boswell, who for a moment had the fear of the General rather than of Johnson before his eyes, replied, "he should think it necessary to fight." "Why then, that solves the question," replied Goldsmith. "No, sir!" thundered out Johnson; "it does not follow that what a man would do, is therefore right." He, however, subsequently went into a discussion to show that there were necessities in the case arising out of the artificial refinement of society, and its proscription of any one who should put up with an affront without fighting a duel. "He then," concluded he, "who fights a duel does not fight from passion against his antagonist, but out of self-defence, to avert the stigma of the world, and to prevent himself from being driven out of society. I could wish there were not that superfluity of refinement; but while such notions prevail, no doubt a man may lawfully fight a duel."

Another question started was, whether people who disagreed on a capital point could live together in friendship. Johnson said they might. Goldsmith said they could not, as they had not the idem velle atque idem nolle—the same likings and aversions. Johnson rejoined, that they must

shun the subject on which they disagreed. "But, sir," said
Goldsmith, "when people live together who have something
as to which they disagree, and which they want to shun,
they will be in the situation mentioned in the story of Blue
Beard: 'you may look into all the chambers but one;' but
we should have the greatest inclination to look into that
chamber, to talk of that subject." "Sir," thundered Johnson, in a loud voice, "I am not saying that *you* could live in
friendship with a man from whom you differ as to some
point; I am only saying that *I* could do it."

Who will not say that Goldsmith had the best of this
petty contest? How just was his remark! how felicitous the
illustration of the blue chamber! how rude and overbearing
was the argumentum ad hominem of Johnson, when he felt
that he had the worst of the argument!

The conversation turned upon ghosts. General Oglethorpe told the story of a Colonel Prendergast, an officer in
the Duke of Marlborough's army, who predicted among his
comrades that he should die on a certain day. The battle
of Malplaquet took place on that day. The Colonel was in
the midst of it, but came out unhurt. The firing had ceased,
and his brother officers jested with him about the fallacy of
his prediction. "The day is not over," replied he, gravely;
"I shall die notwithstanding what you see." His words
proved true. The order for a cessation of firing had not
reached one of the French batteries, and a random shot from
it killed the Colonel on the spot. Among his effects was
found a pocket-book in which he had made a solemn entry,
that Sir John Friend, who had been executed for high treason,
had appeared to him, either in a dream or vision, and predicted that he would meet him on a certain day (the very day
of the battle). Colonel Cecil, who took possession of the
effects of Colonel Prendergast, and read the entry in the

pocket-book, told this story to Pope, the poet, in the presence
of General Oglethorpe.

This story, as related by the General, appears to have
been well received, if not credited, by both Johnson and
Goldsmith, each of whom had something to relate in kind.
Goldsmith's brother, the clergyman in whom he had such
implicit confidence, had assured him of his having seen an
apparition. Johnson also had a friend, old Mr. Cave, the
printer, at St. John's Gate, "an honest man, and a sensible
man," who told him he had seen a ghost; he did not, however,
like to talk of it, and seemed to be in great horror whenever
it was mentioned. "And pray, sir," asked Boswell, "what
did he say was the appearance?" "Why, sir, something of
a shadowy being."

The reader will not be surprised at this superstitious turn
in the conversation of such intelligent men, when he recollects
that, but a few years before this time, all London had been
agitated by the absurd story of the Cock-lane ghost; a matter
which Dr. Johnson had deemed worthy of his serious inves-
tigation, and about which Goldsmith had written a pamphlet.[1]

---

[1] The Cock-lane Ghost was a nine day's wonder of the year 1762; the
result of Dr. Johnson's investigations was the revealing of the imposture.
"The chief impostor, a man of the name of Parsons, had, it should seem,
set his daughter to play the part of the ghost in order to pay out a grudge
against a man who had sued him for a debt. The ghost was made to accuse
this man of poisoning his sister-in-law, and to declare that she should only
be at ease in her mind if he were hanged."—HILL, Boswell's Life of Johnson
I, 406, note 3.

CHAPTER XXXIV

MR. JOSEPH CRADOCK—AN AUTHOR'S CONFIDINGS—AN AMANU-
ENSIS—LIFE AT EDGEWARE—GOLDSMITH CONJURING—GEORGE
COLMAN—THE FANTOCCINI.

Among the agreeable acquaintances made by Goldsmith
about this time was a Mr. Joseph Cradock, a young gentleman of Leicestershire, living at his ease, but disposed to
"make himself uneasy," by meddling with literature and the
theatre; in fact, he had a passion for plays and players, and
had come up to town with a modified translation of Voltaire's
tragedy of "Zobeide," in a view to get it acted. There was
no great difficulty in the case, as he was a man of fortune,
had letters of introduction to persons of note, and was
altogether in a different position from the indigent man of
genius whom managers might harass with impunity. Goldsmith met him at the house of Yates, the actor, and finding
that he was a friend of Lord Clare, soon became sociable
with him. Mutual tastes quickened the intimacy, especially
as they found means of serving each other. Goldsmith wrote
an epilogue for the tragedy of "Zobeide"; and Cradock, who
was an amateur musician, arranged the music for the "Threnodia Augustalis," a Lament on the death of the Princess
Dowager of Wales, the political mistress and patron of Lord
Clare, which Goldsmith had thrown off hastily to please that
nobleman. The tragedy was played with some success at
Covent Garden; the Lament was recited and sung at Mrs.
Cornelys' rooms—a very fashionable resort in Soho Square,
got up by a woman of enterprise of that name. It was in
whimsical parody of those gay and somewhat promiscuous

assemblages that Goldsmith used to call the motley evening parties at his lodgings "little Cornelys."

The "Threnodia Augustalis" was not publicly known to be by Goldsmith until several years after his death.

Cradock was one of the few polite intimates who felt more disposed to sympathize with the generous qualities of the poet than to sport with his eccentricities. He sought his society whenever he came to town, and occasionally had him to his seat in the country. Goldsmith appreciated his sympathy, and unburdened himself to him without reserve. Seeing the lettered ease in which this amateur author was enabled to live, and the time he could bestow on the elaboration of a manuscript, "Ah! Mr. Cradock," cried he, "think of me, that must write a volume every month!" He complained to him of the attempts made by inferior writers, and by others who could scarcely come under that denomination, not only to abuse and depreciate his writings, but to render him ridiculous as a man; perverting every harmless sentiment and action into charges of absurdity, malice, or folly. "Sir," said he, in the fulness of his heart, "I am as a lion baited by curs!"

Another acquaintance, which he made about this time, was a young countryman of the name of M'Donnell, whom he met in a state of destitution, and, of course, befriended. The following grateful recollections of his kindness and his merits were furnished by that person in after years:—

"It was in the year 1772," writes he, "that the death of my elder brother—when in London, on my way to Ireland—left me in a most forlorn situation; I was then about eighteen; I possessed neither friends nor money, nor the means of getting to Ireland, of which or of England I knew scarcely anything, from having so long resided in France. In this situation I had strolled about for two or three days, considering what to do, but unable to come to any determination, when Providence directed me to the Temple Gardens. I threw myself on a seat, and, willing to forget my miseries for a moment, drew out a book; that book was a volume of Boileau. I had not been there long when a gentleman, strolling about, passed near me, and observing, perhaps, something Irish or foreign in my garb or countenance, addressed me: 'Sir, you seem studious; I hope you find this a favorable place to pursue it.' 'Not very studious, sir; I fear it is the want of society that brings me hither; I am solitary and unknown in this metropolis;' and a passage from Cicero—Oratio pro Archia—occurring to me, I quoted it: 'Hæc studia pernoctant nobiscum, peregrinantur, rusticantur.'[1] 'You are a scholar, too, sir, I perceive.' 'A piece of one, sir; but I ought still to have been in the college where I had the good fortune to pick up the little I know.' A good deal of conversation ensued; I told him part of my history, and he, in return, gave his address in the Temple, desiring me to call soon, from which, to my infinite surprise and gratification, I found that the person who thus seemed to take an interest in my fate was my countryman, and a distinguished ornament of letters.

"I did not fail to keep the appointment, and was received in the kindest manner. He told me, smilingly, that he was not rich; that he could do little for me in direct pecuniary aid, but would endeavor to put me in the way of doing something for myself; observing, that he could at least furnish me with advice not wholly useless to a young man placed in the heart of a great metropolis. 'In London,' he continued, 'nothing is to be got for nothing; you must work; and no man who chooses to be industrious need be under obligations

---

[1] "These pursuits keep you company through the night, or when you travel, or when you are in the country."

to another, for here labor of every kind commands its reward.
If you think proper to assist me occasionally as amanuensis,
I shall be obliged, and you will be placed under no obligation,
until something more permanent can be secured for you.'
This employment, which I pursued for some time, was to
translate passages from Buffon, which were abridged or
altered, according to circumstances, for his 'Natural History.'"

Goldsmith's literary tasks were fast getting ahead of him,
and he began now to "toil after them in vain."

Five volumes of the "Natural History" here spoken of
had long since been paid for by Mr. Griffin, yet most of them
were still to be written. His young amanuensis bears testimony to his embarrassments and perplexities, but to the
degree of equanimity with which he bore them:—

"It has been said," observes he, "that he was irritable.
Such may have been the case at times; nay, I believe it was
so; for what with the continual pursuit of authors, printers,
and booksellers, and occasional pecuniary embarrassments,
few could have avoided exhibiting similar marks of impatience. But it was never so towards me. I saw him only
in his bland and kind moods, with a flow, perhaps an over-
flow, of the milk of human kindness for all who were in any
manner dependent upon him. I looked upon him with awe
and veneration, and he upon me as a kind parent upon a
child.

"His manner and address exhibited much frankness and
cordiality, particularly to those with whom he possessed any
degree of intimacy. His good-nature was equally apparent.
You could not dislike the man, although several of his follies
and foibles you might be tempted to condemn. He was
generous and inconsiderate; money with him had little value."

To escape from many of the tormentors just alluded to,

and to devote himself without interruption to his task, Goldsmith took lodgings for the summer at a farm-house near the six-mile stone on the Edgeware road, and carried down his books in two return post-chaises. He used to say he believed the farmer's family thought him an odd character, similar to that in which the *Spectator* appeared to his landlady and her children; he was *The Gentleman*. Boswell tells us that he went to visit him at the place in company with Mickle, translator of the "Lusiad." [1] Goldsmith was not at home. Having a curiosity to see his apartment, however, they went in, and found curious scraps of descriptions of animals scrawled upon the wall with a black-lead pencil.

The farm-house in question is still in existence, though much altered. It stands upon a gentle eminence in Hyde Lane, commanding a pleasant prospect towards Hendon. The room is still pointed out in which "She Stoops to Conquer" was written; a convenient and airy apartment, up one flight of stairs.

Some matter-of-fact traditions concerning the author were furnished, a few years since, by a son of the farmer, who was sixteen years of age at the time Goldsmith resided with his father. Though he had engaged to board with the family, his meals were generally sent to him in his room, in which he passed the most of his time, negligently dressed, with his shirt-collar open, busily engaged in writing. Sometimes, probably when in moods of composition, he would wander into the kitchen, without noticing any one, stand musing with his back to the fire, and then hurry off again to his room, no doubt to commit to paper some thought which had struck him.

Sometimes he strolled about the fields, or was to be seen loitering and reading and musing under the hedges. He was subject to fits of wakefulness, and read much in bed; if

---

[1] A Portuguese epic poem by Camoens.

not disposed to read, he still kept the candle burning; if he wished to extinguish it, and it was out of his reach, he flung his slipper at it, which would be found in the morning near the overturned candlestick and daubed with grease. He was noted here, as everywhere else, for his charitable feelings. No beggar applied to him in vain, and he evinced on all occasions great commiseration for the poor.

He had the use of the parlor to receive and entertain company, and was visited by Sir Joshua Reynolds, Hugh Boyd, the reputed author of "Junius,"[1] Sir William Chambers, and other distinguished characters. He gave occasionally, though rarely, a dinner-party; and on one occasion, when his guests were detained by a thunder-shower, he got up a dance, and carried the merriment late into the night.

As usual, he was the promoter of hilarity among the young, and at one time took the children of the house to see a company of strolling players at Hendon. The greatest amusement to the party, however, was derived from his own jokes on the road and his comments on the performance, which produced infinite laughter among his youthful companions.

Near to his rural retreat at Edgeware, a Mr. Seguin, an Irish merchant, of literary tastes, had country quarters for his family, where Goldsmith was always welcome.

In this family he would indulge in playful and even grotesque humor, and was ready for anything—conversation, music, or a game of romps. He prided himself upon his dancing, and would walk a minuet with Mrs. Seguin, to the infinite amusement of herself and the children, whose shouts of laughter he bore with perfect good-humor. He would sing Irish songs, and the Scotch ballad of "Johnny Arm-

---

[1] The name "Junius" was signed to a series of letters on political subjects, which appeared in the "Public Advertiser," January 21st, 1769, to January 21st, 1772. The authorship of these letters has never been certainly determined, though the evidence strongly points to Sir Philip Francis.

strong." He took the lead in the children's sports of blind-man's-buff, hunt the slipper, &c., or in their games at cards, and was the most noisy of the party, affecting to cheat and to be excessively eager to win; while with children of smaller size he would turn the hind part of his wig before, and play all kinds of tricks to amuse them.

One word as to his musical skill and his performance on the flute, which comes up so invariably in all his fireside revels. He really knew nothing of music scientifically; he had a good ear, and may have played sweetly; but we are told he could not read a note of music. Roubillac, the statuary, once played a trick upon him in this respect. He pretended to score down an air as the poet played it, but put down crotchets and semibreves at random. When he had finished, Goldsmith cast his eye over it and pronounced it correct! It is possible that his execution in music was like his style in writing; in sweetness and melody he may have snatched a grace beyond the reach of art!

He was at all times a capital companion for children, and knew how to fall in with their humors. "I little thought," said Miss Hawkins, the woman grown, "what I should have to boast when Goldsmith taught me to play Jack and Jill by two bits of paper on his fingers." He entertained Mrs. Garrick, we are told, with a whole budget of stories and songs; delivered the "Chimney Sweep" with exquisite taste as a solo; and performed a duet with Garrick of "Old Rose and Burn the Bellows."

"I was only five years old," says the late George Colman, "when Goldsmith one evening, when drinking coffee with my father, took me on his knee and began to play with me, which amiable act I returned with a very smart slap in the face; it must have been a tingler, for I left the marks of my little spiteful paw upon his cheek. This infantile outrage

was followed by summary justice, and I was locked up by
my father in an adjoining room, to undergo solitary imprisonment in the dark.   Here I began to howl and scream most
abominably.   At length a friend appeared to extricate me
from jeopardy; it was the good-natured Doctor himself, with
a lighted candle in his hand, and a smile upon his countenance, which was still partially red from the effects of my
petulance.   I sulked and sobbed, and he fondled and soothed
until I began to brighten.   He seized the propitious moment,
placed three hats upon the carpet, and a shilling under each;
the shillings, he told me, were England, France, and Spain.
'Hey, presto, cockolorum!' cried the Doctor, and, lo! on
uncovering the shillings, they were all found congregated
under one.   I was no politician at the time, and therefore
might not have wondered at the sudden revolution which
brought England, France, and Spain all under one crown;
but, as I was also no conjurer, it amazed me beyond measure.
From that time, whenever the Doctor came to visit my father,

" 'I pluck'd his gown to share the good man's smile;'

a game of romps constantly ensued, and we were always
cordial friends and merry playfellows."

Although Goldsmith made the Edgeware farm-house his
headquarters for the summer, he would absent himself for
weeks at a time on visits to Mr. Cradock, Lord Clare, and
Mr. Langton, at their country-seats.   He would often visit
town, also, to dine and partake of the public amusements.
On one occasion he accompanied Edmund Burke to witness
a performance of the Italian Fantoccini or Puppets, in Panton Street; an exhibition which had hit the caprice of the
town, and was in a great vogue.   The puppets were set in
motion by wires, so well concealed as to be with difficulty
detected.   Boswell, with his usual obtuseness with respect

to Goldsmith, accuses him of being jealous of the puppets! "When Burke," said he, praised the dexterity with which one of them tossed a pike, 'Pshaw,' said Goldsmith *with some warmth*, 'I can do it better myself.'" "The same evening," adds Boswell, "when supping at Burke's lodgings, he broke his shin by attempting to exhibit to the company how much better he could jump over a stick than the puppets."

Goldsmith jealous of puppets! This even passes in absurdity Boswell's charge upon him of being jealous of the beauty of the two Miss Hornecks.

The Panton Street puppets were destined to be a source of further amusement to the town, and of annoyance to the little autocrat of the stage. Foote, the Aristophanes of the English drama, who was always on the alert to turn every subject of popular excitement to account, seeing the success of the Fantoccini, gave out that he should produce a Primitive Puppet-Show at the Haymarket, to be entitled "The Handsome Chambermaid, or Piety in Pattens"; intended to burlesque the *sentimental comedy* which Garrick still maintained at Drury Lane. The idea of a play to be performed in a regular theatre by puppets excited the curiosity and talk of the town. "Will your puppets be as large as life, Mr. Foote?" demanded a lady of rank. "Oh, no, my lady," replied Foote, *"not much larger than Garrick."*

CHAPTER XXXV

Goldsmith returned to town in the autumn (1772), with
his health much disordered. His close fits of sedentary
application, during which he in a manner tied himself to
the mast, had laid the seeds of a lurking malady in his system,
and produced a severe illness in the course of the summer.
Town-life was not favorable to the health either of body or
mind. He could not resist the siren voice of temptation,
which, now that he had become a notoriety, assailed him on
every side. Accordingly we find him launching away in a
career of social dissipation; dining and supping out; at
clubs, at routs, at theatres; he is a guest with Johnson at
the Thrales, and an object of Mrs. Thrale's lively sallies; he
is a lion at Mrs. Vesey's and Mrs. Montagu's, where some of
the high-bred blue-stockings pronounce him a "wild genius,"
and others, peradventure, a "wild Irishman." In the meantime his pecuniary difficulties are increasing upon him, con-
flicting with his proneness to pleasure and expense, and contributing by the harassment of his mind to the wear and tear
of his constitution. His "Animated Nature," though not
finished, has been entirely paid for, and the money spent.
The money advanced by Garrick on Newbery's note still
hangs over him as a debt. The tale on which Newbery had
loaned from two to three hundred pounds previous to the

excursion to Barton, has proved a failure. The bookseller is urgent for the settlement of his complicated account; the perplexed author has nothing to offer him in liquidation but the copyright of the comedy which he has in his portfolio; "Though, to tell you the truth, Frank," said he, "there are great doubts of its success." The offer was accepted, and, like bargains wrung from Goldsmith in times of emergency, turned out a golden speculation to the bookseller.

In this way Goldsmith went on "overrunning the constable," as he termed it; spending everything in advance; working with an overtasked head and weary heart to pay for past pleasures and past extravagance, and at the same time incurring new debts to perpetuate his struggles and darken his future prospects. While the excitement of society and the excitement of composition conspire to keep up a feverishness of the system, he has incurred an unfortunate habit of quacking himself with James's powders, a fashionable panacea of the day.[1]

A farce, produced this year by Garrick, and entitled "The Irish Widow," perpetuates the memory of practical jokes played off a year or two previously upon the alleged vanity of poor, simple-hearted Goldsmith. He was one evening at the house of his friend Burke, when he was beset by a tenth muse,. an Irish widow and authoress, just arrived from Ireland, full of brogue and blunders, and poetic fire and rantipole gentility. She was soliciting subscriptions for her poems, and assailed Goldsmith for his patronage; the great Goldsmith—her countryman, and of course her friend. She overpowered him with eulogiums on his own poems, and then read some of her own, with vehemence of tone and gesture, appealing continually to the great Goldsmith to know how he relished them.

---

[1] See Introduction, p. 45.

Poor Goldsmith did all that a kind-hearted and gallant gentleman could do in such a case; he praised her poems as far as the stomach of his sense would permit—perhaps a little further; he offered her his subscription; and it was not until she had retired with many parting compliments to the great Goldsmith, that he pronounced the poetry which had been inflicted on him execrable. The whole scene had been a hoax got up by Burke for the amusement of his company; and the Irish widow, so admirably performed, had been personated by a Mrs. Balfour, a lady of his connection, of great sprightliness and talent.

We see nothing in the story to establish the alleged vanity of Goldsmith, but we think it tells rather to the disadvantage of Burke,—being unwarrantable under their relations of friendship, and a species of waggery quite beneath his genius.

Croker, in his notes to Boswell, gives another of these practical jokes perpetrated by Burke at the expense of Goldsmith's credulity. It was related to Croker by Colonel O'Moore, of Cloghan Castle, in Ireland, who was a party concerned. The Colonel and Burke, walking one day through Leicester Square on their way to Sir Joshua Reynolds's, with whom they were to dine, observed Goldsmith, who was likewise to be a guest, standing and regarding a crowd which was staring and shouting at some foreign ladies in the window of a hotel. "Observe Goldsmith," said Burke to O'Moore, "and mark what passes between us at Sir Joshua's." They passed on and reached there before him. Burke received Goldsmith with affected reserve and coldness; being pressed to explain the reason, "Really," said he, "I am ashamed to keep company with a person who could act as you have just done in the Square." Goldsmith protested he was ignorant of what was meant. "Why," said Burke, "did you not exclaim, as you were looking up at those women, what stupid beasts the crowd must be for staring with such admiration at those *painted Jezebels*, while a man of your talents passed by unnoticed?" "Surely, surely, my dear friend," cried Goldsmith, with alarm, "surely I did not say so?" "Nay," replied Burke, "if you had not said so, who should I have known it?" "That's true," answered Goldsmith, "I am very sorry—it was very foolish: *I do recollect that something of the kind passed through my mind, but I did not think I had uttered it.*"

It is proper to observe that these jokes were played off by Burke before he had attained the full eminence of his social position, and that he may have felt privileged to take liberties with Goldsmith as his countryman and college associate. It is evident, however, that the peculiarities of the latter, and his guileless simplicity, made him a butt for the broad waggery of some of his associates; while others more polished, though equally perfidious, were on the watch to give currency to his bulls and blunders.

The Stratford jubilee, in honor of Shakspeare, where Boswell had made a fool of himself, was still in every one's mind.[1] It was sportively suggested that a fête should be held at Litchfield in honor of Johnson and Garrick, and that the "Beau's Stratagem" should be played by the members of the Literary Club. "Then," exclaimed Goldsmith, "I

[1] "Boswell wrote a letter signed with his own name to the *London Magazine* for 1769 (p. 451), describing the Jubilee. It is followed by a print of himself 'in the dress of an armed Corsican chief,' and by an account no doubt written by himself. It says: 'Of the most remarkable masks upon this occasion was James Boswell, Esq., in the dress of an armed Corsican chief. He entered the amphitheatre about twelve o'clock. On the front of his cap was embroidered in gold letters, *Viva la Liberta*, and on one side of it was a handsome blue feather and cockade, so that it had an elegant, as well as warlike, appearance. He wore no mask, saying that it was not proper for a gallant Corsican. So soon as he came into the room he drew universal attention.'" Hill's ed. of Boswell's *Johnson*, Vol. II, p. 68. See also below, p. 359.

shall certainly play Scrub.[1]   I should like of all things to try
my hand at that character."   The unwary speech, which
any one else might have made without comment, has been
thought worthy of record as whimsically characteristic.   Beauclerc was extremely apt to circulate anecdotes at his expense,
founded, perhaps, on some trivial incident, but dressed up
with the embellishments of his sarcastic brain.   One relates
to a venerable dish of peas, served up at Sir Joshua's table,
which should have been green, but were any other color.
A wag suggested to Goldsmith in a whisper, that they should
be sent to Hammersmith, as that was the way to *turn-em-
green* (Turnham Green).   Goldsmith, delighted with the
pun, endeavored to repeat it at Burke's table, but missed the
point.   "That is the way to *make* 'em green," said he.   Nobody laughed.   He perceived he was at fault.   "I mean
that is the *road* to turn 'em green."   A dead pause and a
stare;—"whereupon," adds Beauclerc, "he started up disconcerted and abruptly left the table."   This is evidently
one of Beauclerc's caricatures.

On another occasion the poet and Beauclerc were seated
at the theatre next to Lord Shelburne, the minister, whom
political writers thought proper to nickname Malagrida.[2]
"Do you know," said Goldsmith, to his lordship, in the course
of conversation, "that I never could conceive why they call
you Malagrida, *for* Malagrida was a very good sort of man."
This was too good a trip of the tongue for Beauclerc to let
pass: he serves it up in his next letter to Lord Charlemont,
as a specimen of a mode of turning a thought the wrong way,
peculiar to the poet; he makes merry over it with his witty
and sarcastic compeer, Horace Walpole, who pronounces it

---

[1] *The Beaux Stratagem*, to give the original form of the title, was by George
Farquhar (1678-1707).   The character Scrub is servant to a country squire.
[2] Gabriele Malagrida (1689-1761), an Italian Jesuit and popular preacher.
He was convicted of heresy and burned in the year 1761.

"a picture of Goldsmith's whole life." Dr. Johnson alone, when he hears it bandied about as Goldsmith's last blunder, growls forth a friendly defence: "Sir," said he, "it was a mere blunder in emphasis. He meant to say, I wonder they should use Malagrida as a term of reproach." Poor Goldsmith! On such points he was ever doomed to be misinterpreted. Rogers, the poet, meeting in times long subsequent with a survivor from those days, asked him what Goldsmith really was in conversation. The old conventional character was too deeply stamped in the memory of the veteran to be effaced. "Sir," replied the old wiseacre, "*he was a fool. The right word never came to him. If you gave him back a bad shilling, he'd say, Why, it's as good a shilling as ever was born.* You know he ought to have said *coined. Coined,* sir, never entered his head. *He was a fool, sir.*"

We have so many anecdotes in which Goldsmith's simplicity is played upon, that it is quite a treat to meet with one in which he is represented as playing upon the simplicity of others, especially when the victim of his joke is the "Great Cham" himself, whom all others are disposed to hold so much in awe. Goldsmith and Johnson were supping cosily together at a tavern in Dean Street, Soho, kept by Jack Roberts, a singer at Drury Lane, and a protégé of Garrick's. Johnson delighted in these gastronomical *tête-à-têtes,* and was expatiating in high good-humor on a dish of rumps and kidneys, the veins of his forehead swelling with the ardor of mastication. "These," said he, "are pretty little things; but a man must eat a great many of them before he is filled." "Aye; but how many of them," asked Goldsmith, with affected simplicity, "would reach to the moon?" "To the moon! Ah, sir, that, I fear, exceeds your calculation." "Not at all, sir; I think I could tell." "Pray, then, sir, let us hear." "Why, sir, one, *if it were long enough!*" Johnson

growled for a time at finding himself caught in such a
trite schoolboy trap. "Well, sir," cried he at length, "I have
deserved it. I should not have provoked so foolish an
answer by so foolish a question."

Among the many incidents related as illustrative of Goldsmith's vanity and envy is one which occurred one evening
when he was in a drawing-room with a party of ladies, and
a ballad-singer under the window struck up his favorite
song of "Sally Salisbury." "How miserably this woman
sings!" exclaimed he. "Pray, Doctor," said the lady of the
house, "could you do it better?" "Yes, madam, and the
company shall be judges." The company, of course, prepared to be entertained by an absurdity; but their smiles
were wellnigh turned to tears, for he acquitted himself with
a skill and pathos that drew universal applause. He had,
in fact, a delicate ear for music, which had been jarred by
the false notes of the ballad-singer; and there were certain
pathetic ballads, associated with recollections of his childhood,
which were sure to touch the springs of his heart. We have
another story of him, connected with ballad-singing, which is
still more characteristic. He was one evening at the house
of Sir William Chambers, in Berners Street, seated at a
whist table with Sir William, Lady Chambers, and Baretti,
when all at once he threw down his cards, hurried out of the
room and into the street. He returned in an instant, resumed
his seat, and the game went on. Sir William, after a little
hesitation, ventured to ask the cause of his retreat, fearing
he had been overcome by the heat of the room. "Not at
all," replied Goldsmith; "but in truth I could not bear to
hear that unfortunate woman in the street, half singing, half
sobbing, for such tones could only arise from the extremity
of distress: her voice grated painfully on my ear and jarred
my frame, so that I could not rest until I had sent her away."

It was in fact a poor ballad-singer whose cracked voice had been heard by others of the party, but without having the same effect on their sensibilities. It was the reality of his fictitious scene in the story of the "Man in Black"; wherein he describes a woman in rags, with one child in her arms and another on her back, attempting to sing ballads, but with such a mournful voice that it was difficult to determine whether she was singing or crying. "A wretch," he adds, "who, in the deepest distress, still aimed at good-humor, was an object my friend was by no means capable of withstanding." The "Man in Black" gave the poor woman all that he had—a bundle of matches.[1] Goldsmith, it is probable, sent his ballad-singer away rejoicing, with all the money in his pocket.

Ranelagh was at that time greatly in vogue as a place of public entertainment. It was situated near Chelsea; the principal room was a rotunda of great dimensions, with an orchestra in the centre, and tiers of boxes all round. It was a place to which Johnson resorted occasionally. "I am a great friend to public amusements," said he, "for they keep people from vice."* Goldsmith was equally a friend to them, though perhaps not altogether on such moral grounds. He was particularly fond of masquerades, which were then exceedingly popular, and got up at Ranelagh with great expense and magnificence. Sir Joshua Reynolds, who had likewise a taste for such amusements, was sometimes his companion; at other times he went alone; his peculiarities of person and

---

[1] *Citizen of the World*, Letter XXVI.

* "Alas, sir!" said Johnson, speaking, when in another mood, of grand houses, fine gardens, and splendid places of public amusement; "alas, sir! these are only struggles for happiness. When I first entered Ranelagh it gave an expansion and gay sensation to my mind, such as I never experienced anywhere else. But, as Xerxes wept when he reviewed his immense army, and considered that not one of that great multitude would be alive a hundred years afterwards, so it went to my heart to consider that there was not one in all that brilliant circle that was not afraid to go home and think."

manner would soon betray him, whatever might be his disguise, and he would be singled out by wags, acquainted with his foibles, and more successful than himself in maintaining their incognito, as a capital subject to be played upon. Some, pretending not to know him, would decry his writings, and praise those of his contemporaries; others would laud his verses to the skies, but purposely misquote and burlesque them; others would annoy him with parodies; while one young lady, whom he was teasing, as he supposed, with great success and infinite humor, silenced his rather boisterous laughter by quoting his own line about "the loud laugh that speaks the vacant mind." On one occasion he was absolutely driven out of the house by the persevering jokes of a wag, whose complete disguise gave him no means of retaliation.

His name appearing in the newspapers among the distinguished persons present at one of these amusements, his old enemy, Kenrick, immediately addressed to him a copy of anonymous verses, to the following purport:

TO DR. GOLDSMITH;

ON SEEING HIS NAME IN THE LIST OF MUMMERS AT THE LATE
MASQUERADE.

"How widely different, Goldsmith, are the ways
    Of Doctors now, and those of ancient days!
Theirs taught the truth in academic shades,
    Ours in lewd hops and midnight masquerades.
So changed the times! say, philosophic sage,
    Whose genius suits so well this tasteful age,
Is the Pantheon, late a sink obscene,
    Become the fountain of chaste Hippocrene?
Or do thy moral numbers quaintly flow,
    Inspired by th' *Aganippe*[1] of Soho?

    [1] Like Hippocrene, a fountain near Mount Helicon, sacred to the muses.
Soho is a district of London.

Do wisdom's sons gorge cates and vermicelli,
Like beastly Bickerstaffe or bothering Kelly?
Or art thou tired of th' undeserved applause,
Bestowed on bards affecting Virtue's cause?
Is this the good that makes the humble vain?
The good philosophy should not disdain.
If so, let pride dissemble all it can,
A modern sage is still much less than man.''

Goldsmith was keenly sensitive to attacks of the kind,
and meeting Kenrick at the Chapter Coffee-House, called
him to sharp account for taking such liberty with his name,
and calling his morals in question, merely on account of his
being seen at a place of general resort and amusement.   Kenrick shuffled and sneaked, protesting that he meant nothing
derogatory to his private character.   Goldsmith let him know,
however, that he was aware of his having more than once
indulged in attacks of this dastard kind, and intimated that
another such outrage would be followed by personal chastisement.

Kenrick, having played the craven in his presence, avenged
himself as soon as he was gone by complaining of his having
made a wanton attack upon him, and by making coarse comments upon his writings, conversation, and person.

The scurrilous satire of Kenrick, however unmerited, may
have checked Goldsmith's taste for masquerades.   Sir Joshua
Reynolds, calling on the poet one morning, found him walking about his room in somewhat of a reverie, kicking a bundle
of clothes before him like a football.   It proved to be an
expensive masquerade dress, which he said he had been fool
enough to purchase, and as there was no other way of getting
the worth of his money, he was trying to take it out in exercise.

CHAPTER XXXVI

INVITATION TO CHRISTMAS—THE SPRING-VELVET COAT—THE HAY-
MAKING WIG—THE MISCHANCES OF LOO—THE FAIR CULPRIT
—A DANCE WITH THE JESSAMY BRIDE.

From the feverish dissipations of town, Goldsmith is summoned to partake of the genial dissipations of the country.
In the month of December, a letter from Mrs. Bunbury invites
him down to Barton, to pass the Christmas holidays. The
letter is written in the usual playful vein which marks his
intercourse with this charming family. He is to come in his
"smart spring-velvet coat," to bring a new wig to dance with
the haymakers in, and above all to follow the advice of herself
and her sister, (the Jessamy Bride,) in playing loo. This
letter, which plays so archly, yet kindly, with some of poor
Goldsmith's peculiarities, and bespeaks such real ladylike
regard for him, requires a word or two of annotation. The
spring-velvet suit alluded to appears to have been a gallant
adornment, (somewhat in the style of the famous bloom-
colored coat,) in which Goldsmith had figured in the preceding month of May—the season of blossoms: for, on the 21st
of that month, we find the following entry in the chronicle of
Mr. William Filby, tailor: *To your blue velvet suit*, £21 10s.
9d. Also, about the same time, a suit of livery and a crimson
collar for the serving-man. Again we hold the Jessamy
Bride responsible for this gorgeous splendor of wardrobe.

The new wig no doubt is a bag-wig and solitaire, still
highly the mode, and in which Goldsmith is represented as
figuring when in full dress equipped with his sword.

As to the dancing with the haymakers, we presume it

334

alludes to some gambol of the poet, in the course of his former visit to Barton; when he ranged the fields and lawns a chartered libertine, and tumbled into the fishponds.

As to the suggestions about loo, they are in sportive allusion to the Doctor's mode of playing that game in their merry evening parties; affecting the desperate gambler and easy dupe; running counter to all rule; making extravagant ventures; reproaching all others with cowardice; dashing at all hazards at the pool, and getting himself completely loo'd, to the great amusement of the company. The drift of the fair sisters' advice was most probably to tempt him on, and then leave him in the lurch.

With these comments we subjoin Goldsmith's reply to Mrs. Bunbury, a fine piece of off-hand, humorous writing, which has but in late years been given to the public, and which throws a familiar light on the social circle at Barton:

"MADAM,—I read your letter with all that allowance which critical candor could require, but after all find so much to object to, and so much to raise my indignation, that I cannot help giving it a serious answer.—I am not so ignorant, madam, as not to see there are many sarcasms contained in it, and solecisms also. (Solecism is a word that comes from the town of Soleis in Attica, among the Greeks, built by Solon, and applied as we use the word Kidderminster for curtains from a town also of that name;—but this is learning you have no taste for!)—I say, madam, that there are many sarcasms in it, and solecisms also. But not to seem an ill-natured critic, I'll take leave to quote your own words, and give you my remarks upon them as they occur. You begin as follows:

" 'I hope, my good Doctor, you soon will be here,
    And your spring-velvet coat very smart will appear,
    To open our ball the first day of the year.'

"Pray, madam, where did you ever find the epithet 'good,' applied to the title of doctor? Had you called me 'learned doctor,' or 'grave doctor,' or 'noble doctor,' it might be allowable, because they belong to the profession. But, not to cavil at trifles, you talk of my 'spring-velvet coat,' and advise me to wear it the first day in the year, that is, in the middle of winter!—a spring-velvet coat in the middle of winter!!! That would be a solecism indeed! and yet to increase the inconsistency, in another part of your letter you call me a beau. Now, on one side or other, you must be wrong. If I am a beau, I can never think of wearing a spring-velvet in winter; and if I am not a beau, why then, that explains itself. But let me go on to your two next strange lines:—

> " 'And bring with you a wig, that is modish and gay,
> To dance with the girls that are makers of hay.'

"The absurdity of making hay at Christmas you yourself seem sensible of: you say your sister will laugh; and so indeed she well may! The Latins have an expression for a contemptuous kind of laughter, 'naso contemnere adunco;' that is, to laugh with a crooked nose. She may laugh at you in the manner of the ancients if she thinks fit. But now I come to the most extraordinary of all extraordinary propositions,—which is, to take your and your sister's advice in playing at loo. The presumption of the offer raises my indignation beyond the bounds of prose; it inspires me at once with verse and resentment. I take advice! and from whom? You shall hear.

> "First, let me suppose, what may shortly be true,
> The company set, and the word to be Loo:
> All smirking, and pleasant, and big with adventure,
> And ogling the stake which is fix'd in the centre.

Round and round go the cards, while I inwardly damn
At never once finding a visit from Pam.[1]
I lay down my stake, apparently cool,
While the harpies about me all pocket the pool.
I fret in my gizzard, yet, cautious and sly,
I wish all my friends may be bolder than I:
Yet still they sit snug, not a creature will aim
By losing their money to venture at fame.
'Tis in vain that at niggardly caution I scold,
'Tis in vain that I flatter the brave and the bold:
All play their own way, and they think me an ass,   .
'What does Mrs. Bunbury?' . . 'I, Sir? I pass.'
'Pray what does Miss Horneck? take courage, come do.'
'Who, I?—let me see, sir, why I must pass too.'
Mr. Bunbury frets, and I fret like the devil,
To see them so cowardly, lucky, and civil.
Yet still I sit snug, and continue to sigh on,
Till, made by my losses as bold as a lion,
I venture at all, while my avarice regards
The whole pool as my own. . . 'Come, give me five cards.'
'Well done!' cry the ladies; 'ah, Doctor, that's good!
The pool's very rich, . . ah! the Doctor is loo'd!'
Thus foil'd in my courage, on all sides perplext,
I ask for advice from the lady that's next:
'Pray, ma'am, be so good as to give your advice;
Don't you think the best way is to venture for't twice?'
'I advise,' cries the lady, 'to try it, I own. . .
Ah! the Doctor is loo'd! Come, Doctor, put down.'
Thus, playing, and playing, I still grow more eager,
And so bold, and so bold, I'm at last a bold beggar.
Now, ladies, I ask, if law-matters you're skill'd in,
Whether crimes such as yours should not come before
      Fielding:[2]

---

[1] Pam is the name of the highest card in the game of Loo; Pope in the *Rape of the Lock*, Canto III, l. 61 mentions the game of Loo:

> "Even mighty Pam that Kings and Queens overthrew
> And mow'd down armies in the fights of Loo,
> Sad chance of war! now destitute of aid,
> Falls undistinguish'd by the victor spade.

[2] Henry Fielding, the novelist, was appointed justice of the peace for the district of Westminster in London in 1748.

For giving advice that is not worth a straw,
May well be call'd picking of pockets in law;
And picking of pockets, with which I now charge ye,
Is, by quinto Elizabeth, Death without Clergy.[1]
What justice, when both to the Old Bailey brought!
By the gods, I'll enjoy it, tho' 'tis but in thought!
Both are placed at the bar, with all proper decorum,
With bunches of fennel, and nosegays before 'em;
Both cover their faces with mobs and all that,
But the judge bids them, angrily, take off their hat.
When uncover'd a buzz of inquiry runs round,
'Pray what are their crimes?' . . 'They've been pilfering
      found.'
'But, pray, who have they pilfer'd?' . . 'A doctor, I
      hear.'
'*What, yon solemn-faced, odd-looking man that stands
      near?*'
'The same.' . . 'What a pity! how does it surprise one,
Two handsomer culprits I never set eyes on!'
Then their friends all come round me with cringing and
      leering,
To melt me to pity, and soften my swearing.
First Sir Charles advances with phrases well-strung,
'Consider, dear Doctor, the girls are but young.'
'The younger the worse,' I return him again,
'It shows that their habits are all dyed in grain.'
'But then they're so handsome, one's bosom it grieves.'
'What signifies *handsome*, when people are thieves?'
'But where is your justice? their cases are hard.'
'What signifies *justice?* I want the *reward.*'

" 'There's the parish of Edmonton offers forty pounds;
there's the parish of St. Leonard Shoreditch offers forty
pounds; there's the parish of Tyburn, from the Hog-in-the-

---

[1] This legal learning is of course playful; "quinto Elizabeth" would
mean a decree of the fifth year of Elizabeth's reign. In old English law
ecclesiastics, and later all persons who could read, were granted special
privileges, notably that of being tried for criminal offences in ecclesiastical
courts instead of secular courts; this was called the privilege or benefit of
clergy. Note the meaning of English *clerk* as related to *clergy.*

pound to St. Giles's watch-house, offers forty pounds,—I shall have all that if I convict them!'—

> " 'But consider their case, . . it may yet be your own!
> And see how they kneel! Is your heart made of stone?'
> This moves: . . so at last I agree to relent,
> For ten pounds in hand, and ten pounds to be spent.'

"I challenge you all to answer this: I tell you, you cannot. It cuts deep. But now for the rest of the letter: and next— but I want room—so I believe I shall battle the rest out at Barton some day next week.—I don't value you all!   O. G."

We regret that we have no record of this Christmas visit to Barton; that the poet had no Boswell to follow at his heels, and take note of all his sayings and doings. We can only picture him in our minds, casting off all care; enacting the lord of misrule; presiding at the Christmas revels; providing all kinds of merriment; keeping the card-table in an uproar, and finally opening the ball on the first day of the year in his spring-velvet suit, with the Jessamy Bride for a partner.

CHAPTER XXXVII

The gay life depicted in the two last chapters, while it
kept Goldsmith in a state of continual excitement, aggravated the malady which was impairing his constitution; yet
his increasing perplexities in money-matters drove him to
the dissipation of society as a relief from solitary care. The
delays of the theatre added to those perplexities. He had
long since finished his new comedy, yet the year 1772 passed
away without his being able to get it on the stage. No one,
uninitiated in the interior of a theatre, that little world of
traps and trickery, can have any idea of the obstacles and
perplexities multiplied in the way of the most eminent and
successful author by the mismanagement of managers, the
jealousies and intrigues of rival authors, and the fantastic
and impertinent caprices of actors. A long and baffling
negotiation was carried on between Goldsmith and Colman,
the manager of Covent Garden; who retained the play in his
hands until the middle of January, (1773,) without coming
to a decision. The theatrical season was rapidly passing
away, and Goldsmith's pecuniary difficulties were augment-
ing and pressing on him. We may judge of his anxiety by
the following letter:—

" To George Colman, Esq.
"DEAR SIR,—

"I entreat you'll relieve me from that state of suspense in which I have been kept for a long time. Whatever objections you have made or shall make to my play, I will endeavor to remove and not argue about them. To bring in any new judges either of its merits or faults I can never submit to. Upon a former occasion, when my other play was before Mr. Garrick, he offered to bring me before Mr. Whitehead's tribunal, but I refused the proposal with indignation: I hope I shall not experience as harsh treatment from you as from him. I have, as you know, a large sum of money to make up shortly; by accepting my play, I can readily satisfy my creditor that way; at any rate, I must look about to some certainty to be prepared. For God's sake take the play, and let us make the best of it, and let me have the same measure, at least, which you have given as bad plays as mine.

"I am, your friend and servant,
"OLIVER GOLDSMITH."

Colman returned the manuscript with the blank sides of the leaves scored with disparaging comments, and suggested alterations, but with the intimation that the faith of the theatre should be kept, and the play acted notwithstanding. Goldsmith submitted the criticisms to some of his friends, who pronounced them trivial, unfair, and contemptible, and intimated that Colman, being a dramatic writer himself, might be actuated by jealousy. The play was then sent, with Colman's comments written on it, to Garrick; but he had scarce sent it when Johnson interfered, represented the evil that might result from an apparent rejection of it by Covent Garden, and undertook to go forthwith to Colman,

and have a talk with him on the subject. Goldsmith, therefore, penned the following note to Garrick:—

"DEAR SIR,—
    "I ask many pardons for the trouble I gave you yesterday.
Upon more mature deliberation, and the advice of a sensible
friend, I began to think it indelicate in me to throw upon you
the odium of confirming Mr. Colman's sentence. I therefore
request you will send my play back by my servant; for having been assured of having it acted at the other house, though
I confess yours in every respect more to my wish, yet it would
be folly in me to forego an advantage which lies in my power
of appealing from Mr. Colman's opinion to the judgment of
the town. I entreat, if not too late, you will keep this affair
a secret for some time.
        "I am, dear sir, your very humble servant,
                            "OLIVER GOLDSMITH."

    The negotiation of Johnson with the manager of Covent
Garden was effective. "Colman," he says, "was prevailed
on at last, by much solicitation, nay, a kind of force," to
bring forward the comedy. Still the manager was ungenerous, or at least indiscreet enough to express his opinion that
it would not reach a second representation. The plot, he
said, was bad, and the interest not sustained; "it dwindled,
and dwindled, and at last went out like the snuff of a candle."
The effect of his croaking was soon apparent within the walls
of the theatre. Two of the most popular actors, Woodward
and Gentleman Smith, to whom the parts of Tony Lumpkin
and Young Marlow were assigned, refused to act them; one
of them alleging, in excuse, the evil predictions of the manager.
Goldsmith was advised to postpone the performance of his
play until he could get these important parts well supplied.

"No," said he, "I would sooner that my play were damned by bad players than merely saved by good acting."

Quick was substituted for Woodward in Tony Lumpkin, and Lee Lewis, the harlequin of the theatre, for Gentleman Smith in Young Marlow; and both did justice to their parts.

Great interest was taken by Goldsmith's friends in the success of his piece. The rehearsals were attended by Johnson, Cradock, Murphy, Reynolds, and his sister, and the whole Horneck connection, including, of course, the *Jessamy Bride*, whose presence may have contributed to flutter the anxious heart of the author. The rehearsals went off with great applause; but that Colman attributed to the partiality of friends. He continued to croak, and refused to risk any expense in new scenery or dresses on a play which he was sure would prove a failure.

The time was at hand for the first representation, and as yet the comedy was without a title. "We are all in labor for a name for Goldy's play," said Johnson, who, as usual, took a kind of fatherly protecting interest in poor Goldsmith's affairs. "The Old House a New Inn" was thought of for a time, but still did not please. Sir Joshua Reynolds proposed "The Belle's Strategem," an elegant title, but not considered applicable, the perplexities of the comedy being produced by the mistakes of the hero, not the stratagem of the heroine. The name was afterwards adopted by Mrs. Cowley for one of her comedies. "The Mistakes of a Night" was the title at length fixed upon, to which Goldsmith prefixed the words, "She Stoops to Conquer."

The evil bodings of Colman still continued: they were even communicated in the box-office to the servant of the Duke of Gloucester, who was sent to engage a box. Never did the play of a popular writer struggle into existence through more difficulties.

In the meantime Foote's "Primitive Puppet-Show," entitled the "Handsome Housemaid, or Piety on Pattens," had
been brought out at the Haymarket on the 15th of February.
All the world, fashionable and unfashionable, had crowded
to the theatre. The street was thronged with equipages,—
the doors were stormed by the mob. The burlesque was
completely successful, and sentimental comedy received its
quietus. Even Garrick, who had recently befriended it, now
gave it a kick, as he saw it going down-hill, and sent Goldsmith a humorous prologue to help his comedy of the opposite
school. Garrick and Goldsmith, however, were now on very
cordial terms, to which the social meetings in the circle of the
Hornecks and Bunburys may have contributed.

On the 15th of March the new comedy was to be performed. Those who had stood up for its merits, and been
irritated and disgusted by the treatment it had received from
the manager, determined to muster their forces, and aid in
giving it a good launch upon the town. The particulars of
this confederation, and of its triumphant success, are amus-
ingly told by Cumberland in his memoirs.

"We were not over-sanguine of success, but perfectly
determined to struggle hard for our author. We accordingly
assembled our strength at the Shakspeare Tavern, in a considerable body, for an early dinner, where Samuel Johnson
took the chair at the head of a long table, and was the life
and soul of the corps; the poet took post silently by his side,
with the Burkes, Sir Joshua Reynolds, Fitzherbert, Caleb
Whitefoord, and a phalanx of North British, predetermined
applauders, under the banner of Major Mills,—all good men
and true. Our illustrious president was in inimitable glee;
and poor Goldsmith that day took all his raillery as patiently
and complacently as my friend Boswell would have done any
day or every day of his life. In the meantime we did not

forget our duty; and though we had a better comedy going, in which Johnson was chief actor, we betook ourselves in good time to our separate and allotted posts, and waited the awful drawing up of the curtain. As our stations were pre-concerted, so were our signals for plaudits arranged and determined upon in a manner that gave every one his cue where to look for them, and how to follow them up.

"We had among us a very worthy and efficient member, long since lost to his friends and the world at large, Adam Drummond, of amiable memory, who was gifted by nature with the most sonorous, and at the same time the most contagious laugh that ever echoed from the human lungs. The neighing of the horse of the son of Hystaspes[1] was a whisper to it; the whole thunder of the theatre could not drown it. This kind and ingenious friend fairly forewarned us that he knew no more when to give his fire than the cannon did that was planted on a battery. He desired, therefore, to have a flapper at his elbow, and I had the honor to be deputed to that office. I planted him in an upper box, pretty nearly over the stage, in full view of the pit and galleries, and perfectly well situated to give the echo all its play through the hollows and recesses of the theatre. The success of our manœuvre was complete. All eyes were upon Johnson, who sat in a front row of a side-box; and when he laughed, everybody thought themselves warranted to roar. In the meantime, my friend followed signals with a rattle so irresistibly comic, that, when he had repeated it several times, the attention of the spectators was so engrossed by his person and performances, that the progress of the play seemed

---

[1] A satrap of Persia who lived about 550 B.C. He was the father of Darius I. Darius and others, according to Herodotus, conspired to dethrone a certain ruler, and agreed that he of the conspirators whose horse should first neigh at the rising of the sun, should possess the kingdom. Through the contrivance of his groom, Darius managed to win the wager.

likely to become a secondary object, and I found it prudent to insinuate to him that he might halt his music without any prejudice to the author; but alas! it was now too late to rein him in; he had laughed upon my signal where he found no joke, and now, unluckily, he fancied that he found a joke in almost everything that was said; so that nothing in nature could be more mal-apropos than some of his bursts every now and then were. These were dangerous moments, for the pit began to take umbrage; but we carried our point through, and triumphed not only over Colman's judgment, but our own."

Much of this statement has been condemned as exaggerated or discolored. Cumberland's memoirs have generally been characterized as partaking of romance, and in the present instance he had particular motives for tampering with the truth. He was a dramatic writer himself, jealous of the success of a rival, and anxious to have it attributed to the private management of friends. According to various accounts, public and private, such management was unnecessary, for the piece was "received throughout with the greatest acclamations."

Goldsmith, in the present instance, had not dared, as on a former occasion, to be present at the first performance. He had been so overcome by his apprehensions that, at the preparatory dinner, he could hardly utter a word, and was so choked that he could not swallow a mouthful. When his friends trooped to the theatre, he stole away to St. James's Park: there he was found by a friend, between seven and eight o'clock, wandering up and down the Mall like a troubled spirit. With difficulty he was persuaded to go to the theatre, where his presence might be important should any alteration be necessary. He arrived at the opening of the fifth act, and made his way behind the scenes. Just as he entered there

was a slight hiss at the improbability of Tony Lumpkin's
trick on his mother, in persuading her she was forty miles
off, on Crackskull Common, though she had been trundled
about on her own grounds. "What's that? what's that!"
cried Goldsmith to the manager, in great agitation. "Pshaw!
Doctor," replied Colman, sarcastically, "don't be frightened
at a squib, when we've been sitting these two hours on a barrel
of gunpowder!" Though of a most forgiving nature, Goldsmith did not easily forget this ungracious and ill-timed
sally.

If Colman was indeed actuated by the paltry motives
ascribed to him in his treatment of this play, he was most
amply punished by its success, and by the taunts, epigrams,
and censures levelled at him through the press, in which his
false prophecies were jeered at, his critical judgment called
in question, and he was openly taxed with literary jealousy.
So galling and unremitting was the fire, that he at length
wrote to Goldsmith, entreating him "to take him off the rack
of the newspapers"; in the meantime, to escape the laugh
that was raised about him in the theatrical world of London,
he took refuge in Bath during the triumphant career of the
comedy.

The following is one of the many squibs which assailed
the ears of the manager:—

TO GEORGE COLMAN, ESQ.,

ON THE SUCCESS OF DR. GOLDSMITH'S NEW COMEDY

"Come, Coley, doff those mourning weeds,
    Nor thus with jokes be flamm'd;
Tho' Goldsmith's present play succeeds,
    His next may still be damn'd.

"As this has 'scaped without a fall.
    To sink his next prepare;

New actors hire from Wapping Wall,[1]
And dresses from Rag Fair.

"For scenes let tatter'd blankets fly,
The prologue Kelly write;
Then swear again the piece must die
Before the author's night.

"Should these tricks fail, the lucky elf
To bring to lasting shame,
E'en write *the best you can yourself*,
And print it in *his name*."

The solitary hiss, which had startled Goldsmith, was ascribed by some of the newspaper scribblers to Cumberland himself, who was "manifestly miserable" at the delight of the audience, or to Ossian Macpherson, who was hostile to the whole Johnson clique, or to Goldsmith's dramatic rival, Kelly. The following is one of the epigrams which appeared:—

"At Dr. Goldsmith's merry play,
All the spectators laugh, they say;
The assertion, sir, I must deny,
For Cumberland and Kelly cry.
Ride si sapis."[2]

Another, addressed to Goldsmith, alludes to Kelly's early apprenticeship to stay-making:—

" 'If Kelly finds fault with the *shape* of your muse,
And thinks that too loosely it plays,
He surely, dear Doctor, will never refuse
To make it a new *Pair of Stays!*"

Cradock had returned to the country before the production of the play; the following letter, written just after the performance, gives an additional picture of the thorns which beset an author in the path of theatrical literature:—

---

[1] A district along the Thames, the haunt of sailors and rough characters generally.

[2] Laugh if you are wise.

"My Dear Sir,—

"The play has met with a success much beyond your expectations or mine. I thank you sincerely for your epilogue, which, however, could not be used, but with your permission shall be printed. The story in short is this. Murphy sent me rather the outline of an epilogue than an epilogue, which was to be sung by Miss Catley, and which she approved; Mrs. Bulkley, hearing this, insisted on throwing up her part" (*Miss Hardcastle*) "unless, according to the custom of the theatre, she were permitted to speak the epilogue. In this embarrassment I thought of making a quarrelling epilogue between Catley and her, debating *who* should speak the epilogue; but then Miss Catley refused after I had taken the trouble of drawing it out. I was then at a loss indeed; an epilogue was to be made, and for none but Mrs. Bulkley. I made one, and Colman thought it too bad to be spoken; I was obliged, therefore, to try a fourth time, and I made a very mawkish thing, as you'll shortly see. Such is the history of my stage adventures, and which I have at last done with I cannot help saying that I am very sick of the stage; and though I believe I shall get three tolerable benefits, yet I shall, on the whole, be a loser, even in a pecuniary light; my ease and comfort I certainly lost while it was in agitation.

"I am, my dear Cradock, your obliged and obedient servant,   OLIVER GOLDSMITH.

"P. S.—Present my most humble respects to Mrs. Cradock."

Johnson, who had taken such a conspicuous part in promoting the interest of poor "Goldy," was triumphant at the success of the piece. "I know of no comedy for many years," said he, "that has so much exhilarated an audience; that has answered so much the great end of comedy—making an audience merry."

Goldsmith was happy, also, in gleaning applause from less authoritative sources. Northcote, the painter, then a youthful pupil of Sir Joshua Reynolds, and Ralph, Sir Joshua's confidential man, had taken their stations in the gallery to lead the applause in that quarter. Goldsmith asked Northcote's opinion of the play. The youth modestly declared he could not presume to judge on such matters. "Did it make you laugh?" "Oh, exceedingly!" "That is all I require," replied Goldsmith; and rewarded him for his criticism by box-tickets for his first benefit-night.

The comedy was immediately put to press, and dedicated to Johnson in the following grateful and affectionate terms:—

"In inscribing this slight performance to you, I do not mean so much to compliment you as myself. It may do me some honor to inform the public that I have lived many years in intimacy with you. It may serve the interests of mankind also to inform them, that the greatest wit may be found in a character, without impairing the most unaffected piety."

The copyright was transferred to Mr. Newbery, according to agreement, whose profits on the sale of the work far exceeded the debts for which the author in his perplexities had preëngaged it. The sum which accrued to Goldsmith from his benefit-nights afforded but a slight palliation of his pecuniary difficulties. His friends, while they exulted in his success, little knew of his continually increasing embarrassments, and of the anxiety of mind which kept tasking his pen while it impaired the ease and freedom of spirit necessary to felicitous composition.

CHAPTER XXXVIII

The triumphant success of "She Stoops to Conquer" brought forth, of course, those carpings and cavillings of underling scribblers, which are the thorns and briers in the path of successful authors. Goldsmith, though easily nettled by attacks of the kind, was at present too well satisfied with the reception of his comedy to heed them; but the following anonymous letter, which appeared in a public paper, was not to be taken with equal equanimity:—

(For the London Packet)

"TO DR. GOLDSMITH.

"Vous vous noyez par vanité[1]

"SIR,—The happy knack which you have learned of puffing your own compositions provokes me to come forth. You have not been the editor of newspapers and magazines not to discover the trick of literary *humbug;* but the gauze is so thin that the very foolish part of the world see through it, and discover the doctor's monkey-face and cloven foot. Your poetic vanity is as unpardonable as your personal. Would man believe it, and will woman bear it, to be told that for hours the Great Goldsmith will stand surveying his grotesque orang-outang's figure in a pier-glass? Was but the lovely H—k as much enamored, you would not sigh, my gentle swain, in vain. But your vanity is preposterous. How will this same bard of Bedlam ring the changes in the praise of

---

[1] Your vanity will be the end of you.

Goldy! But what has he to be either proud or vain of? 'The Traveller' is a flimsy poem, built upon false principles—principles diametrically opposite to liberty. What is 'The Good-natured Man' but a poor, water-gruel dramatic dose? What is 'The Deserted Village' but a pretty poem of easy numbers, without fancy, dignity, genius, or fire? And, pray, what may be the last *speaking pantomime*, so praised by the Doctor himself, but an incoherent piece of stuff, the figure of a woman with a fish's tail, without plot, incident, or intrigue? We are made to laugh at stale, dull jokes, wherein we mistake pleasantry for wit, and grimace for humor; wherein every scene is unnatural and inconsistent with the rules, the laws of nature and of the drama; viz.: two gentlemen come to a man of fortune's house, eat, drink, &c., and take it for an inn. The one is intended as a lover for the daughter: he talks with her for some hours; and, when he sees her again in a different dress, he treats her as a bar-girl, and swears she squinted. He abuses the master of the house, and threatens to kick him out of his own doors. The squire whom we are told is to be a fool, proves to be the most sensible being of the piece; and he makes out a whole act by bidding his mother lie close behind a bush, persuading her that his father, her own husband, is a highwayman, and that he has come to cut their throats; and, to give his cousin ,an opportunity to go off, he drives his mother over hedges, ditches, and through ponds. There is not, sweet, sucking Johnson, a natural stroke in the whole play but the young fellow's giving the stolen jewels to the mother, supposing her to be the landlady. That Mr. Colman did no justice to this piece, I honestly allow; that he told all his friends it would be damned, I positively aver; and, from such ungenerous insinuations, without a dramatic merit, it rose to public notice, and it is now the ton to go and see it, though I never

saw a person that either liked it or approved it, any more
than the absurd plot of Home's tragedy of 'Alonzo.' Mr.
Goldsmith, correct your arrogance, reduce your vanity, and
endeavor to believe, as a man, you are of the plainest sort,—
and as an author, but a mortal piece of mediocrity.

> "Brise le miroir infidèle
> Qui vous cache la vérité.[1]

"TOM TICKLE."

It would be difficult to devise a letter more calculated to
wound the peculiar sensibilities of Goldsmith. The attacks
upon him as an author, though annoying enough, he could
have tolerated; but then the allusion to his "grotesque" person; to his studious attempts to adorn it; and, above all, to
his being an unsuccessful admirer of the lovely H—k (the
Jessamy Bride), struck rudely upon the most sensitive part
of his highly sensitive nature. The paragraph, it is said,
was first pointed out to him by an officious friend, an Irishman, who told him he was bound in honor to resent it; but
he needed no such prompting. He was in a high state of
excitement and indignation, and, accompanied by his friend,
who is said to have been a Captain Higgins, of the marines,
he repaired to Paternoster Row, to the shop of Evans, the
publisher, whom he supposed to be the editor of the paper.
Evans was summoned by his shopman from an adjoining
room. Goldsmith announced his name. "I have called,"
added he, " in consequence of a scurrilous attack made upon .
me, and an unwarrantable liberty taken with the name of a
young lady. As for myself, I care little; but her name must
not be sported with."
Evans professed utter ignorance of the matter, and said
he would speak to the editor. He stooped to examine a file

---

[1] Shatter the faithless mirror that conceals the truth from you.

of the paper, in search of the offensive article; whereupon Goldsmith's friend gave him a signal, that now was a favorable moment for the exercise of his cane. The hint was taken as quick as given, and the cane was vigorously applied to the back of the stooping publisher. The latter rallied in an instant, and, being a stout, high-blooded Welshman, returned the blows with interest. A lamp hanging overhead was broken, and sent down a shower of oil upon the combatants; but the battle raged with unceasing fury. The shopman ran off for a constable; but Dr. Kenrick, who happened to be in the adjacent room, sallied forth, interfered between the combatants, and put an end to the affray. He conducted Goldsmith to a coach, in exceedingly battered and tattered plight, and accompanied him home, soothing him with much mock commiseration, though he was generally suspected, and on good grounds, to be the author of the libel.

Evans immediately instituted a suit against Goldsmith for an assault, but was ultimately prevailed upon to compromise the matter, the poet contributing fifty pounds to the Welsh charity.

Newspapers made themselves, as may well be supposed, exceedingly merry with the combat. Some censured him severely for invading the sanctity of a man's own house; others accused him of having, in his former capacity of editor of a magazine, been guilty of the very offences that he now resented in others. This drew from him the following vindication:—

" To the Public.

"Lest it should be supposed that I have been willing to correct in others an abuse of which I have been guilty myself, I beg leave to declare, that, in all my life, I never wrote or dictated a single paragraph, letter, or essay in a newspaper, except a few moral essays under the character of a Chinese, about ten years ago, in the 'Ledger,' and a letter, to which I signed my name, in the 'St. James's Chronicle.' If the liberty of the press, therefore, has been abused, I have had no hand in it.

"I have always considered the press as the protector of our freedom, as a watchful guardian, capable of uniting the weak against the encroachments of power. What concerns the public most properly admits of a public discussion. But, of late, the press has turned from defending public interests to making inroads upon private life; from combating the strong to overwhelming the feeble. No condition is now too obscure for its abuse, and the protector has become the tyrant of the people. In this manner the freedom of the press is beginning to sow the seeds of its own dissolution; the great must oppose it from principle, and the weak from fear; till at last every rank of mankind shall be found to give up its benefits, content with security from insults.

"How to put a stop to this licentiousness, by which all are indiscriminately abused, and by which vice consequently escapes in the general censure, I am unable to tell; all I could wish is, that, as the law gives us no protection against the injury, so it should give calumniators no shelter after having provoked correction. The insults which we receive before the public, by being more open, are the more distressing; by treating them with silent contempt we do not pay a sufficient deference to the opinion of the world. By recurring to legal redress we too often expose the weakness of the law, which only serves to increase our mortification by failing to relieve us. In short, every man should singly consider himself as the guardian of the liberty of the press, and, as far as his influence can extend, should endeavor to prevent its licentiousness becoming at last the grave of its freedom.

"OLIVER GOLDSMITH."

Boswell, who had just arrived in town, met with this article in a newspaper which he found at Dr. Johnson's. The Doctor was from home at the time, and Bozzy and Mrs. Williams,[1] in a critical conference over the letter, determined from the style that it must have been written by tbe lexicographer himself. The latter on his return soon undeceived them. "Sir," said he to Boswell, "Goldsmith would no more have asked me to write such a thing as that for him than he would have asked me to feed him with a spoon, or do anything else that denoted his imbecility. Sir, had he shown it to any one friend, he would not have been allowed to publish it. He has, indeed, done it very well; but it is a foolish thing well done. I suppose he has been so much elated with the success of his new comedy, that he has thought everything that concerned him must be of importance to the public."

---

[1] Mrs. Williams was a pensioner of Dr. Johnson's and a member of his household.

CHAPTER XXXIX

The return of Boswell to town to his task of noting down
the conversations of Johnson, enables us to glean from his
journal some scanty notices of Goldsmith. It was now
Holy-Week, a time during which Johnson was particularly
solemn in his manner and strict in his devotions. Boswell,
who was the imitator of the great moralist in everything,
assumed, of course, an extra devoutness on the present
occasion. "He had an odd mock solemnity of tone and
manner," said Miss Burney,[1] (afterwards Madame
D'Arblay,) "which he had acquired from constantly thinking, and imitating Dr. Johnson." It would seem that he
undertook to deal out some second-hand homilies, *à la
Johnson,* for the edification of Goldsmith during Holy-Week.
The poet, whatever might be his religious feeling, had no
disposition to be schooled by so shallow an apostle. "Sir,"
said he in reply, "as I take my shoes from the shoemaker,
and my coat from the tailor, so I take my religion from the
priest."

Boswell treasured up the reply in his memory or his mem-
orandum-book. A few days afterwards, the 9th of April, he
kept Good Friday with Dr. Johnson, in orthodox style;
breakfasted with him on tea and cross-buns; went to church
with him morning and evening; fasted in the interval, and

---

[1] Frances Burney (1752-1840), author of *Evelina* and other novels.

read with him in the Greek Testament: then, in the piety of his heart, complained of the sore rebuff he had met with in the course of his religious exhortations to the poet, and lamented that the latter should indulge in "this loose way of talking." "Sir," replied Johnson, "Goldsmith knows nothing—he has made up his mind about nothing."

This reply seems to have gratified the lurking jealousy of Boswell, and he has recorded it in his journal. Johnson, however, with respect to Goldsmith, and indeed with respect to everybody else, blew hot as well as cold, according to the humor he was in. Boswell, who was astonished and piqued at the continually increasing celebrity of the poet, observed some time after to Johnson, in a tone of surprise, that Goldsmith had acquired more fame than all the officers of the last war who were not generals. "Why, sir," answered Johnson, his old feeling of good-will working uppermost, "you will find ten thousand fit to do what they did, before you find one to do what Goldsmith has done. You must consider that a thing is valued according to its rarity. A pebble that paves the street is in itself more useful than the diamond upon a lady's finger."

On the 13th of April we find Goldsmith and Johnson at the table of old General Oglethorpe, discussing the question of the degeneracy of the human race. Goldsmith asserts the fact, and attributes it to the influence of luxury. Johnson denies the fact, and observes, that, even admitting it, luxury could not be the cause. It reached but a small proportion of the human race. Soldiers, on sixpence a day, could not indulge in luxuries; the poor and laboring classes, forming the great mass of mankind, were out of its sphere. Wherever it could reach them, it strengthened them and rendered them prolific. The conversation was not of particular force or point as reported by Boswell; the dinner-party was a very small one, in which there was no provocation to intellectual display.

After dinner they took tea with the ladies, where we find poor Goldsmith happy and at home, singing Tony Lumpkin's song of the "Three Jolly Pigeons," and another, called the "Humors of Ballamaguery," to a very pretty Irish tune. It was to have been introduced in "She Stoops to Conquer," but was left out, as the actress who played the heroine could not sing.

It was in these genial moments that the sunshine of Goldsmith's nature would break out, and he would say and do a thousand whimsical and agreeable things that made him the life of the strictly social circle. Johnson, with whom conversation was everything, used to judge Goldsmith too much by his own colloquial standard, and undervalue him for being less provided than himself with acquired facts, the ammunition of the tongue and often the mere lumber of the memory; others, however, valued him for the native felicity of his thoughts, however carelessly expressed, and for certain goodfellow qualities, less calculated to dazzle than to endear. "It is amazing," said Johnson one day, after he himself had been talking like an oracle; "it is amazing how little Goldsmith knows; he seldom comes where he is not more ignorant than any one else." "Yet," replied Sir Joshua Reynolds, with affectionate promptness, "there is no man whose company is more *liked*."

Two or three days after the dinner at General Oglethorpe's, Goldsmith met Johnson again at the table of General Paoli, the hero of Corsica.[1] Martinelli, of Florence,

---

[1] Pasquale di Paoli (1726-1807), a celebrated Corsican general. He defended the cause of Corsica against the French, but after his defeat at the battle of Ponte Nuovo in 1769 he retired to England. In 1789 he was recalled from exile and given command over Corsica; in 1794 he transferred the sovereignty of the island to England. He died near London in 1807. Boswell toadied to Paoli much as he did to Johnson. See above, p. 327.

author of an Italian History of England, was among the
guests; as was Boswell, to whom we are indebted for
minutes of the conversation which took place. The question
was debated whether Martinelli should continue his history
down to that day. "To be sure he should," said Goldsmith.
"No, sir," cried Johnson, "it would give great offence. He
would have to tell of almost all the living great what they
did not wish told." Goldsmith.—"It may, perhaps, be
necessary for a native to be more cautious; but a foreigner,
who comes among us without prejudice, may be considered
as holding the place of a judge, and may speak his mind
freely." Johnson.—"Sir, a foreigner, when he sends a work
from the press, ought to be on his guard against catching the
error and mistaken enthusiasm of the people among whom
he happens to be." Goldsmith.—"Sir, he wants only to sell
his history, and to tell truth; one an honest, the other a
laudable motive." Johnson.—"Sir, they are both laudable
motives. It is laudable in a man to wish to live by his
labors; but he should write so as he may *live* by them, not
so as he may be knocked on the head. I would advise him
to be at Calais before he publishes his history of the present
age. A foreigner who attaches himself to a political party
in this country is in the worst state that can be imagined; he
is looked upon as a mere intermeddler. A native may do it
from interest." Boswell.—"Or principle." Goldsmith.—
"There are people who tell a hundred political lies every
day, and are not hurt by it. Surely, then, one may tell truth
with perfect safety." Johnson.—"Why, sir, in the first
place, he who tells a hundred lies has disarmed the force of
his lies. But, besides, a man had rather have a hundred
lies told of him than one truth which he does not wish to be
told." Goldsmith.—"For my part, I'd tell the truth, and
shame the devil." Johnson.—"Yes, sir, but the devil will

be angry. I wish to shame the devil as much as you do, but I should choose to be out of the reach of his claws." Goldsmith.—"His claws can do you no hurt where you have the shield of truth."

This last reply was one of Goldsmith's lucky hits, and closed the argument in his favor.

"We talked," writes Boswell, "of the King's coming to see Goldsmith's new play." "I wish he would," said Goldsmith, adding, however, with an affected indifference, "not that it would do me the least good." "Well, then," cried Johnson, laughing, "let us say it would do *him* good. No, sir, this affectation will not pass,—it is mighty idle. In such a state as ours, who would not wish to please the chief magistrate?"

"I *do* wish to please him," rejoined Goldsmith. "I remember a line in Dryden:—

"'And every poet is the monarch's friend;'

it ought to be reversed." "Nay," said Johnson, "there are finer lines in Dryden on this subject:

"'For colleges on bounteous kings depend,
  And never rebel was to arts a friend.'"

General Paoli observed that "successful rebels might be." "Happy rebellions," interjected Martinelli. "We have no such phrase," cried Goldsmith. "But have you not the thing?" asked Paoli. "Yes," replied Goldsmith, "all our *happy* revolutions. They have hurt our constitution, and *will* hurt it, till we mend it by another HAPPY REVOLUTION." This was a sturdy sally of Jacobitism, that quite surprised Boswell, but must have been relished by Johnson.

General Paoli mentioned a passage in the play, which had been construed into a compliment to a lady of distinction, whose marriage with the Duke of Cumberland had excited

the strong disapprobation of the King as a mesalliance.
Boswell, to draw Goldsmith out, pretended to think the
compliment unintentional. The poet smiled and hesitated.
The General came to his relief. "Monsieur Goldsmith,"
said he, "est comme la mer, qui jette des perles et beaucoup
d'autres belles choses, sans s'en appercevoir." (Mr. Goldsmith is like the sea, which casts forth pearls and many
other beautiful things without perceiving it.)

"Tres-bien dit, et tres-élégamment," (very well said, and
very elegantly,) exclaimed Goldsmith, delighted with so
beautiful a compliment from such a quarter.

Johnson spoke disparagingly of the learning of Mr.
Harris, of Salisbury, and doubted his being a good Grecian.
"He is what is much better," cried Goldsmith, with prompt
good-nature,—"he is a worthy, humane man." "Nay, sir,"
rejoined the logical Johnson, "that is not to the purpose of
our argument; that will prove that he can play upon the
fiddle as well as Giardini,[1] as that he is an eminent
Grecian." Goldsmith found he had got into a scrape, and
seized upon Giardini to help him out of it. "The greatest
musical performers," said he, dexterously turning the conversation, "have but small emoluments; Giardini, I am told,
does not get above seven hundred a year." "That is indeed
but little for a man to get," observed Johnson, "who does
best that which so many endeavor to do. There is nothing,
I think, in which the power of art is shown so much as in
playing on the fiddle. In all other things we can do something at first. Any man will forge a bar of iron, if you give
him a hammer; not so well as a smith, but tolerably. A
man will saw a piece of wood, and make a box, though a

---

[1] Felice Giardini (1716-1796), a celebrated violinist and composer. He
spent some years in London and was, for a time, one of the managers of the
King's Theatre.

clumsy one; but give him a fiddle and fiddlestick and he can do nothing."

This, upon the whole, though reported by the one-sided Boswell, is a tolerable specimen of the conversations of Goldsmith and Johnson; the former heedless, often illogical, always on the kind-hearted side of the question, and prone to redeem himself by lucky hits; the latter closely argumentative, studiously sententious, often profound, and sometimes laboriously prosaic.

They had an argument a few days later at Mr. Thrale's table, on the subject of suicide. "Do you think, sir," said Boswell, "that all who commit suicide are mad?" "Sir," replied Johnson, "they are not often universally disordered in their intellects, but one passion presses so upon them that they yield to it, and commit suicide, as a passionate man will stab another. I have often thought," added he, "that after a man has taken the resolution to kill himself, it is not courage in him to do anything, however desperate, because he has nothing to fear." "I don't see that," observed Goldsmith. "Nay, but, my dear sir," rejoined Johnson, "why should you not see what every one else does?" "It is," replied Goldsmith, "for fear of something that he has resolved to kill himself; and will not that timid disposition restrain him?" "It does not signify," pursued Johnson, "that the fear of something made him resolve; it is upon the state of his mind, after the resolution is taken, that I argue. Suppose a man, either from fear, or pride, or conscience, or whatever motive, has resolved to kill himself; when once the resolution is taken he has nothing to fear. He may then go and take the King of Prussia by the nose at the head of his army. He cannot fear the rack who is determined to kill himself." Boswell reports no more of the discussion, though Goldsmith might have continued it with advantage: for the very timid disposition, which through fear of something was impelling the man to commit suicide, might restrain him from an act involving the punishment of the rack, more terrible to him than death itself.

It is to be regretted in all these reports by Boswell, we have scarcely anything but the remarks of Johnson; it is only by accident that he now and then gives us the observations of others, when they are necessary to explain or set off those of his hero. "When in *that presence*," says Miss Burney, "he was unobservant, if not contemptuous of every one else. In truth, when he met with Dr. Johnson, he commonly forbore even answering anything that was said, or attending to anything that went forward, lest he should miss the smallest sound from that voice, to which he paid such exclusive, though merited homage. But the moment that voice burst forth, the attention which it excited on Mr. Boswell amounted almost to pain. His eyes goggled with eagerness; he leant his ear almost on the shoulder of the Doctor; and his mouth dropped open to catch every syllable that might be uttered; nay, he seemed not only to dread losing a word, but to be anxious not to miss a breathing, as if hoping from it latently, or mystically, some information."

On one occasion the Doctor detected Boswell, or Bozzy, as he called him, eavesdropping behind his chair, as he was conversing with Miss Burney at Mr. Thrale's table. "What are you doing there, sir?" cried he, turning round angrily, and clapping his hand upon his knee. "Go to the table, sir."

Boswell obeyed with an air of affright and submission, which raised a smile on every face. Scarce had he taken his seat, however, at a distance, than, impatient to get again at the side of Johnson, he rose and was running off in quest of something to show him, when the Doctor roared after him authoritatively, "What are you thinking of, sir? Why do

you get up before the cloth is removed? Come back to
your place, sir;"—and the obsequious spaniel did as he was
commanded.—"Running about in the middle of meals!"
muttered the Doctor, pursing his mouth at the same time to
restrain his rising risibility.

Boswell got another rebuff from Johnson, which would
have demolished any other man. He had been teasing him
with many direct questions, such as, "What did you do,
sir?—What did you say, sir?" until the great philologist
became perfectly enraged. "I will not be put to the *question!*" roared he. "Don't you consider, sir, that these are
not the manners of a gentleman? I will not be baited with
what and *why;*—What is this? What is that? Why is a
cow's tail long? Why is a fox's tail bushy?" "Why, sir,"
replied pilgarlick, "you are so good that I venture to
trouble you." "Sir," replied Johnson, "my being so *good* is
no reason why you should be so *ill*." "You have but two
topics, sir," exclaimed he on another occasion, "yourself and
me, and I am sick of both."

Boswell's inveterate disposition to *toad*, was a sore cause
of mortification to his father, the old laird of Auchinleck,
(or Affleck.) He had been annoyed by his extravagant
devotion to Paoli, but then he was something of a military
hero; but this tagging at the heels of Dr. Johnson, whom
he considered a kind of pedagogue, set his Scotch blood in a
ferment. "There's nae hope for Jamie, mon," said he to a
friend;—"Jamie is gaen clean gyte. What do you think,
mon? He's done wi' Paoli; he's off wi' the landlouping
scoundrel of a Corsican; and whose tail do you think he has
pinn'd himself to now, mon? A *dominie*, mon; an auld
dominie; he keeped a schule, and cau'd it an acaadamy."

We shall show in the next chapter that Jamie's devotion
to the dominie did not go unrewarded.

CHAPTER XL

The Literary Club (as we have termed the club in Gerard Street, though it took that name some time later) had now been in existence several years. Johnson was exceedingly chary at first of its exclusiveness, and opposed to its being augmented in number. Not long after its institution, Sir Joshua Reynolds was speaking of it to Garrick. "I like it much," said little David, briskly; "I think I shall be of you." "When Sir Joshua mentioned this to Dr. Johnson," says Boswell, "he was much displeased with the actor's conceit. *'He'll be of us?'* growled he. 'How does he know we will *permit* him? The first duke in England has no right to hold such language.'"

When Sir John Hawkins spoke favorably of Garrick's pretensions, "Sir," replied Johnson, "he will disturb us by his buffoonery." In the same spirit he declared to Mr. Thrale, that, if Garrick should apply for admission, he would black-ball him. "Who, sir?" exclaimed Thrale, with surprise; "Mr. Garrick—your friend, your companion—black-ball him!" "Why, sir," replied Johnson, "I love my little David dearly—better than all or any of his flatterers do; but surely one ought to sit in a society like ours,

"'Unelbowed by a gamester, pimp, or player.'"

The exclusion from the club was a sore mortification to Garrick, though he bore it without complaining. He could not help continually to ask questions about it—what was going on there—whether he was ever the subject of conversation. By degrees the rigor of the club relaxed: some of the members grew negligent. Beauclerc lost his right of membership by neglecting to attend. On his marriage, however, with Lady Diana Spencer, daughter of the Duke of Marlborough, and recently divorced from Viscount Bolingbroke, he had claimed and regained his seat in the club. The number of members had likewise been augmented. The proposition to increase it originated with Goldsmith. "It would give," he thought, "an agreeable variety to their meetings; for there can be nothing new amongst us," said he; "we have travelled over each other's minds." Johnson was piqued at the suggestion. "Sir," said he, "you have not travelled over my mind, I promise you." Sir Joshua, less confident in the exhaustless fecundity of his mind, felt and acknowledged the force of Goldsmith's suggestion. Several new members, therefore, had been added; the first, to his great joy, was David Garrick. Goldsmith, who was now on cordial terms with him, had zealously promoted his election, and Johnson had given it his warm approbation. Another new member was Beauclerc's friend, Lord Charlemont; and a still more important one was Mr. (afterwards Sir William) Jones, the famous Orientalist, at that time a young lawyer of the Temple and a distinguished scholar.

To the great astonishment of the club, Johnson now proposed his devoted follower, Boswell, as a member. He did it in a note addressed to Goldsmith, who presided on the evening of the 23d of April. The nomination was seconded by Beauclerc. According to the rules of the club, the ballot would take place at the next meeting (on the 30th); there was an intervening week, therefore, in which to discuss the pretensions of the candidate. We may easily imagine the discussions that took place. Boswell had made himself absurd in such a variety of ways that the very idea of his admission was exceedingly irksome to some of the members. "The honor of being elected into the Turk's Head Club," said the Bishop of St. Asaph, "is not inferior to that of being representative of Westminster and Surrey;" what had Boswell done to merit such an honor? What chance had he of gaining it? The answer was simple: he had been the persevering worshipper, if not sycophant of Johnson. The great lexicographer had a heart to be won by apparent affection; he stood forth authoritatively in support of his vassal. If asked to state the merits of the candidate, he summed them up in an indefinite but comprehensive word of his own coining:—he was *clubable*. He moreover gave significant hints that if Boswell were kept out he should oppose the admission of any other candidate. No further opposition was made; in fact none of the members had been so fastidious and exclusive in regard to the club as Johnson himself; and if he were pleased, they were easily satisfied: besides, they knew that, with all his faults, Boswell was a cheerful companion, and possessed lively social qualities.

On Friday, when the ballot was to take place, Beauclerc gave a dinner, at his house in the Adelphi, where Boswell met several of the members who were favorable to his election. After dinner the latter adjourned to the club, leaving Boswell in company with Lady Di Beauclerc until the fate of his election should be known. He sat, he says, in a state of anxiety which even the charming conversation of Lady Di could not entirely dissipate. It was not long before tidings were brought of his election, and he was conducted to the place of meeting, where, beside the company he had met at dinner, Burke, Dr. Nugent, Garrick, Goldsmith, and Mr. William Jones were waiting to receive him. The club, notwithstanding all its learned dignity in the eyes of the world, could at times "unbend and play the fool" as well as less important bodies. Some of its jocose conversations have at times leaked out, and a society in which Goldsmith could venture to sing his song of "an old woman tossed in a blanket," could not be so very staid in its gravity. We may suppose, therefore, the jokes that had been passing among the members while awaiting the arrival of Boswell. Beau-clerc himself could not have repressed his disposition for a sarcastic pleasantry. At least we have a right to presume all this from the conduct of Dr. Johnson himself.

With all his gravity he possessed a deep fund of quiet humor, and felt a kind of whimsical responsibility to protect the club from the absurd propensities of the very questionable associate he had thus inflicted on them. Rising, therefore, as Boswell entered, he advanced with a very doctorial air, placed himself behind a chair, on which he leaned as on a desk or pulpit, and then delivered, *ex cathedra*, a mock solemn charge, pointing out the conduct expected from him as a good member of the club; what he was to do, and especially what he was to avoid; including in the latter, no doubt, all those petty, prying, questioning, gossiping, bab-bling habits which had so often grieved the spirit of the lexi-cographer. It is to be regretted that Boswell has never thought proper to note down the particulars of this charge, which, from the well-known characters and positions of the parties, might have furnished a parallel to the noted charge of Launcelot Gobbo to his dog.[1]

---

[1] *Two Gentlemen of Verona*, Act II, Sc. iii.; Irving makes a mistake in the name, which should be Launce, Launcelot Gobbo being a character in the *Merchant of Venice*.

CHAPTER XLI

A few days after the serio-comic scene of the elevation of
Boswell into the Literary Club, we find that indefatigable
biographer giving particulars of a dinner at the Dilly's,
booksellers, in the Poultry, at which he met Goldsmith and
Johnson, with several other literary characters. His anecdotes of the conversation, of course, go to glorify Dr. Johnson; for, as he observes in his biography, "his conversation
alone, or what led to it, or was interwoven with it, is the
business of this work." Still on the present, as on other
occasions, he gives unintentional and perhaps unavoidable
gleams of Goldsmith's good sense, which show that the latter
only wanted a less prejudiced and more impartial reporter, to
put down the charge of colloquial incapacity so unjustly fixed
upon him. The conversation turned upon the natural history of birds, a beautiful subject, on which the poet, from his
recent studies, his habits of observation, and his natural
tastes, must have talked with instruction and feeling; yet,
though we have much of what Johnson said, we have only a
casual remark or two of Goldsmith. One was on the migration of swallows, which he pronounced partial; "the stronger
ones," said he, "migrate, the others do not."

Johnson denied to the brute creation the faculty of reason.
"Birds," said he, "build by instinct; they never improve; they
build their first nest as well as any one they ever build."

"Yet we see," observed Goldsmith, "if you take away a bird's-nest with the eggs in it, she will make a slighter nest and lay again." "Sir," replied Johnson, "that is because at first she has full time, and makes her nest deliberately. In the case you mention, she is pressed to lay, and must, therefore, make her nest quickly, and consequently it will be slight." "The nidification of birds," rejoined Goldsmith, "is what is least known in natural history, though one of the most curious things in it." While conversation was going on in this placid, agreeable, and instructive manner, the eternal meddler and busybody, Boswell, must intrude to put in a brawl. The Dillys were dissenters; two of their guests were dissenting clergymen; another, Mr. Toplady, was a clergyman of the established church. Johnson himself was a zealous, uncompromising churchman. None but a marplot like Boswell would have thought, on such an occasion and in such company, to broach the subject of religious toleration; but, as has been well observed, "it was his perverse inclination to introduce subjects that he hoped would produce difference and debate." In the present instance he gained his point. An animated dispute immediately arose, in which, according to Boswell's report, Johnson monopolized the greater part of the conversation; not always treating the dissenting clergymen with the greatest courtesy, and even once wounding the feelings of the mild and amiable Bennet Langton by his harshness.

Goldsmith mingled a little in the dispute and with some advantage, but was cut short by flat contradictions when most in the right. He sat for a time silent but impatient under such overbearing dogmatism, though Boswell, with his usual misinterpretation, attributes his "restless agitation" to a wish *to get in and shine*. "Finding himself excluded," continues Boswell, "he had taken his hat to go away, but remained for a time with it in his hand, like a gamester who at the end of a long night lingers for a little while to see if he can have a favorable opportunity to finish with success." Once he was beginning to speak, when he was overpowered by the loud voice of Johnson, who was at the opposite end of the table, and did not perceive his attempt; whereupon he threw down, as it were, his hat and his argument, and, darting an angry glance at Johnson, exclaimed in a bitter tone, "*Take it.*"

Just then one of the disputants was beginning to speak, when Johnson uttering some sound, as if about to interrupt him, Goldsmith, according to Boswell, seized the opportunity to vent his own *envy and spleen* under pretext of supporting another person. "Sir," said he to Johnson, "the gentleman has heard you patiently for an hour; pray allow us now to hear him." It was a reproof in the lexicographer's own style, and he may have felt that he merited it; but he was not accustomed to be reproved. "Sir " said he, sternly, "I was not interrupting the gentleman; I was only giving him a signal of my attention. Sir, *you are impertinent.*" Goldsmith made no reply but after some time went away, having another engagement.

That evening as Boswell was on the way with Johnson and Langton to the club, he seized the occasion to make some disparaging remarks on Goldsmith, which he thought would just then be acceptable to the great lexicographer. "It was a pity," he said, "that Goldsmith would on every occasion endeavor to shine, by which he so often exposed himself." Langton contrasted him with Addison, how, content with the fame of his writings, acknowledged himself unfit for conversation; and on being taxed by a lady with silence in company, replied, "Madam, I have but ninepence in ready money, but I can draw for a thousand pounds."

To this Boswell rejoined that Goldsmith had a great deal of gold in his cabinet, but was always taking out his purse. "Yes, sir," chuckled Johnson, "and that so often an empty purse."

By the time Johnson arrived at the club, however, his angry feelings had subsided, and his native generosity and sense of justice had got the uppermost. He found Goldsmith in company with Burke, Garrick, and other members, but sitting silent and apart, "brooding," as Boswell says, "over the reprimand he had received." Johnson's good heart yearned towards him; and knowing his placable nature, "I'll make Goldsmith forgive me," whispered he; then, with a loud voice, "Dr. Goldsmith," said he, "something passed to-day where you and I dined,—*I ask your pardon.*" The ire of the poet was extinguished in an instant, and his grateful affection for the magnanimous though sometimes overbearing moralist rushed to his heart. "It must be much from you, sir," said he, "that I take ill!" "And so," adds, Boswell, "the difference was over, and they were on as easy terms as ever, and Goldsmith rattled away as usual." We do not think these stories tell to the poet's disadvantage, even though related by Boswell.

Goldsmith, with all his modesty, could not be ignorant of his proper merit, and must have felt annoyed at times at being undervalued and elbowed aside by light-minded or dull men, in their blind and exclusive homage to the literary autocrat. It was a fine reproof he gave to Boswell on one occasion, for talking of Johnson as entitled to the honor of exclusive superiority. "Sir, you are for making a monarchy what should be a republic." On another occasion, when he was conversing in company with great vivacity, and apparently to the satisfaction of those around him, an honest Swiss who sat near, one George Michael Moser, keeper of the

Royal Academy, perceiving Dr. Johnson rolling himself as
if about to speak, exclaimed, "Stay, stay! Toctor Shonson is
going to say something." "And are you sure, sir," replied
Goldsmith, sharply, "that *you* can comprehend what he
says?"

This clever rebuke, which gives the main zest to the anecdote, is omitted by Boswell, who probably did not perceive
the point of it.

He relates another anecdote of the kind on the authority
of Johnson himself. The latter and Goldsmith were one
evening in company with the Rev. George Graham, a master of Eton, who, notwithstanding the sobriety of his cloth,
had got intoxicated "to about the pitch of looking at one
man and talking to another." "Doctor," cried he, in an
ecstasy of devotion and good-will, but goggling by mistake
upon Goldsmith, "I should be glad to see you at Eton."
"I shall be glad to wait upon you," replied Goldsmith.
"No, no!" cried the other, eagerly; "'tis not you I mean,
Doctor *Minor*, 'tis Doctor *Major* there." "You may easily
conceive," said Johnson, in relating the anecdote, "what
effect this had upon Goldsmith, who was irascible as a
hornet." The only comment, however, which he is said to
have made, partakes more of quaint and dry humor than
bitterness. "That Graham," said he, "is enough to make
one commit suicide." What more could be said to express
the intolerable nuisance of a consummate *bore?*

We have now given the last scenes between Goldsmith
and Johnson which stand recorded by Boswell. The latter
called on the poet, a few days after the dinner at Dilly's, to
take leave of him prior to departing for Scotland; yet, even
in this last interview, he contrives to get up a charge of
"jealousy and envy." Goldsmith, he would fain persuade
us, is very angry that Johnson is going to travel with him in

Scotland, and endeavors to persuade him that he will be a dead weight "to lug along through the Highlands and Hebrides." Any one else, knowing the character and habits of Johnson, would have thought the same; and no one but Boswell would have supposed his office of bear-leader to the *ursa major* a thing to be envied.*

---

*One of Peter Pindar's (Dr. Wolcot) most amusing *jeux d'esprit* is his congratulatory epistle to Boswell on this tour, of which we subjoin a few lines.

> "O Boswell, Bozzy, Bruce, whate'er thy name,
> Thou mighty shark for anecdote and fame;
> Thou jackal, leading lion Johnson forth,
> To eat McPherson 'midst his native north;
> To frighten grave professors with his roar,
> And shake the Hebrides from shore to shore.
>
> .   .   .   .
>
> Bless'd be thy labors, most adventurous Bozzy,
> Bold rival of Sir John and Dame Piozzi,[1]
> Heavens! with what laurels shall thy head be crown'd!
> A grove, a forest, shall thy ears surround!
> Yes, whilst the Rambler shall a comet blaze,
> And gild a world of darkness with his rays,
> Thee, too, that world with wonderment shall hail,
> A lively, bouncing cracker at his tail!"

[1] By Sir John is probably meant Sir John Hawkesworth who wrote a life of Johnson. Dame Piozzi is Mrs. Thrale, Piozzi being the name of her second husband. Johnson lived for many years in the Thrale household; in 1786 and 1788 Mrs. Thrale published two volumes of reminiscences of Johnson. The Rambler is of course Johnson himself.

CHAPTER XLII

PROJECT OF A DICTIONARY OF ARTS AND SCIENCES—DISAPPOINT-
MENT—NEGLIGENT AUTHORSHIP—APPLICATION FOR A PEN-
SION—BEATTIE'S ESSAY ON TRUTH—PUBLIC ADULATION—A
HIGH-MINDED REBUKE.

The works which Goldsmith had still in hand being
already paid for, and the money gone, some new scheme
must be devised to provide for the past and the future,—for
impending debts which threatened to crush him, and
expenses which were continually increasing. He now projected a work of greater compass than any he had yet
undertaken: a Dictionary of Arts and Sciences on a comprehensive scale, which was to occupy a number of volumes.
For this he received promise of assistance from several
powerful hands. Johnson was to contribute an article on
ethics; Burke, an abstract of his "Essay on the Sublime and
Beautiful," an essay on the Berkleyan system of philosophy,
and others on political science; Sir Joshua Reynolds, an
essay on painting; and Garrick, while he undertook on his
own part to furnish an essay on acting, engaged Dr. Burney
to contribute an article on music. Here was a great array
of talent positively engaged, while other writers of eminence
were to be sought for the various departments of science.
Goldsmith was to edit the whole. An undertaking of this
kind, while it did not incessantly task and exhaust his
inventive powers by original composition, would give agreeable and profitable exercise to his taste and judgment in
selecting, compiling, and arranging, and he calculated to
diffuse over the whole the acknowledged graces of his style.

He drew up a prospectus of the plan, which is said by

Bishop Percy, who saw it, to have been written with uncommon ability, and to have had that perspicuity and elegance for which his writings are remarkable. This paper, unfortunately, is no longer in existence.

Goldsmith's expectations, always sanguine respecting any new plan, were raised to an extraordinary height by the present project; and well they might be, when we consider the powerful coadjutors already pledged. They were doomed, however, to complete disappointment. Davies, the bibliopole of Russell Street, lets us into the secret of this failure. "The booksellers," said he, "notwithstanding they had a very good opinion of his abilities, yet were startled at the bulk, importance, and expense of so great an undertaking, the fate of which was to depend upon the industry of a man with whose indolence of temper and method of procrastination they had long been acquainted."

Goldsmith certainly gave reason for some such distrust by the heedlessness with which he conducted his literary undertakings. Those unfinished, but paid for, would be suspended to make way for some job that was to provide for present necessities. Those thus hastily taken up would be as hastily executed, and the whole, however pressing, would be shoved aside and left "at loose ends," on some sudden call to social enjoyment or recreation.

Cradock tells us that on one occasion, when Goldsmith was hard at work on his "Natural History," he sent to Dr. Percy and himself, entreating them to finish some pages of his work which lay upon his table, and for which the press was urgent, he being detained by other engagements at Windsor. They met by appointment at his chambers in the Temple, where they found everything in disorder, and costly books lying scattered about on the tables and on the floor; many of the books on natural history which he had recently

consulted lay open among uncorrected proof-sheets. The
subject in hand, and from which he had suddenly broken
off, related to birds. "Do you know anything about birds?"
asked Dr. Percy, smiling. "Not an atom," replied Cradock; "do you?" "Not I! I scarcely know a goose from
a swan; however, let us try what we can do." They set to
work and completed their friendly task. Goldsmith, however, when he came to revise it, made such alterations that
they could neither of them recognize their own share. The
engagement at Windsor, which had thus caused Goldsmith
to break off suddenly from his multifarious engagements,
was a party of pleasure with some literary ladies. Another
anecdote was current, illustrative of the carelessness with
which he executed works requiring accuracy and research.
On the 22d of June he had received payment in advance
for a "Grecian History" in two volumes, though only one
was finished. As he was pushing on doggedly at the second
volume, Gibbon, the historian, called in. "You are the
man of all others I wish to see," cried the poet, glad to be
saved the trouble of reference to his books. "What was the
name of that Indian king who gave Alexander the Great so
much trouble?" "Montezuma," replied Gibbon, sportively.
The heedless author was about committing the name to
paper without reflection, when Gibbon pretended to recollect himself, and gave the true name, Porus.

This story, very probably, was a sportive exaggeration;
but it was a multiplicity of anecdotes like this and the preceding one, some true and some false, which had impaired
the confidence of booksellers in Goldsmith as a man to be
relied on for a task requiring wide and accurate research,
and close and long-continued application. The project of
the "Universal Dictionary," therefore, met with no encouragement, and fell through.

The failure of this scheme, on which he had built such spacious hopes, sank deep into Goldsmith's heart. He was still further grieved and mortified by the failure of an effort made by some of his friends to obtain for him a pension from government. There had been a talk of the disposition of the ministry to extend the bounty of the crown to distinguished literary men in pecuniary difficulty, without regard to their political creed: when the merits and claims of Goldsmith, however, were laid before them, they met no favor. The sin of sturdy independence lay at his door. He had refused to become a ministerial hack when offered a *carte blanche* by Parson Scott, the cabinet emissary. The wondering parson had left him in poverty and "*his garret*," and there the ministry were disposed to suffer him to remain.

In the meantime Dr. Beattie comes out with his "Essay on Truth," and all the orthodox world are thrown into a paroxysm of contagious ecstasy. He is cried up as the great champion of Christianity against the attacks of modern philosophers and infidels; he is fêted and flattered in every way. He receives at Oxford the honorary degree of Doctor of Civil Law, at the same time with Sir Joshua Reynolds. The King sends for him, praises his Essay, and gives him a pension of two hundred pounds.

Goldsmith feels more acutely the denial of a pension to himself when one has thus been given unsolicited to a man he might without vanity consider so much his inferior. He was not one to conceal his feelings. "Here's such a stir," said he one day at Thrale's table, "about a fellow that has written one book, and I have written so many!"

"Ah, Doctor!" exclaimed Johnson, in one of his caustic moods, "there go two-and-forty sixpences, you know, to one guinea." This is one of the cuts at poor Goldsmith in which Johnson went contrary to head and heart in his love for saying what is called a "good thing." No one knew better than himself the comparative superiority of the writings of Goldsmith; but the jingle of the sixpences and the guinea was not to be resisted.

"Everybody," exclaimed Mrs. Thrale, "loves Dr. Beattie, but Goldsmith, who says he cannot bear the sight of so much applause as they all bestow upon him. Did he not tell us so himself, no one would believe he was so exceedingly ill-natured."

He told them so himself because he was too open and unreserved to disguise his feelings, and because he really considered the praise lavished on Beattie extravagant, as in fact it was. It was all, of course, set down to sheer envy and uncharitableness. To add to his annoyance, he found his friend, Sir Joshua Reynolds, joining in the universal adulation. He had painted a full-length portrait of Beattie decked in the doctor's robes in which he had figured at Oxford, with the "Essay on Truth" under his arm and the angel of truth at his side, while Voltaire figured as one of the demons of infidelity, sophistry, and falsehood, driven into utter darkness.

Goldsmith had known Voltaire in early life; he had been his admirer and his biographer; he grieved to find him receiving such an insult from the classic pencil of his friend. "It is unworthy of you," said he to Sir Joshua, "to debase so high a genius as Voltaire before so mean a writer as Beattie. Beattie and his book will be forgotten in ten years, while Voltaire's fame will last forever. Take care it does not perpetuate this picture to the shame of such a man as you." This noble and high-minded rebuke is the only instance on record of any reproachful words between the poet and the painter; and we are happy to find that it did not destroy the harmony of their intercourse.

CHAPTER XLIII

TOIL WITHOUT HOPE—THE POET IN THE GREEN ROOM; IN THE FLOWER-GARDEN; AT VAUXHALL; DISSIPATION WITHOUT GAY-ETY—CRADOCK IN TOWN; FRIENDLY SYMPATHY; A PARTING SCENE; AN INVITATION TO PLEASURE.

Thwarted in the plans and disappointed in the hopes which had recently cheered and animated him, Goldsmith found the labor at his half-finished tasks doubly irksome from the consciousness that the completion of them could not relieve him from his pecuniary embarrassments. His impaired health, also, rendered him less capable than formerly of sedentary application, and continual perplexities disturbed the flow of thought necessary for original composition. He lost his usual gayety and good-humor, and became at times, peevish and irritable. Too proud of spirit to seek sympathy or relief from his friends, for the pecuniary difficulties he had brought upon himself by his errors and extravagance, and unwilling, perhaps, to make known their amount, he buried his cares and anxieties in his own bosom, and endeavored in company to keep up his usual air of gayety and unconcern. This gave his conduct an appearance of fitfulness and caprice, varying suddenly from moodiness to mirth, and from silent gravity to shallow laughter; causing surprise and ridicule in those who were not aware of the sickness of heart which lay beneath.

His poetical reputation, too, was sometimes a disadvantage to him; it drew upon him a notoriety which he was not always in the mood or the vein to act up to. "Good heavens, Mr. Foote," exclaimed an actress at the Haymarket Theatre, "what a humdrum kind of man Dr. Goldsmith appears in our green-room compared with the figure he makes in his poetry!" "The reason of that, madam," replied Foote, "is because the Muses are better company than the players."

Beauclerc's letters to his friend, Lord Charlemont, who was absent in Ireland, give us now and then an indication of the whereabout of the poet during the present year. "I have been but once to the club since you left England," writes he, "we were entertained, as usual, with Goldsmith's absurdity." With Beauclerc everything was absurd that was not polished and pointed. In another letter he threatens, unless Lord Charlemont returns to England, to bring over the whole club, and let them loose upon him to drive him home by their peculiar habits of annoyance;—Johnson shall spoil his books; Goldsmith shall *pull his flowers;* and last, and most intolerable of all, Boswell shall—talk to him. It would appear that the poet, who had a passion for flowers, was apt to pass much of his time in the garden when on a visit to a country-seat, much to the detriment of the flower-beds and the despair of the gardener.

The summer wore heavily away with Goldsmith. He had not his usual solace of a country retreat; his health was impaired and his spirits depressed. Sir Joshua Reynolds, who perceived the state of his mind, kindly gave him much of his company. In the course of their interchange of thought, Goldsmith suggested to him the story of Ugolino,[1] as a subject for his pencil. The painting founded on it remains a memento of their friendship.

On the 4th of August we find them together at Vauxhall,

---

[1] Two famous versions of the story of Ugolino are those by Dante, *Inferno*, XXXIII, and Chaucer, *Monk's Tale*, in the *Canterbury Tales*. According to the story Ugolino of Pisa is imprisoned by a political enemy, together with his four sons, who die of starvation one after the other before the eyes of their father.

at that time a place in high vogue, and which had once been to Goldsmith a scene of Oriental splendor and delight. We have, in fact, in the "Citizen of the World," a picture of it as it had struck him in former years and in his happier moods. "Upon entering the gardens," says the Chinese philosopher, "I found every sense occupied with more than expected pleasure: the lights everywhere glimmering through the scarcely moving trees; the full-bodied concert bursting on the stillness of the night; the natural concert of the birds in the more retired part of the grove, vying with that which was formed by art; the company gayly dressed, looking satisfaction, and the tables spread with various delicacies,— all conspired to fill my imagination with the visionary happiness of the Arabian law-giver,[1] and lifted me into an ecstasy of admiration."*

Everything now, however, is seen with different eyes; with him it is dissipation without pleasure; and he finds it impossible any longer, by mingling in the gay and giddy throng of apparently prosperous and happy beings, to escape from the carking care which is clinging to his heart.

His kind friend, Cradock, came up to town towards autumn, when all the fashionable world was in the country, to give his wife the benefit of a skilful dentist. He took lodgings in Norfolk Street, to be in Goldsmith's neighborhood, and passed most of his mornings with him. "I found him," he says, "much altered and at times very low. He wished me to look over and revise some of his works; but, with a select friend or two, I was more pressing that he should publish by subscription his two celebrated poems of the 'Traveller' and the 'Deserted Village,' with notes." The idea of Cradock was, that the subscription would enable

---

[1] The allusion is to the paradise of Mohammed.
* *Citizen of the World.* Letter LXXI.

wealthy persons, favorable to Goldsmith, to contribute to his pecuniary relief without wounding his pride. "Goldsmith," said he, "readily gave up to me his private copies, and said, 'Pray do what you please with them.' But whilst he sat near me, he rather submitted to than encouraged my zealous proceedings.

"I one morning called upon him, however, and found him infinitely better than I had expected; and, in a kind of exulting style, he exclaimed, 'Here are some of the best of my prose writings; *I have been hard at work since midnight,* and I desire you to examine them.' 'These,' said I, 'are excellent indeed.' 'They are,' replied he, 'intended as an introduction to a body of arts and sciences.'"

Poor Goldsmith was, in fact, gathering together the fragments of his shipwreck; the notes and essays, and memoranda collected for his dictionary, and proposed to found on them a work in two volumes, to be entitled "A Survey of Experimental Philosophy."

The plan of the subscription came to nothing, and the projected survey never was executed. The head might yet devise, but the heart was failing him; his talent at hoping, which gave him buoyancy to carry out his enterprises, was almost at an end.

Cradock's farewell-scene with him is told in a simple but touching manner.

"The day before I was to set out for Leicestershire, I insisted upon his dining with us. He replied, 'I will, but on one condition, that you will not ask me to eat anything.' 'Nay,' said I, 'this answer is absolutely unkind, for I had hoped, as we are supplied from the Crown and Anchor, that you would have named something you might have relished.' 'Well,' was the reply, 'if you will but explain it to Mrs. Cradock, I will certainly wait upon you.'

"The Doctor found, as usual, at my apartments, newspapers and pamphlets, and with a pen and ink he amused
himself as well as he could. I had ordered from the tavern
some fish, a roasted joint of lamb, and a tart; and the
Doctor either sat down or walked about just as he pleased.
After dinner he took some wine with biscuits; but I was
obliged soon to leave him for a while, as I had matters to
settle prior to my next day's journey. On my return, coffee
was ready, and the Doctor appeared more cheerful (for Mrs.
Cradock was always rather a favorite with him), and in the
evening he endeavored to talk and remark as usual, but all
was force. He stayed till midnight, and I insisted on seeing
him safe home, and we most cordially shook hands at the
Temple-gate." Cradock little thought that this was to be
their final parting. He looked back to it with mournful
recollections in after-years, and lamented that he had not
remained longer in town, at every inconvenience, to solace
the poor broken-spirited poet.

The latter continued in town all the autumn. At the
opening of the Opera-House, on the 20th of November,
Mrs. Yates, an actress whom he held in great esteem, delivered a poetical exordium of his composition. Beauclerc, in
a letter to Lord Charlemont, pronounced it very good, and
predicted that it would soon be in all the papers. It does
not appear, however, to have been ever published. In his fitful
state of mind Goldsmith may have taken no care about it, and
thus it has been lost to the world, although it was received
with great applause by a crowded and brilliant audience.

A gleam of sunshine breaks through the gloom that was
gathering over the poet. Towards the end of the year he
receives another Christmas invitation to Barton. A country
Christmas!—with all the cordiality of the fireside circle, and
the joyous revelry of the oaken hall,—what a contrast to the

loneliness of a bachelor's chambers in the Temple! It is
not to be resisted. But how is poor Goldsmith to raise the
ways and means? His purse is empty; his booksellers are
already in advance to him. As a last resource, he applies to
Garrick. Their mutual intimacy at Barton may have suggested him as an alternative. The old loan of forty pounds
has never been paid; and Newbery's note, pledged as a
security, has never been taken up. An additional loan of
sixty pounds is now asked for, thus increasing the loan to
one hundred; to insure the payment, he now offers, besides
Newbery's note, the transfer of the comedy of the "Good-
natured Man" to Drury Lane, with such alterations as Garrick may suggest. Garrick, in reply, evades the offer of the
altered comedy, alludes significantly to a new one which
Goldsmith had talked of writing for him, and offers to furnish the money required on his own acceptance.

The reply of Goldsmith bespeaks a heart brimful of gratitude and overflowing with fond anticipations of Barton and
the smiles of its fair residents. "My dear friend," writes he,
"I thank you. I wish I could do something to serve you.
I shall have a comedy for you in a season, or two at farthest,
that I believe will be worth your acceptance, for I fancy I
will make it a fine thing. You shall have the refusal. . . .
I will draw upon you one month after date for sixty pounds,
and your acceptance will be ready money, *part of which I
want to go down to Barton with*. May God preserve my
honest little man, for he has my heart. Ever,

"OLIVER GOLDSMITH."

And having thus scrambled together a little pocket-money,
by hard contrivance, poor Goldsmith turns his back upon
care and trouble, and Temple quarters, to forget for a time
his desolate bachelorhood in the family circle and a Christmas fireside at Barton.

CHAPTER XLIV

The Barton festivities are over; Christmas, with all its
home-felt revelry of the heart, has passed like a dream; the
Jessamy Bride has beamed her last smile upon the poor
poet, and the early part of 1774 finds him in his now dreary
bachelor abode in the Temple, toiling fitfully and hopelessly
at a multiplicity of tasks. His "Animated Nature," so long
delayed, so often interrupted, is at length announced for
publication, though it has yet to receive a few finishing
touches. He is preparing a third "History of England," to
be compressed and condensed in one volume, for the use of
schools. He is revising his "Inquiry into Polite Learning,"
for which he receives the pittance of five guineas, much
needed in his present scantiness of purse; he is arranging
his "Survey of Experimental Philosophy," and he is translating the "Comic Romance" of Scarron. Such is a part of
the various labors of a drudging, depressing kind, by which
his head is made weary and his heart faint. "If there is a
mental drudgery," says Sir Walter Scott, "which lowers the
spirits and lacerates the nerves, like the toil of a slave, it is
that which is exacted by literary composition, when the heart
is not in unison with the work upon which the head is
employed. Add to the unhappy author's task sickness,

sorrow, or the pressure of unfavorable circumstances, and the labor of the bondsman becomes light in comparison." Goldsmith again makes an effort to rally his spirits by going into gay society. "Our Club," writes Beauclerc to Charlemont, on the 12th of February, "has dwindled away to nothing. Sir Joshua and Goldsmith have got into such a round of pleasures that they have no time." This shows how little Beauclerc was the companion of the poet's mind, or could judge of him below the surface. Reynolds, the kind participator in joyless dissipation, could have told a different story of his companion's heart-sick gayety.

In this forced mood Goldsmith gave entertainments in his chambers in the Temple; the last of which was a dinner to Johnson, Reynolds, and others of his intimates, who partook with sorrow and reluctance of his imprudent hospitality. The first course vexed them by its needless profusion. When a second, equally extravagant, was served up, Johnson and Reynolds declined to partake of it; the rest of the company understanding their motives, followed their example, and the dishes went from the table untasted. Goldsmith felt sensibly this silent and well-intended rebuke.

The gayeties of society, however, cannot medicine for any length of time a mind diseased.[1] Wearied by the distractions and harassed by the expenses of a town life, which he had not the discretion to regulate, Goldsmith took the resolution, too tardily adopted, of retiring to the serene quiet, and cheap and healthful pleasures of the country, and of passing only two months of the year in London. He accordingly made arrangements to sell his right in the Temple chambers, and in the month of March retired to his country quarters at Hyde, there to devote himself to toil. At this dispirited juncture, when inspiration seemed to be at

---

[1] See *Macbeth* V, iii, 40, "Canst thou not minister to a mind diseased?"

an end, and the poetic fire extinguished, a spark fell on his
combustible imagination and set it in a blaze.

He belonged to a temporary association of men of talent,
some of them members of the Literary Club, who dined
together occasionally at the St. James's Coffee-House. At
these dinners, as usual, he was one of the last to arrive. On
one occasion, when he was more dilatory than usual, a whim
seized the company to write epitaphs on him, as "The late
Dr. Goldsmith," and several were thrown off in a playful
vein, hitting off his peculiarities. The only one extant was
written by Garrick, and has been preserved, very probably,
by its pungency:—

> "Here lies poet Goldsmith, for shortness called Noll,
> Who wrote like an angel, but talked like poor poll."

Goldsmith did not relish the sarcasm, especially as coming from such a quarter. He was not very ready at repartee;
but he took his time, and in the interval of his various tasks
concocted a series of epigrammatic sketches, under the title
of "Retaliation," in which the characters of his distinguished
intimates were admirably hit off, with a mixture of generous
praise and good-humored raillery. In fact the poem, for its
graphic truth, its nice discrimination, its terse good sense,
and its shrewd knowledge of the world, must have electrified
the club almost as much as the first appearance of "The
Traveller," and let them still deeper into the character and
talents of the man they had been accustomed to consider as
their butt. "Retaliation," in a word, closed his accounts
with the club, and balanced all his previous deficiencies.

The portrait of David Garrick is one of the most elaborate in the poem. When the poet came to touch it off, he
had some lurking piques to gratify, which the recent attack
had revived. He may have forgotten David's cavalier treat-

ment of him, in the early days of his comparative obscurity;
he may have forgiven his refusal of his plays; but Garrick
had been capricious in his conduct in the times of their
recent intercourse: sometimes treating him with gross familiarity, at other times affecting dignity and reserve, and
assuming airs of superiority; frequently he had been facetious
and witty in company at his expense, and lastly he had been
guilty of the couplet just quoted.   Goldsmith, therefore,
touched off the lights and shadows of his character with a
free hand, and at the same time gave a side-hit at his old
rival, Kelly, and his critical persecutor, Kenrick, in making
them sycophantic satellites of the actor.   Goldsmith, however, was void of gall even in his revenge, and his very
satire was more humorous than caustic:—

> "Here lies David Garrick, describe him who can,
> An abridgement of all that was pleasant in man;
> As an actor, confess'd without rival to shine;
> As a wit, if not first, in the very first line:
> Yet, with talents like these, and an excellent heart,
> The man had his failings, a dupe to his art.
> Like an ill-judging beauty, his colors he spread,
> And beplaster'd with rouge his own natural red.
> On the stage he was natural, simple, affecting;
> 'Twas only that when he was off he was acting.
> With no reason on earth to go out of his way,
> He turn'd and he varied full ten times a day:
> Though secure of our hearts, yet confoundedly sick
> If they were not his own by finessing and trick:
> He cast off his friends as a huntsman his pack,
> For he knew, when he pleased, he could whistle them back.
> Of praise a mere glutton, he swallow'd what came,
> And the puff of a dunce he mistook it for fame;
> Till his relish, grown callous almost to disease,
> Who pepper'd the highest was surest to please.
> But let us be candid, and speak out our mind,
> If dunces applauded, he paid them in kind.

Ye Kenricks, ye Kellys, and Woodfalls so grave,
What a commerce was yours, while you got and you gave!
How did Grub Street reëcho the shouts that you raised
While he was be-Rosciused and you were be-praised!
But peace to his spirit, wherever it flies,
To act as an angel and mix with the skies:
Those poets who owe their best fame to his skill,
Shall still be his flatterers, go where he will;
Old Shakspeare receive him with praise and with love,
And Beaumonts and Bens be his Kellys above."[1]

This portion of "Retaliation" soon brought a retort from
Garrick, which we insert, as giving something of a likeness
of Goldsmith, though in broad caricature:—

"Here, Hermes, says Jove, who with nectar was mellow,
Go fetch me some clay—I will make an odd fellow:
Right and wrong shall be jumbled, much gold and some dross,
Without cause be he pleased, without cause be he cross;
Be sure, as I work, to throw in contradictions,
A great love of truth, yet a mind turn'd to fictions;
Now mix these ingredients, which, warm'd in the baking,
Turn'd to *learning* and *gaming*, *religion* and *raking*.
With the love of a wench let his writings be chaste;
Tip his tongue with strange matter, his lips with fine taste:
That the rake and the poet o'er all may prevail.
Set fire to the head and set fire to the tail;
For the joy of each sex on the world I'll bestow it,
This scholar, rake, Christian, dupe, gamester, and poet.
Though a mixture so odd, he shall merit great fame,
And among brother mortals be Goldsmith his name;
When on earth this strange meteor no more shall appear,
You, *Hermes*, shall fetch him, to make us sport here."

The charge of raking, so repeatedly advanced in the foregoing lines, must be considered a sportive one, founded, per-

---

[1] Francis Beaumont (1584-1616), a writer of plays and one of the chief of
Shakspere's successors; "Bens" refers to the dramatist Ben Jonson (1573-
1637).

haps, on an incident or two within Garrick's knowledge, but
not borne out by the course of Goldsmith's life. He seems
to have had a tender sentiment for the sex, but perfectly free
from libertinism. Neither was he an habitual gamester.
The strictest scrutiny has detected no settled vice of the
kind. He was fond of a game of cards but an unskilful
and careless player. Cards in those days were universally
introduced into society. High play was, in fact, a fashionable amusement, as at one time was deep drinking; and a
man might occasionally lose large sums, and be beguiled
into deep potations, without incurring the character of a
gamester or a drunkard. Poor Goldsmith, on his advent
into high society, assumed fine notions with fine clothes; he
was thrown occasionally among high players, men of fortune
who could sport their cool hundred as carelessly as his early
comrades at Ballymahon could their half-crowns. Being at
all times magnificent in money-matters, he may have played
with them in their own way, without considering that what
was sport to them to him was ruin. Indeed, part of his
financial embarrassments may have arisen from losses of the
kind, incurred inadvertently, not in the indulgence of a
habit. "I do not believe Goldsmith to have deserved the
name of gamester," said one of his contemporaries; "he
liked cards very well, as other people do, and lost and won
occasionally, but as far as I saw or heard, and I had many
opportunities of hearing, never any considerable sum. If he
gamed with any one, it was probably with Beauclerc, but I
do not know that such was the case."

"Retaliation," as we have already observed, was thrown
off in parts, at intervals, and was never completed. Some
characters, originally intended to be introduced, remained
unattempted; others were but partially sketched—such as
the one of Reynolds, the friend of his heart, and which he

commenced with a felicity which makes us regret that it
should remain unfinished.

> "Here Reynolds is laid, and to tell you my mind,
> He has not left a wiser or better behind.
> His pencil was striking, resistless, and grand;
> His manners were gentle, complying, and bland;
> Still born to improve us in every part,
> His pencil our faces, his manners our heart.
> To coxcombs averse, yet most civilly steering,
> When they judged without skill he was still hard of hearing:
> When they talked of their Raphaels, Correggios, and stuff,
> He shifted his trumpet and only took snuff.
> By flattery unspoiled"——

The friendly portrait stood unfinished on the easel; the
hand of the artist had failed! An access of a local complaint, under which he had suffered for some time past, added
to a general prostration of health, brought Goldsmith back
to town before he had well settled himself in the country.
The local complaint subsided, but was followed by a low nervous fever. He was not aware of his critical situation, and
intended to be at the club on the 25th of March, on which
occasion Charles Fox, Sir Charles Bunbury (one of the Horneck connection), and two other new members were to be
present. In the afternoon, however, he felt so unwell as to
take to his bed, and his symptoms soon acquired sufficient
force to keep him there. His malady fluctuated for several
days, and hopes were entertained of his recovery, but they
proved fallacious. He had skilful medical aid and faithful
nursing, but he would not follow the advice of his physicians,
and persisted in the use of James's powders, which he had
once found beneficial, but which were now injurious to him.
His appetite was gone, his strength failed him, but his mind
remained clear, and was perhaps too active for his frame.
Anxieties and disappointments which had previously sapped

his constitution, doubtless aggravated his present complaint and rendered him sleepless. In reply to an inquiry of his physician, he acknowledged that his mind was ill at ease. This was his last reply: he was too weak to talk, and in general took no notice of what was said to him. He sank at last into a deep sleep, and it was hoped a favorable crisis had arrived. He awoke, however, in strong convulsions, which continued without intermission until he expired, on the fourth of April, at five o'clock in the morning; being in the forty-sixth year of his age.

His death was a shock to the literary world, and a deep affliction to a wide circle of intimates and friends; for, with all his foibles and peculiarities, he was fully as much beloved as he was admired. Burke, on hearing the news, burst into tears. Sir Joshua Reynolds threw by his pencil for the day, and grieved more than he had done in times of great family distress. "I was abroad at the time of his death," writes Dr. M'Donnell, the youth whom when in distress he had employed as an amanuensis, "and I wept bitterly when the intelligence first reached me. A blank came over my heart as if I had lost one of my nearest relatives, and was followed for some days by a feeling of despondency." Johnson felt the blow deeply and gloomily. In writing some time afterwards to Boswell, he observed, "Of poor Dr. Goldsmith there is little to be told more than the papers have made public. He died of a fever, made, I am afraid, more violent by uneasiness of mind. His debts began to be heavy, and all his resources were exhausted. Sir Joshua is of opinion that he owed no less than two thousand pounds. Was ever poet so trusted before?"

Among his debts were seventy-nine pounds due to his tailor, Mr. William Filby, from whom he had received a new suit but a few days before his death. "My father," said the younger Filby, "though a loser to that amount, attributed no blame to Goldsmith; he had been a good customer, and, had he lived, would have paid every farthing." Others of his tradespeople evinced the same confidence in his integrity, notwithstanding his heedlessness. Two sister milliners in Temple Lane, who had been accustomed to deal with him, were concerned when told, some time before his death, of his pecuniary embarrassments. "Oh, sir," said they to Mr. Cradock, "sooner persuade him to let us work for him gratis than apply to any other; we are sure he will pay us when he can."

On the stairs of his apartment there was the lamentation of the old and infirm, and the sobbing of women; poor objects of his charity, to whom he had never turned a deaf ear, even when struggling himself with poverty.

But there was one mourner whose enthusiasm for his memory, could it have been foreseen, might have soothed the bitterness of death. After the coffin had been screwed down, a lock of his hair was requested for a lady, a particular friend, who wished to preserve it as a remembrance. It was the beautiful Mary Horneck—the Jessamy Bride. The coffin was opened again, and a lock of hair cut off; which she treasured to her dying day. Poor Goldsmith! could he have foreseen that such a memorial of him was to be thus cherished!

One word more concerning this lady, to whom we have so often ventured to advert. She survived almost to the present day. Hazlitt met her at Northcote's painting-room, about twenty years since, as Mrs. Gwyn, the widow of a General Gwyn of the army. She was at that time upwards of seventy years of age. Still, he said, she was beautiful, beautiful even in years. After she was gone, Hazlitt remarked how handsome she still was. "I do not know," said Northcote, "why she is so kind as to come to see me, except that I am the last link in the chain that connects her with all those she most esteemed when young—Johnson, Reynolds, Goldsmith—and remind her of the most delightful period of her life." "Not only so," observed Hazlitt, "but you remember what she was at twenty; and you thus bring back to her the triumphs of her youth—that pride of beauty, which must be the more fondly cherished as it has no external vouchers, and lives chiefly in the bosom of its once lovely possessor. In her, however, the Graces had triumphed over time; she was one of Ninon de l'Enclos's[1] people, of the last of the immortals. I could almost fancy the shade of Goldsmith in the room, looking round with complacency."

The Jessamy Bride survived her sister upwards of forty years, and died in 1840, within a few days of completing her eighty-eighth year. "She had gone through all the stages of life," says Northcote, "and had lent a grace to each." However gayly she may have sported with the half-concealed admiration of the poor awkward poet in the heyday of her youth and beauty, and however much it may have been made a subject of teasing by her youthful companions, she evidently prided herself in after-years upon having been an object of his affectionate regard; it certainly rendered her interesting throughout life in the eyes of his admirers, and has hung a poetical wreath above her grave.

---

[1] Ninon de L'Enclos (1615-1705), a leader of the social life of Paris in one of its gayest and freest periods. She remained the mistress and chief attraction of a brilliant *salon* up to the last years of her long life.

CHAPTER XLV

In the warm feeling of the moment, while the remains of the poet were scarce cold, it was determined by his friends to honor them by a public funeral and a tomb in Westminster Abbey. His very pall-bearers were designated: Lord Shelburne, Lord Lowth, Sir Joshua Reynolds; the Hon. Mr. Beauclerc, Mr. Burke, and David Garrick. This feeling cooled down, however, when it was discovered that he died in debt, and had not left wherewithal to pay for such expensive obsequies. Five days after his death, therefore, at five o'clock of Saturday evening, the 9th of April, he was privately interred in the burying-ground of the Temple Church; a few persons attending as mourners, among whom we do not find specified any of his peculiar and distinguished friends. The chief mourner was Sir Joshua Reynolds's nephew, Palmer, afterwards Dean of Cashel. One person, however, from whom it was but little to be expected, attended the funeral and evinced real sorrow on the occasion. This was Hugh Kelly, once the dramatic rival of the deceased, and often, it is said, his anonymous assailant in the newspapers. If he had really been guilty of this basest of literary offences, he was punished by the stings of remorse, for we are told that he shed bitter tears over the grave of the man he had injured. His tardy atonement only provoked the lash of some unknown satirist, as the following lines will show:—

"Hence Kelly, who years, without honor or shame,
Had been sticking his bodkin in Oliver's fame,

Who thought, like the Tartar, by this to inherit
His genius, his learning, simplicity, spirit;
Now sets every feature to weep o'er his fate,
And acts as a mourner to blubber in state."

One base wretch deserves to be mentioned, the reptile
Kenrick, who, after having repeatedly slandered Goldsmith,
while living, had the audacity to insult his memory when
dead. The following distich is sufficient to show his malig-
nancy, and to hold him up to execration:—

'By his own art, who justly died,
A, blund'ring, artless suicide:
Share, earthworms, share, since now he's dead,
His megrim, maggot-bitten head."

This scurrilous epitaph produced a burst of public indignation, that awed for a time even the infamous Kenrick into
silence. On the other hand, the press teemed with tributes
in verse and prose to the memory of the deceased; all evinc-
ing the mingled feeling of admiration for the author and
affection for the man.

Not long after his death the Literary Club set on foot a
subscription, and raised a fund to erect a monument to his
memory, in Westminster Abbey. It was executed by Nolle-
kens, and consisted simply of a bust of the poet in profile, in
high relief, in a medallion, and was placed in the area of a
pointed arch, over the south door in Poet's Corner, between
the monuments of Gay and the Duke of Argyle. Johnson
furnished a Latin epitaph, which was read at the table of
Sir Joshua Reynolds, where several members of the club and
other friends of the deceased were present. Though considered by them a masterly composition, they thought the
literary character of the poet not defined with sufficient
exactness, and they preferred that the epitaph should be in
English rather than Latin, as "the memory of so eminent

an English writer ought to be perpetuated in the language to which his works were likely to be so lasting an ornament."

These objections were reduced to writing, to be respectfully submitted to Johnson, but such was the awe entertained of his frown, that every one shrank from putting his name first to the instrument; whereupon their names were written about it in a circle, making what mutinous sailors call a Round Robin. Johnson received it half graciously, half grimly. "He was willing," he said, "to modify the sense of the epitaph in any manner the gentlemen pleased; *but he never would consent to disgrace the walls of Westminster Abbey with an English inscription.*" Seeing the names of Dr. Warton and Edmund Burke among the signers, "he wondered," he said, "that Joe Warton, a scholar by profession, should be such a fool; and should have thought that Mund Burke would have had more sense." The following is the epitaph as it stands inscribed on a white marble tablet beneath the bust:—

"OLIVARII GOLDSMITH,

Poetæ, Physici, Historici,
Qui nullum ferè scribendi genus
Non tetigit,
Nullum quod tetigit non ornavit:
Sive risus essent movendi,
Sive lacrymæ,
Affectuum potens at lenis dominator:
Ingenio sublimis, vividus, versatilis,
Oratione grandis, nitidus, venustus:
Hoc monumento memoriam coluit
Sodalium amor,
Amicorum fides,
Lectorum veneratio.
Natus in Hiberniâ Forniæ Longfordiensis,
In loco cui nomen Pallas,
Nov. xxix. MDCCXXXI. ;

Eblanæ literis institutus;
Obiit Londini,*
April iv. MDCCLXXIV.†"

We shall not pretend to follow these anecdotes of the life
of Goldsmith with any critical dissertation on his writings;
their merits have long since been fully discussed, and their
station in the scale of literary merit permanently established.
They have outlasted generations of works of higher power
and wider scope, and will continue to outlast succeeding
generations, for they have that magic charm of style by which
works are embalmed to perpetuity. Neither shall we attempt
a regular analysis of the character of the poet, but will indulge
in a few desultory remarks, in addition to those scattered
throughout the preceding chapters.

Never was the trite, because sage apophthegm, that "The

---

*The following translation is from Croker's edition of Boswell's "John-
son":—

"OF OLIVER GOLDSMITH—

A Poet, Naturalist, and Historian,
Who left scarcely any style of writing
Untouched,
And touched nothing that he did not adorn:
Of all the passions,
Whether smiles were to be moved
Or tears,
A powerful yet gentle master;
In genius, sublime, vivid, versatile,
In style, elevated, clear, elegant—
The love of companions,
The fidelity of friends,
And the veneration of readers,
Have by this monument honored the memory.
He was born in Ireland,
At a place called Pallas,
[In the parish] of Forney, [and county] of Longford,
On the 29th Nov., 1731.
Educated at [the University of] Dublin,
And died in London,
4th April, 1774.

† Not correct. The true date of birth was 10th Nov. 1728, as given on
page 56.

child is father to the man," more fully verified than in the case of Goldsmith. He is shy, awkward, and blundering in childhood, yet full of sensibility; he is a butt for the jeers and jokes of his companions, but apt to surprise and confound them by sudden and witty repartees; he is dull and stupid at his tasks, yet an eager and intelligent devourer of the travelling tales and campaigning stories of his half military pedagogue; he may be a dunce, but he is already a rhymer; and his early scintillations of poetry awaken the expectations of his friends. He seems from infancy to have been compounded of two natures, one bright, the other blundering; or to have had fairy gifts laid in his cradle by the "good people" who haunted his birthplace, the old goblin mansion on the banks of the Inny.

He carries with him the wayward elfin spirit, if we may so term it, throughout his career. His fairy gifts are of no avail at school, academy, or college: they unfit him for close study and practical science, and render him heedless of everything that does not address itself to his poetical imagination and genial and festive feelings; they dispose him to break away from restraint, to stroll about hedges, green lanes, and haunted streams, to revel with jovial companions, or to rove the country like a gypsy in quest of odd adventures.

As if confiding in these delusive gifts, he takes no heed of the present nor care for the future, lays no regular and solid foundation of knowledge, follows out no plan, adopts and discards those recommended by his friends, at one time prepares for the ministry, next turns to the law, and then fixes upon medicine. He repairs to Edinburgh, the great emporium of medical science, but the fairy gifts accompany him; he idles and frolics away his time there, imbibing only such knowledge as is agreeable to him; makes an excursion to the poetical regions of the Highlands; and having walked

the hospitals for the customary time, sets off to ramble over
the Continent, in quest of novelty rather than knowledge.
His whole tour is a poetical one. He fancies he is playing
the philosopher while he is really playing the poet; and
though professedly he attends lectures and visits foreign
universities, so deficient is he on his return, in the studies for
which he set out, that he fails in an examination as a surgeon's
mate; and while figuring as a doctor of medicine, is outvied
on a point of practice by his apothecary. Baffled in every
regular pursuit, after trying in vain some of the humbler
callings of commonplace life, he is driven almost by chance
to the exercise of his pen, and here the fairy gifts come to his
assistance. For a long time, however, he seems unaware of
the magic properties of that pen: he uses it only as a make-
shift until he can find a *legitimate* means of support. He is
not a learned man, and can write but meagrely and at second-
hand on learned subjects; but he has a quick convertible
talent that seizes lightly on the points of knowledge necessary
to the illustration of a theme: his writings for a time are
desultory, the fruits of what he has seen and felt, or what he
has recently and hastily read; but his gifted pen transmutes
everything into gold, and his own genial nature reflects its
sunshine through his pages.

Still unaware of his powers he throws off his writings
anonymously, to go with the writings of less favored men;
and it is a long time, and after a bitter struggle with poverty
and humiliation, before he acquires confidence in his literary
talent as a means of support, and begins to dream of reputation.

From this time his pen is a wand of power in his hand,
and he has only to use it discreetly, to make it competent to
all his wants. But discretion is not a part of Goldsmith's
nature; and it seems the property of these fairy gifts to be

accompanied by moods and temperaments to render their effect precarious. The heedlessness of his early days; his disposition for social enjoyment; his habit of throwing the present on the neck of the future, still continue. His expenses forerun his means; he incurs debts on the faith of what his magic pen is to produce, and then, under the pressure of his debts, sacrifices its productions for prices far below their value. It is a redeeming circumstance in his prodigality that it is lavished oftener upon others than upon himself: he gives without thought or stint, and is the continual dupe of his benevolence and his trustfulness in human nature. We may say of him as he says of one of his heroes, "He could not stifle the natural impulse which he had to do good, but frequently borrowed money to relieve the distressed; and when he knew not conveniently where to borrow, he has been observed to shed tears as he passed through the wretched suppliants who attended his gate." . . .

"His simplicity in trusting persons whom he had no previous reasons to place confidence in, seems to be one of those lights of his character which, while they impeach his understanding, do honor to his benevolence. The low and the timid are ever suspicious; but a heart impressed with honorable sentiments, expects from others sympathetic sincerity."*

His heedlessness in pecuniary matters, which had rendered his life a struggle with poverty even in the days of his obscurity, rendered the struggle still more intense when his fairy gifts had elevated him into the society of the wealthy and luxurious, and imposed on his simple and generous spirit fancied obligations to a more ample and bounteous display.

"How comes it," says a recent and ingenious critic, "that in all the miry paths of life which he had trod, no speck ever

---

* Goldsmith's Life of Nash.

sullied the robe of his modest and graceful Muse? How amidst all the love of inferior company, which never to the last forsook him, did he keep his genius so free from every touch of vulgarity?"

We answer that it was owing to the innate purity and goodness of his nature; there was nothing in it that assimilated to vice and vulgarity. Though his circumstances often compelled him to associate with the poor, they never could betray him into companionship with the depraved. His relish for humor and for the study of character, as we have before observed, brought him often into convivial company of a vulgar kind; but he discriminated between their vulgarity and their amusing qualities, or rather wrought from the whole those familiar pictures of life which form the staple of his most popular writings.

Much, too, of this intact purity of heart may be ascribed to the lessons of his infancy under the paternal roof; to the gentle, benevolent, elevated, unworldly maxims of his father, who "passing rich with forty pounds a year," infused a spirit into his child which riches could not deprave nor poverty degrade. Much of his boyhood, too, had been passed in the household of his uncle, the amiable and generous Contarine; where he talked of literature with the good pastor, and practised music with his daughter, and delighted them both by his juvenile attempts at poetry. These early associations breathed a grace and refinement into his mind and tuned it up, after the rough sports on the green, or the frolics at the tavern. These led him to turn from the roaring glees of the club, to listen to the harp of his cousin Jane; and from the rustic triumph of "throwing sledge," to a stroll with his flute along the pastoral banks of the Inny.

The gentle spirit of his father walked with him through life, a pure and virtuous monitor; and in all the vicissitudes of his career we find him ever more chastened in mind by the sweet and holy recollections of the home of his infancy.

It has been questioned whether he really had any religious feeling. Those who raise the question have never considered well his writings; his "Vicar of Wakefield," and his pictures of the Village Pastor, present religion under its most endearing forms, and with a feeling that could only flow from the deep convictions of the heart. When his fair travelling companions at Paris urged him to read the Church Service on a Sunday, he replied that "he was not worthy to do it." He had seen in early life the sacred offices performed by his father and his brother with a solemnity which had sanctified them in his memory; how could he presume to undertake such functions? His religion has been called in question by Johnson and by Boswell: he certainly had not the gloomy hypochondriacal piety of the one, nor the babbling mouth-piety of the other; but the spirit of Christian charity, breathed forth in his writings and illustrated in his conduct, give us reason to believe he had the indwelling religion of the soul.

We have made sufficient comments in the preceding chapters on his conduct in elevated circles of literature and fashion. The fairy gifts which took him there were not accompanied by the gifts and graces necessary to sustain him in that artificial sphere. He can neither play the learned sage with Johnson, nor the fine gentleman with Beauclerc; though he has a mind replete with wisdom and natural shrewdness, and a spirit free from vulgarity. The blunders of a fertile but hurried intellect, and the awkward display of the student assuming the man of fashion, fix on him a character for absurdity and vanity which, like the charge of lunacy, it is hard to disprove, however weak the grounds of the charge and strong the facts in opposition to it.

In truth, he is never truly in his place in these learned and fashionable circles, which talk and live for display. It is not the kind of society he craves. His heart yearns for domestic life; it craves familiar, confiding intercourse, family firesides, the guileless and happy company of children; these bring out the heartiest and sweetest sympathies of his nature.

"Had it been his fate," says the critic we have already quoted, "to meet a woman who could have loved him, despite his faults, and respected him despite his foibles, we cannot but think that his life and his genius would have been much more harmonious; his desultory affections would have been concentrated, his craving self-love appeased, his pursuits more settled, his character more solid. A nature like Goldsmith's, so affectionate, so confiding—so susceptible to simple, innocent enjoyments—so dependent on others for the sunshine of existence, does not flower if deprived of the atmosphere of home."

The cravings of his heart in this respect are evident, we think, throughout his career; and if we have dwelt with more significancy than others upon his intercourse with the beautiful Horneck family, it is because we fancied we could detect, amid his playful attentions to one of its members, a lurking sentiment of tenderness, kept down by conscious poverty and a humiliating idea of personal defects. A hopeless feeling of this kind—the last a man would communicate to his friends—might account for much of that fitfulness of conduct, and that gathering melancholy, remarked, but not comprehended by his associates, during the last year or two of his life; and may have been one of the troubles of the mind which aggravated his last illness, and only terminated with his death.

We shall conclude these desultory remarks with a few which have been used by us on a former occasion. From the general tone of Goldsmith's biography, it is evident that his faults, at the worst, were but negative, while his merits were great and decided. He was no one's enemy but his own; his errors, in the main, inflicted evil on none but himself, and were so blended with humorous and even affecting circumstances, as to disarm anger and conciliate kindness. Where eminent talent is united to spotless virtue, we are awed and dazzled into admiration, but our admiration is apt to be cold and reverential; while there is something in the harmless infirmities of a good and great, but erring individual, that pleads touchingly to our nature; and we turn more kindly towards the object of our idolatry, when we find that, like ourselves, he is mortal and is frail. The epithet so often heard, and in such kindly tones, of "poor Goldsmith," speaks volumes. Few, who consider the real compound of admirable and whimsical qualities which form his character, would wish to prune away his eccentricities, trim its grotesque luxuriance, and clip it down to the decent formalities of rigid virtue. "Let not his frailties be remembered," said Johnson; "he was a very great man." But, for our part, we rather say, "Let them be remembered," since their tendency is to endear; and we question whether he himself would not feel gratified in hearing his reader, after dwelling with admiration on the proofs of his greatness, close the volume with the kind-hearted phrase, so fondly and familiarly ejaculated, of "POOR GOLDSMITH."

THE END

APPENDIX

Irving naturally has much to say of Boswell's ill-natured criticisms of Goldsmith, and for these he has ascribed a

Adverse criticisms of Goldsmith. fairly sufficient motive. Boswell, however, did not stand alone among Goldsmith's contemporaries in his contemptuous estimate of Goldsmith's character; witness Walpole, whose characterization of Goldsmith as an "inspired idiot" received a new lease of life from Carlyle, in his *Essay on Boswell's Johnson.* "Yet," concludes Carlyle, "on the whole, there is no evil in the 'goose-berry fool'; but rather much good; of a finer, if of a weaker, sort than Johnson's." With these distinctly hostile estimates by Boswell, Walpole, and Carlyle, may be compared the following more judicial summary of the character of Goldsmith by Macaulay:

"His associates seem to have regarded him with kindness, which, in spite of their admiration of his writings, was not

Macaulay on Goldsmith. unmixed with contempt. In truth, there was in his character much to love, but very little to respect. His heart was soft even to weakness: he was so generous that he quite forgot to be just: he forgave injuries so readily that he might be said to invite them; and was so liberal to beggars that he had nothing left for his tailor and his butcher. He was vain, sensual, frivolous, profuse, improvident. One vice of a darker shade was imputed to him, envy. But there is not

the least reason to believe that this bad passion, though it
sometimes made him wince and utter fretful exclamations,
ever impelled him to injure by wicked arts the reputation of
any of his rivals. The truth probably is, that he was not
more envious, but merely less prudent, than his neighbours."
—*Essay on Oliver Goldsmith.*

On the other hand, it must not be supposed
Scott on Goldsmith.   that Irving stands alone in his generous
characterization of Goldsmith. Sir Walter
Scott says of him:

"He was a friend to virtue, and in his most playful pages
never forgets what is due to it. A gentleness, delicacy and
purity of feeling distinguishes whatever he wrote, and bears
a correspondence to the generosity of a disposition which
knew no bounds but his last guinea. It was an attribute
almost essential to such a temper, that he wanted the proper
guards of firmness and decision, and permitted, even when
aware of their worthlessness, the intrusions of cunning and
of effrontery. . . . With this cullibility of temper was
mixed a hasty and eager jealousy of his own personal consequence: he unwillingly admitted that anything was done
better than he himself could have performed it; and sometimes made himself ridiculous by hastily undertaking to distinguish himself upon subjects which he did not understand.
But with these weaknesses, and with that of carelessness in
his own affairs, terminates all that censure can say of Goldsmith. The folly of submitting to imposition may be well
balanced with the universality of his benevolence, and the
wit which his writings evince, more than counterbalance his
defects in conversation, if these could be of consequence to
the present and future generations."—*Biographical and Critical Notices of Eminent Novelists by Walter Scott: Oliver
Goldsmith.*

And at the conclusion of his essay on Goldsmith in his *English Humorists*, Thackeray sums up his subject in the following eloquent words:

Thackeray on Goldsmith. "Think of him reckless, thriftless, vain if you like—but merciful, gentle, generous, full of love and pity. He passes out of our life, and goes to render his account beyond it. Think of the poor pensioners weeping at his grave; think of the noble spirits that admired and deplored him; think of the righteous pen that wrote his epitaph—and of the wonderful and unanimous response of affection with which the world has paid back the love he gave it. His humor delighting us still; his song fresh and beautiful as when first he charmed with it; his words in all our mouths; his very weaknesses beloved and familiar—his benevolent spirit seems still to smile upon us: to do gentle kindnesses: to succor with sweet charity: to soothe, caress, and forgive: to plead with the fortunate for the unhappy and the poor."

It would be easy to add indefinitely to the above appreciations, but it must suffice to note the following paragraphs, the one from De Quincey (*The Eighteenth Century in Scholarship and Literature*), and the second from Dobson's *Life of Goldsmith*.

De Quincey on Goldsmith.

"Goldsmith's own precipitancy, his overmastering defect in proper reserve, in self-control, and in presence of mind, falling in with the habitual undervaluation of many amongst his associates, placed him at a great disadvantage in animated conversation. His very truthfulness, his simplicity, his frankness, his hurry of feeling all told against him. They betrayed him into inconsiderate expressions that lent a color of plausibility to the malicious ridicule of those who disliked him the more, from being compelled, after all, to respect him. His own understanding oftentimes sided with his disparagers.

He *saw* that he had been in the wrong; whilst secretly he *felt* that his meaning—if properly explained—had been right. Defrauded in this way, and by his own coöperation, of distinctions that naturally belonged to him, he was driven unconsciously to attempt some restoration of the balance, by claiming for a moment distinctions to which he had no real pretensions. The whole was a prick of sorrow, and of sorrowing perplexity. He felt that no justice had been done to him, and that he himself had made an opening for the wrong. The result he saw, but the process he could not disentangle; and in the confusion of his distress, natural irritation threw him upon blind efforts to recover his ground by unfounded claims, when claims so well-founded had been maliciously disallowed."

"It would be easy to multiply examples of that strange mingling of strength and weakness—of genius and *gaucherie* —which went to make up Goldsmith's char-
Dobson on Goldsmith. acter. Yet the advantage would remain with its gentler and more lovable aspects, and the 'over-word' would still be the compassionate verdict: 'Let not his frailties be remembered, for he was a very great man.'"

INDEX OF INTRODUCTION AND ANNOTATIONS

www.ingramcontent.com/pod-product-compliance
Lightning Source LLC
Chambersburg PA
CBHW030351030726
47497CB00002B/286